East-West Monograph Series 5

SDI and European Security

Regina Cowen
Peter Rajcsanyi
Vladimir Bilandzic

with an Introduction by
F. Stephen Larrabee

WESTVIEW PRESS • BOULDER, COLORADO

 Institute for East-West Security Studies

This publication is made possible through the generous support of the Ford Foundation.

Distributed by Westview Press
5500 Central Avenue
Boulder, Colorado 80301

Library of Congress Cataloging-in-Publication Data
Cowen, Regina H. E.
   SDI and European security.

   (East-West monograph series; #5)
   1. Europe—National security.   2. Strategic Defense Initiative.   1. Bilandzic, Vladimir, 1946–
II. Rajcsanyi, Peter M.   III. Title.   IV. Series.
UA646.C74   1988   355'.03304   87-35290
ISBN 0-913449-07-5
   0-8133-0662-0 (Westview)

Printed in the United States of America

ii

TABLE OF CONTENTS

Preface

European concerns about strategic defense and its impact on the stability of the East-West strategic balance have been the subject of frequent and lively discussion at the Institute for East-West Security Studies in the more than four years since President Reagan announced his Strategic Defense Initiative (SDI) in March 1983. The three essays in this monograph, written by former Institute Fellows from the United Kingdom, Hungary and Yugoslavia, look at the Strategic Defense Initiative from specifically European perspectives and emphasize the consequences of SDI for *Europe*.

The monograph fills an important gap in the literature on the subject which has tended to overlook the European implications of strategic defense. In addition, the chapters present three contrasting European perspectives—one from a NATO country, one from a Warsaw Treaty nation, and one from a neutral/nonaligned state—in accordance with the Institute's aim of treating security issues from a broad East-West perspective.

The authors are well qualified to comment on the impact of strategic defense for Europe. Regina Cowen, from the United Kingdom, a Resident Fellow at the Institute in 1985-1986, is a specialist on European defense issues currently working as a Research Associate at the Stockholm International Peace Research Institute. Peter Rajcsanyi, from Hungary, a Resident Fellow in 1984-1985 and again for part of 1986, is a specialist on transatlantic relations now with the Central Committee staff of the Hungarian Socialist Workers Party. Vladimir Bilandzic from Yugoslavia, a Resident Fellow in 1983 and 1984-1985, is a Senior Research Associate at the Institute of International Politics and Economics in Belgrade, and has been a member of the Yugoslav delegation to the CSCE talks on European security in both Madrid and Vienna.

The authors would like to thank the Institute staff, particularly Vice President and Director of Studies F. Stephen Larrabee, for their encouragement and comments throughout, and the East-West Fellows at the Institute from 1984 to 1986, who played such an instrumental role in creating the stimulating intellectual atmosphere from which these essays emerged.

The authors' stay at the Institute was made possible through the generosity of The Ford Foundation and the Alfried Krupp von Bohlen und Halbach-Foundation in Essen. The Institute also gratefully acknowledges the support of The Ford Foundation for the publication and dissemination of this study. The views expressed in this monograph are solely those of the authors and should not be ascribed to the funders of this study or the Institute. The Institute for East-West Security Studies is pleased to sponsor the publication of this monograph as a contribution to the debate in both East and West about this critical issue of international security.

John Edwin Mroz
President
Institute for East-West
  Security Studies
New York
October 1987

Introduction

F. STEPHEN LARRABEE

Since its official inauguration on March 23, 1983, by President Reagan, the Strategic Defense Initiative (SDI) has been a subject of considerable controversy. Most studies, especially in the United States, have concentrated on issues related to SDI's technical feasibility and its impact on the security of the two superpowers. Very little consideration has been given to European perceptions and the impact that any deployment of strategic defenses might have for Europe. Indeed, President Reagan's speech announcing SDI was made without any consultation with America's West European allies and only briefly mentioned them. Yet as the essays in this volume make clear, the development of strategic defenses is of vital concern to Europeans as well.

This volume, part of a series of ongoing projects undertaken by the Institute to analyze the implications of defensive systems for East-West security,[1] seeks to fill this void. The essays in the volume look at the problem of SDI from specifically "European" perspectives and emphasize the implications of SDI *for Europe*. The authors, all Europeans and former Fellows at the Institute, represent different political perspectives—NATO, the Warsaw Treaty Organization and the neutral/nonaligned. Indeed, this is one of the unique features of the volume. While all three authors are concerned with the broad political-strategic implications of SDI, the focus of each chapter is different. Regina Cowen, a defense analyst from the United Kingdom, looks at the place of SDI in the evolution of U.S. strategic doctrine and the implications for the Atlantic alliance; Peter Rajcsanyi from Hungary

---

1. F. Stephen Larrabee, "SDI: Implikationen fuer Abruestung und die Ost-West-Beziehungen," in Hartmut Buehl, ed., *Strategiediscussion* (Bonn: Verlag E.S. Mitter und Son, 1987), pp. 293–318; Robert S. Crawford, "SDI und der amerikanische Kongress," *Europa Archiv*, Folge 8/1987, pp. 237–246; and Ian Cuthbertson, *The Anti-Tactical Ballistic Missile Defense Issue and European Security*, Occasional Paper Number 7 (New York: Institute for East-West Security Studies, forthcoming).

trates on the implications of SDI for U.S.-Soviet relations and arms control; and Vladimir Bilandzic from Yugoslavia analyzes European attitudes and responses to SDI, including those of the neutral/ nonaligned countries.

Technology vs. Politics

What is perhaps most striking about the essays in the volume is the degree to which the authors, despite their diverse political-ideological backgrounds, share certain basic attitudes. The first is a tendency to see security in broad *political* terms rather than in strictly military or technological terms. This tendency differentiates Europeans from Americans. As Christoph Bertram has pointed out, the experience of Europeans leads them to conclude that security is, above all, "a political task."[2] Thus, as he notes, Europeans tend to ask more often than Americans what the *political* consequences of a new weapons system are likely to be. They suspect that whatever new sophisticated weapons systems are introduced the political problems will be the same.

This basic "European mindset" is strongly reflected in the contributions to this volume. All three authors, their very different political-ideological backgrounds notwithstanding, are profoundly skeptical about SDI's ability to contribute to greater security; all three see the basic problem as a *political* rather than a technological one; all three are concerned about the impact SDI will have on the broad political framework of East-West relations.

The views of the three authors coincide on a number of other points as well. Both Cowen and Rajcsanyi see SDI not as a break with the past but as part of a general evolution of U.S. strategy. SDI, as Cowen argues, is not a revolutionary concept. She sees the concern with active defenses as "part of a larger debate on U.S. strategy." In her view President Reagan's speech on March 23 "merely increased the prominence of active defenses within that debate." Similarly, Rajcsanyi regards SDI as part of a larger search for greater flexibility in U.S. strategic doctrine and as an evolutionary response to the problem of increasing ICBM vulnerability, while Bilandzic sees its

---

2. Christoph Bertram, "Strategic Defense and the Western Alliance," *Weapons in Space*, Volume II, *Daedalus* (Summer 1985), p. 280.

21015   Item:

BELM   Date:12/13/89   Fund:

1            $11.85   190

COWEN
SDI & EUROPEAN SECURITY

WESTVIEW PR.
Req. by: 12/13/90

T

origins in the disenchantment of both superpowers, particularly the United States, with the strategy of mutual assured destruction (MAD).

Another common point is the central importance that each author attaches to the Anti-Ballistic Missile (ABM) Treaty. While each concedes that the treaty contains ambiguities, all regard it as an important cornerstone of strategic stability. Rajcsanyi, for instance, sees the Reagan administration's determination to go forward with field tests in the early 1990s as a major challenge to strategic stability, a view echoed by Bilandzic. If the Reagan administration proceeds with such tests, Rajcsanyi argues, the Soviet Union will have no choice but to respond. This could open up a dangerous and highly destabilizing offense-defense race. He cautions, however, that the USSR is not likely to respond by emulating the U.S. SDI program, but rather by developing a variety of countermeasures designed to overcome the defense.

Cowen also is concerned about the impact of SDI on strategic stability. She points out that a less than perfect defense—the only thing feasible within the next decade—would increase Soviet incentives for preemption in a conflict. As she points out, placing the Soviet Union in a position in which its leaders have to fear the loss of their retaliatory forces through a U.S. preemptive strike might make it imperative for Moscow to act preventively. Rather than bolstering deterrence, she warns, such a posture would undermine it.

Cowen's analysis highlights one of the main weaknesses of SDI: its unilateral character. As she points out, SDI was launched and has proceeded "as if the Soviet Union did not exist." Yet, as Reagan administration officials themselves acknowledge, if SDI is to succeed, it will require a high degree of Soviet cooperation. Its success, at least in the short run, is contingent upon constraining and reducing the number of offensive warheads.

This in turn highlights the important role of arms control and the need for greater political cooperation. As Cowen points out, the world beyond the ABM Treaty is one of profound conceptual uncertainty. It is unlikely that technology will resolve this debate. The only way to address and perhaps resolve these uncertainties lies in the political field. What is required, as she notes, is a cooperative relationship at the political level that takes account of this reality and reinforces it through policy. Unilateral strategic actions are likely to reduce rather than enhance the possibility for developing such a cooperative political relationship.

The European Dimension

As all three essays underscore, SDI has important implications not just for U.S.-Soviet relations but for Europe as well. This is particularly true for America's West European allies, who (with the exception of France) are dependent upon the U.S. nuclear guarantee for their ultimate security. Thus any effort to replace this guarantee with a new system of security based on strategic defense cannot but have important implications for their security.

The debate on strategic defense in the United States, however, has tended to be conducted without much concern for European perceptions. As noted at the outset, the West European allies were not even consulted before President Reagan launched his initiative. The lack of consultation and coordination was undoubtedly one of the chief reasons for the largely negative initial reaction to SDI in many West European quarters. (Indeed, the manner in which SDI was presented seems to be a classic example of how *not* to conduct alliance diplomacy.) But even if there had been greater consultation, it is unlikely that the West European attitude would have been highly supportive of the initiative. The lack of consultation was irritating. But the real basis of West European concerns lies much deeper. They are imbedded, as Cowen's essay points out, in the very nature of extended deterrence itself.

Many West Europeans see in SDI a profound challenge to the very essence of the Atlantic alliance. They fear that it will lead to the emergence of "two separate zones of security" and strengthen a trend toward a "Fortress America" mentality in the United States. Moreover, they are convinced that their security rests on *American vulnerability* and that the United States will remain vitally concerned about Western Europe only so long as America's own survival is at stake. SDI therefore threatens to undermine what Christoph Bertram has called the "basic bargain" of the Atlantic alliance—the idea of shared risk.[3] To many West Europeans it suggests that the United States wants to escape the risk of a European conflict—or keep it limited to Europe.

The Reagan administration has sought to counter these fears by offering to extend the defense to Europe. But even if the United States were to extend its defensive shield to Western Europe, the basic problem would remain: the security ladder of potential escalation to the strategic nuclear level, the core of NATO's strategy of flexible re-

---

3. For a good discussion of this point see Bertram, "Strategic Defense and the Atlantic Alliance," pp. 294–295.

sponse, would be broken. In addition, Western Europe would still face a threat from other nuclear weapons such as artillery, aircraft and cruise missiles.

A second West European concern relates to the potential impact of SDI on detente and arms control. Given its geographic proximity to the Soviet Union, Western Europe has a vested stake in detente and arms control. The United States can always retreat into "splendid isolation," as it has done several times in the past. For Western Europe this is not an option. Thus the West Europeans generally support arms control—as much for political as military reasons. Within this context, the ABM Treaty plays a key role. The treaty is seen by many West Europeans as the cornerstone of the arms control regime established by the two superpowers in the early 1970s. Thus the West European governments of NATO have generally opposed actions which might lead to its violation or erosion, such as the Reagan administration's effort to adopt a "broad" interpretation of the treaty.

A third and related concern is the impact that any deployment of SDI might have on the French and British nuclear forces. The credibility of these forces depends on their ability to penetrate Soviet defenses, which are currently constrained by the ABM Treaty. Were the ABM Treaty to be either formally abrogated or, through unilateral action, effectively become a dead letter, the Soviet Union would be able to significantly expand its defenses, eroding the capability of the French and British nuclear forces. While both countries could take measures to restore that credibility, these measures would be costly and might provoke an intensified domestic debate, particularly in Great Britain.

A fourth concern relates to resources. Many Europeans fear that SDI could siphon off funds that would otherwise go to NATO-related defense, especially conventional forces. This is particularly true if the United States begins to address the budget deficit seriously, as inevitably it must. Strengthening conventional forces, however, will become all the more important if there is an INF agreement eliminating all medium- and short-range nuclear missiles in Europe. Thus SDI could increase the need for difficult tradeoffs and lead to greater pressure on West European governments to do more in the conventional area at a time when they face severe economic and demographic constraints.

A final concern is technological. Many West Europeans fear that SDI will exacerbate the technological gap between the United States and its West European allies.[4] The desire to counter such a develop-

4. See in particular Konrad Seitz, "SDI: The Technological Challenge for Europe," *The World Today*, August–September 1985, pp. 154–157.

ment has been one of the main factors behind the creation of the Eureka program, which is designed to give new impetus to West European technological cooperation in the non-military area. At the same time several West European countries, notably Great Britain and West Germany, have agreed to participate in the SDI research program in the hope of sharing in the technological spinoffs. To what extent these hopes will be realized remains to be seen. The initial results, however, have not been particularly encouraging.

On the political level, the West European reaction to date has largely been one of damage limitation. As Bilandzic's essay points out, the allies have essentially adopted a "wait and see" attitude, hoping either that the problem will somehow go away after Reagan departs or that it will be resolved by an arms control agreement between the two superpowers. While they have been willing to give conditional support to the research program, they have expressed reservations about any future deployment, insisting that any decision to proceed with deployment should be a subject of consultation and negotiation.

SDI, however, is not simply an issue between the United States and its West European allies. As the contributions by Rajcsanyi and Bilandzic make clear, the East European and neutral/nonaligned countries also have a stake, albeit a less direct one, in the outcome. An intensification of the arms race, as Rajcsanyi notes, would inevitably have a spillover effect on Eastern Europe, increasing pressure for higher defense spending and diverting much-needed resources away from the tasks of economic modernization, which is a top priority for many of these countries. Moreover, heightened tension between the superpowers would make an expansion of political contacts between both parts of Europe more difficult. A relaxation of tension, on the other hand, would make such contacts easier.

The same is true of the neutral/nonaligned. While not directly involved, they too would be adversely affected by any downturn in U.S.-Soviet relations and an intensified arms race. Hence, they too have an interest in more stable relations between the superpowers and preventing an intensification of the military competition between the two blocs. This is particularly true, as Bilandzic points out, for a country like Yugoslavia, which is located in a geographic area that has traditionally been a victim of great-power politics.

Bilandzic's essay highlights the degree to which the neutral/nonaligned countries in recent years have begun to concern themselves more forcefully with broad security issues formerly considered beyond their purview. At the same time it underscores one of the distinctive features of international politics in the nuclear age: the degree to which security is today increasingly interlinked and interdependent.

Nuclear weapons have blurred the significance of the traditional geographic boundaries of the nation-state. Today no state in Europe, even one which is neutral or nonaligned, could escape the consequences of a nuclear conflict. Hence, the neutral/nonaligned countries have increasingly pressed to expand the security dialogue beyond the bilateral and bloc context to multilateral fora where they have an opportunity to make their voice heard on important security issues.

SDI and Arms Control

One of the major concerns of all three authors in this volume is the impact of SDI on arms control. And justifiably so. While the two superpowers have narrowed their differences considerably on strategic offensive forces and intermediate-range forces, they still remain fundamentally at loggerheads over SDI. At the October 1986 Reykjavik summit Soviet leader Mikhail Gorbachev and President Reagan agreed in principle to a 50-percent cut in strategic offensive forces. Gorbachev, however, tied this to a commitment not to withdraw from the ABM Treaty for a period of ten years, to be followed by discussions on how to proceed at the end of this period. While he agreed that research on SDI could go forward, he insisted that such research be restricted to "laboratory research" and that testing of space-based "elements" should be prohibited. President Reagan, on the other hand, favored a ten-year extension of the ABM Treaty, at the end of which both sides would be free to deploy defenses. Since Reykjavik the United States has modified its position, reducing the time period for withdrawal from ten to seven years (until 1994)—mainly to allow the United States to undertake certain SDI-related tests which it hopes to be able to conduct by 1993-1994.

In the last year, in fact, the administration's SDI program has undergone a gradual reorientation—away from its original focus on exotic systems such as laser and particle beams toward a "near-term deployment option" which would rely on kinetic energy weapons (KEW).[5] The system would be based on land-based interceptors and "smart rocks"—rockets fired from orbiting platforms in space with warheads equipped with heat-seeking sensors that track and destroy missiles on impact. This limited system could probably be deployed in six to eight years. However, it would violate the ABM Treaty, which pro-

5. See Douglas C. Waller and James C. Bruce, "SDI's Covert Reorientation," *Arms Control Today* 17, No. 5 (June 1987), pp. 2–8.

hibits the testing and deployment of ABM systems or their components based in space.

The current reorientation of the program appears to be driven more by political considerations than strategic logic. One of the main motives behind the push for near-term deployment of such a system appears to be a desire to bind the hands of the next president and pave the way for the erosion of the ABM Treaty, which advocates of near-term deployment see as a major obstacle to moving forward with SDI. In addition, many conservative supporters of SDI appear to believe that highly visible demonstrations are needed to maintain Congressional support for funding SDI. The repeated change of priorities, however, inhibits serious, stable research. At the same time, many experts believe that the goal of 1994 set for near-term deployment is unrealistic and overly ambitious.[6]

Doubts about the administration's approach to SDI have been reinforced by an authoritative report released by the American Physical Society in April 1987, which concluded that a decade or more will be needed to resolve key technical questions regarding the development of a sophisticated defense against Soviet missiles.[7] This means that any phased deployment of kinetic weapons followed by a system based on lasers and particle beams would be decades away. At best such a system based on kinetic weapons could only be an additional deterrent to attack, not a system that would meet President Reagan's goal. These considerations raise serious questions about the wisdom of proceeding with near-term deployment. Were the United States to proceed down this path it would be committing itself to spend hundreds of billions of dollars to build a defense before knowing whether survivable and effective second-generation defenses can be developed.

The conclusions of the American Physical Society report also have important implications for arms control. In effect, the report suggests that it is possible to have arms control and a vigorous research program on SDI since the type of technologies needed to support President Reagan's original vision will not be ready to be tested for several

---

6. See in particular Harold Brown, "Too Much, Too Soon," *Arms Control Today* 17, No. 4 (May 1987), pp. 2–3.

7. Philip M. Boffey, "Physicists Express 'Star Wars' Doubt; Long Delays Seen," *The New York Times*, April 23, 1987. The full title of the report is *Science and Technology of Directed Energy Weapons: Report of The American Physical Society Study Group* (April 1987).

decades. In principle, therefore, some sort of "grand compromise," which would trade deep cuts in offensive forces for some constraints on SDI, could be possible. Such a deal would allow the United States to proceed with an arms control dialogue with the Soviet Union while still maintaining a robust SDI research program within the framework of the ABM Treaty.

Nuclear Deterrence in Transition

SDI, however, must be seen within the larger context of changing attitudes and policy toward nuclear deterrence in general. Developments since Reykjavik, including the progress made toward an agreement eliminating medium- and short-range missiles in Europe, have reinforced the centrality of these concerns. The long-term psychological and political impact of such an INF agreement along the lines currently proposed is likely to be profound, particularly for Western Europe. The elimination of all medium- and short-range weapons from Europe will make NATO's strategy of flexible response harder to implement and may even require some changes in the strategy itself. At the same time a reduced reliance on nuclear weapons for deterrence will make the need to address the disparities between NATO and the Warsaw Pact at the conventional level all the more urgent. Thus conventional arms control, dormant for over a decade, could be given new impetus.

An INF agreement is also likely to have an effect on the structure of NATO, leading to a closer harmonization of West European defense policies and a strengthening of the European pillar within NATO. There have been several signs of such a trend already. One has been the greater consciousness about the need for an integrated European defense effort. Another has been increased French-West German military cooperation, reflected in particular in the decision in June 1987 to form a joint French-West German brigade under a French commander outside the framework of NATO. A third sign has been the quiet effort by France and Britain to step up their military cooperation.

These developments are part of a general trend, discussed by Regina Cowen in her chapter, toward a greater "Europeanization" of NATO. To be sure, this trend began well before Reykjavik, as the three authors' discussion of alliance reactions to SDI indicates. But developments since Reykjavik have given this trend greater momentum and its various aspects reflect West European unease with the directions of American policy. If this unease continues to grow—with ambivalence toward SDI, reservations about a double-zero INF agreement for Europe, and apprehension about the general conduct of U.S. security policy—it could have important security implications over the long run.

In short, East-West relations seem to be entering a new period in which some of the basic assumptions of postwar politics are being challenged. SDI is a part of this larger process of change. Managing this process of change, especially for Europe, will present a major challenge to governments in both East and West and require "new thinking" and greater cooperation on both sides.

1

The Strategic Defense Initiative and the Atlantic Alliance: Doctrines versus Security

REGINA COWEN

Prologue

President Reagan's Strategic Defense Initiative has raised profound questions about the possibility of transforming the present security system from an offense-dominated deterrence structure to a defense-dominated posture. Most analyses thus far have been concerned with the technical feasibility of a ballistic missile defense (BMD) system; the strategic instabilities which a move towards defensive systems are likely to create; potential Soviet countermeasures, both offensive and defensive; political and military opportunity costs; and the impact of BMD research upon the continued viability of the 1972 Anti-Ballistic Missile (ABM) Treaty and the prospects for offensive nuclear reductions. Almost all analysts share one particular handicap: the vague official U.S. definition of SDI and the related fact that no one knows what SDI is going to be. This paper is an attempt to investigate what SDI could most likely turn out to be. The analysis tests the hypothesis that SDI represents not a departure from the traditional tenets of the U.S. strategic debate but that the revival of the BMD debate was a timely and evolutionary development of U.S. strategic thinking. Part I makes the case for this hypothesis by reviewing the evolution of U.S. strategic theory. The purpose of Part I is to remove the SDI issue from much of the day-to-day events surrounding it, which will allow a broader SDI picture to emerge. The assumption is that only if the speculative nature of such technical questions as "Is the technology going to work or not" is not the primary purpose of the analysis will it be possible to recognize what the BMD debate really represents within the U.S. and the European security contexts.

Part II analyzes the European context of the SDI debate. It suggests that the myth of strategic nuclear policy is perpetuated in the doctrine and strategy of extended deterrence. While this is the core argument in Part II, the focus of the discussion is again directed at the ways and means employed to achieve a politically credible strategy and the peculiar political and military reality that has been created. This analysis provides the backdrop to the subsequent discussion of how SDI is perceived in Europe.

Part I: The Evolution of U.S. Strategic Theory

Four years have passed since President Reagan so dramatically launched the Strategic Defense Initiative. The initial surge of criticism of the style in which SDI was introduced to a wider public forum and of the "imminent" strategic pitfalls it was believed to cause have given way to a more reflective evaluation of the Reagan administration's research program. In part, the subsidence of the more passionate critiques that flooded the media until relatively recently is due to a growing recognition on the part of SDI critics that whatever SDI turns out to be, we are on the verge of entering a new era of international security. Seemingly overnight, strategic defenses as a basis for national defense policy planning were given a new lease on life. Hardly anyone familiar with U.S. political organization and processes and the world of strategic analysis believes at this stage that SDI can disappear in a cloud of smoke, making possible a return to the "blissful" state of affairs prior to 1983. Even if such an unlikely event came about—that is, the disappearance of SDI—the past four years have given us a glimpse of the world beyond the ABM Treaty, and whether we like what we see or not, this world has begun to encroach upon us.

Since 1983, the views of SDI supporters have undergone change, too. The early enthusiasm about the seemingly vast opportunities offered by new and emerging technologies for purposes of strategic defense has given way to a much more sober assessment of the probable limitations even of yet unknown technologies. The idea of the perfect defensive shield, although remaining the stated official objective of SDI efforts, has in fact generated a host of lesser yet equally desirable roles for strategic defenses. The increasingly detectable emphasis on the short- and medium-term goals of SDI and the benefits derived from technologically less comprehensive defensive capabilities is largely due to the fact that the president's speech was not made in a political vacuum. Indeed, the president raised the issue of strategic defenses at a time when the existing U.S. defense community and the ongoing discussion of the future of the U.S. deterrent force and policy provided a most fertile environment for serious consideration of strategic defenses. In order to understand the process of conceptualization that SDI has undergone since 1983 and the reasons for its persisting momentum, it is important to analyze its role and place in U.S. strategic thinking.

It is beyond the scope of this study to undertake a substantial discussion of the evolution of U.S. strategic doctrine and nuclear strategy. Suffice it therefore to analyze the dominant traits of U.S. strategic doctrine and highlight the persisting tensions between doctrine and strategy.

Almost as soon as the notion of nuclear strategy was formulated into national security policy in the late 1940s and early 1950s, a debate arose over what nuclear deterrence is, how it operates and what kind of nuclear forces it requires. This debate is still going on, and it is doubtful that these issues can ever be resolved to the satisfaction of all concerned. During the course of this debate, two distinct schools of thought have emerged. Each fundamentally disagrees with the other on how nuclear deterrence helps to prevent nuclear war. As Colin Gray and Keith Payne aptly wrote in 1983, "The real debate concerns the optimal method of ensuring deterrence, not which side most convincingly opposes nuclear war. . . ."[1] In other words, the strategic debate is about methods of policy planning, not about the principle of deterrence as the basis of U.S. security policy. It is well understood that the credibility of any deterrence posture prescribes the use of nuclear weapons. Where the two schools mainly differ is on the level of credibility required to deter the Soviet Union and under what circumstances nuclear weapons would actually be used. The subsequent analysis looks at each school's strengths and weaknesses.

The proponents of the first school subscribe to mutual assured destruction (MAD), based on the vulnerability to nuclear attack of U.S. and Soviet societies and the possession of retaliatory nuclear forces by both sides. Assured destruction became mutual when the Soviet Union gained the ability to inflict unacceptable damage upon the United States in retaliation to a U.S. first strike. MAD assumes that no rational leader would initiate a first strike against the other country because his society would in turn suffer unacceptable levels

1. Colin S. Gray and Keith B. Payne, "Nuclear Strategy: Is There a Future?" *The Washington Quarterly* 6, No. 3 (Summer 1983), p. 56.

of damage. Credibility of the MAD doctrine is believed to derive from the sheer enormity of the retaliatory threat and the suicidal nature of a nuclear first strike. With regard to force planning, the MAD logic is equally simple. A relatively small force of invulnerable nuclear weapons, perhaps even of large yields, would be all that is required to inflict unimaginable destruction on the Russian people should their leaders ever consider forgoing reasoned judgment. The attractive logic of MAD theory is matched in its purity by the complexity of the real world and its persistent deviation from the prescriptions of MAD. Even MAD adherents will admit that there has hardly ever been a period of time since 1945 in which MAD theory alone was the guide to U.S. strategic policy. Like "massive retaliation," MAD's counterpart in military strategy, MAD policy was changed as soon as it was expounded.

Mutual assured destruction as strategic policy is unsatisfactory on several grounds. First, it is overly prescriptive. MAD assumes that only the worst kind of retaliatory threat assures strategic stability and, further, that only a massive first strike needs to be deterred. Both assumptions may not be justified. Deterring the biggest threat does not automatically enable the United States to deter any contingency short of that. Also, threatening devastation even in retaliation is not a policy but a political straitjacket. MAD prescribes certainty of response but does little to enable the United States to use the tools of MAD, that is, nuclear weapons, in a more discriminating deterrence policy. Second, MAD does provide for a very unequivocal peacetime posture. But should war nevertheless break out, perhaps through miscalculation of intentions or mismanagement of a crisis, MAD gives no alternative but to carry out a suicidal threat. No policy-maker relishes the prospect of so monumental a decision. Third, while MAD retains a great deal of credibility as a response to a Soviet attack upon the United States, it is highly questionable whether such a posture deters either a limited nuclear or even a conventional attack on Western Europe. There is a growing consensus in the Western defense community that it does not. The defense literature provides innumerable scenarios of aggression in Europe and possible U.S. responses—these are well known and need no further elaboration here. Fact is, mutual assured destruction as deterrence policy is a limited construct with potentially disastrous consequences.

The second school of deterrence attempts to 'correct' some of MAD's greatest shortcomings. First, it takes account of the possibility of lesser threats. Indeed, most of its proponents would agree that the lesser threats are the more likely ones a deterrence policy has to cope with.

Second, it addresses the problem of deterrence failure. Although one is an issue of peacetime posture and the other one of military response in time of war, both complement each other. Deterrence of a lesser threat demands forces tailored to achieve the deterring effect desired. On the other hand, should deterrence break down through aggression on a limited scale, the military forces to meet such limited aggression are available. In other words, a differentiated spectrum of deterrence capabilities adds credibility to deterrence as a whole and provides military options.

The quest for credible military options began in the early 1950s. As far as is known, specifically military options first became part of official U.S. defense policy with Secretary of Defense Robert McNamara's Single Integrated Operations Plan 63 of 1961-1962. From this date, a steady elaboration of the military options themselves and the role they should play in U.S. deterrence policy has taken place: Secretary of Defense James Schlesinger's 1974 National Security Decisions Memorandum (NSDM) 242, President Carter's Presidential Directive (PD) 59 in 1979 and, most recently, President Reagan's National Security Decision Directive (NSDD) 13 in 1981.[2] Paul Nitze recalls that

> when President Reagan assumed office, existing U.S. deterrence policy called for maintenance of a range of nuclear response options and set a goal of terminating any war on terms most favorable for the nation.[3]

The second part of this quotation highlights one of the most questioned implications of a policy based on nuclear options. Military options only make sense if derived from a notion of using them in order to win the war. This is a worrying development to those who see it as a trend towards returning to pre-1945 concepts of deterrence and warfighting. They fear that once nuclear weapons are perceived as usable instruments of war, much like a military aircraft or a tank, they begin to undermine the very concept of deterrence they are meant to preserve.

Militarily usable options and a strategy that aims to conclude any war on terms favorable to the United States could be not only destabilizing but, from a conceptual point of view, a poor substitute for

---

2. Fred Kaplan, *The Wizards of Armageddon* (New York: Simon and Schuster, 1983), pp. 371–391.

3. Paul H. Nitze, "U.S. Strategic Force Structures: The Challenge Ahead," U.S. Department of State, *Current Policy*, No. 794, p. 1.

mutual assured destruction. MAD policy, after all, was criticized for its inability to appreciate threats and responses other than those commonly associated only with worst-case analyses. To devise military options for distinctly identifiable levels of conflict and have confidence in one's ability and opportunity to execute such options in a nuclear war environment requires a degree of command, control and communication (C^3) hitherto unprecedented. Desmond Ball and many others over recent years have very ably demonstrated the operational demands made upon a warfighting strategy and have invariably reached the conclusion that the technical problems associated with the controlled use of nuclear weapons alone are so formidable that a national policy based on nuclear options is sheer folly.[4]

There is an even more basic challenge to the nuclear options school. Control of nuclear war assumes a cooperative adversary. So does MAD, it could be argued. But a nuclear option strategy whose purpose after all is to respond to a limited attack in a controlled and limited fashion needs to be perceived as such by the Soviet Union. Targeting Soviet missiles and command and control facilities instead of cities may tell the Soviet Union in peacetime that we would spare their cities in the first round of retaliation, but who is to say that neither we nor they will change existing assumptions of strategic warfare once war has broken out? Could the Soviets be sure that our peacetime pronouncements on nuclear strategy would be a true guide to our assessment of a war situation? Moreover, how could we ensure that they are sure? We cannot. The simple fact is that no one knows how to fight a war with nuclear weapons. Neither can anyone be sure to control a nuclear exchange early enough for an observer to recognize the difference between the closing stages of limited nuclear options and the beginning of assured destruction. Here lies the crux of the matter. Due to the many and varied uncertainties of nuclear warfare, rapid escalation to an all-out nuclear exchange always remains within the realm of possibility. In effect, it could be argued that the quest for credible nuclear options has failed not for lack of effort, but because there are none, and even if there were, an elaborate peacetime strategy could not adequately predict our behavior in war, not for ourselves and not for the Soviets. If this is indeed the case, have we merely

---

4. Desmond Ball, "Can Nuclear War be Controlled?" *Adelphi Papers* 169 (London: International Institute for Strategic Studies, 1981); Desmond Ball, "Targeting for Strategic Deterrence," *Adelphi Papers* 185 (London: International Institute for Strategic Studies, 1983).

engaged in a futile attempt to replace our big bluff (assured destruction) with ever more sophisticated but equally incredible smaller bluffs? Has strategic debate in the West come full circle? After a voluminous study of strategic matters, Lawrence Freedman concludes that we do not have a nuclear strategy (although the length of his study seems to attest to our increased understanding as to why we do not have one).[5]

If a policy of assured destruction seems absurd, and if planning to meet lesser contingencies does not resolve the fundamental problem of still having to fight a nuclear war should deterrence break down, why do we and the Soviets still have this paramount need to invent a nuclear strategy? Thus far, this study has primarily focused on the evolution of deterrence from a security or national survival aspect. Yet it is well known that deterrence has not only an immediate security dimension but also a broader political context. It is suggested here that the need for nuclear strategy stems as much from political as from security concerns.

The military relationship between the United States and the Soviet Union is based on the technical fact that one side can inflict unacceptable damage upon the other and suffer equal destruction in return. Mutual assured destruction has become a condition of the nuclear age. In effect, MAD is no longer a policy option but part of the security environment within which both the United States and the Soviet Union formulate their respective security policies. The political rivalry between these two powers is expressed most visibly in the field of nuclear strategy, in part because the Soviet Union's competitiveness is limited to this field. Each side tries to score political points through military means. In a recent speech, West German Defense Minister Manfred Woerner expressed this phenomenon succinctly:

> The fact remains that since 1945 the conflicts between highly industrialized and nuclear armed states are carried out exclusively in the field of options. . . . There the attempt is made to shape the other side's will through military instruments of power. This struggle costs money but no lives, it is bloodless but no less fierce.[6]

5. Lawrence Freedman, *The Evolution of Nuclear Strategy* (New York: St. Martin's Press, 1981), pp. 372–400.

6. Manfred Woerner, "Strategie in Wandel, Grundrichtungen und Eckwerte der Strategie aus dem Blickwinkel der Bundesrepublik Deutschland," Der Bundesminister der Verteidigung, *Material fuer die Presse*, Bonn, XXIII/6 (February 26, 1986), p. 10.

Undoubtedly, a major Soviet military technological breakthrough, perhaps in the area of anti-submarine warfare, could seriously undermine the military credibility of the submarine-based leg of the U.S. strategic triad. In time of crisis, the United States might then severely doubt its ability to rely on sea-based systems as retaliatory forces. In other words, military advances by the Russians do matter militarily for the United States. The point here is, however, that what the other side does also matters politically.

Consider, for example, the debate that began in the late 1970s over the potential vulnerability of U.S. land-based strategic nuclear systems to a Soviet first strike. ICBM MIRVing and improved warhead accuracy had made these systems both militarily attractive and cost-effective targets. One SS-18 with ten warheads, it was suggested, could theoretically destroy thirty Minuteman III ICBM warheads in their silos. Given the well-known technical uncertainties of effective and controlled nuclear use, U.S. ICBM vulnerability may be of lesser military but greater political significance; in other words, conceding even a theoretical first-strike capability to the Soviet Union is politically nonviable. As long as nuclear weapons are the unit of exchange, the strategic currency, between the United States and the Soviet Union, one side will have to match the military options created by the other irrespective of whether these new options make military sense. Such, for example, was the reasoning behind stationing Pershing II and cruise missiles in Western Europe. At the time there were many who argued that U.S. use of new long-range INF systems was no more a likely course of action in the defense of Europe than that of using U.S. strategic systems.

At the beginning of the 1980s the existing strategic debate in the United States turned into an extremely strenuous exercise. A disenchantment with arms control as a moderating force in the nuclear arms race was shared by the political left and right. European peace movements and the U.S. freeze campaign challenged many aspects of the conventional defense wisdom. The Soviet invasion of Afghanistan that had prompted President Carter to withdraw SALT II from deliberations in the Senate was cause for many to call for a comprehensive reassessment of relations with the Soviet Union. At the same time, the U.S. domestic political atmosphere began to change. The post-Vietnam era that had paralyzed American confidence for most of the 1970s made way for a new spirit of enterprise, ready to face old and new challenges with determination. Ronald Reagan's landslide victory in the 1980 presidential election epitomized the 'new' America.

This spirit of newfound resolve was not shared by the defense community. Indeed, strategic debate had reached an all-time low. As discussed above, the search for selective nuclear options had only led its proponents full circle: MAD was and is a stark reality. Despite the apparent logic which rules that anything short of mutual assured destruction must, by definition, be more rational than MAD itself, selective nuclear options remained a highly controversial issue. And yet, the new domestic spirit made the political role of options imperative. The unprecedented military buildup during the first Reagan administration, the harsh rhetoric towards the Soviet Union, the emerging doubts about the role of arms control as a part of U.S. security policy, and a deeply felt rejection of the Soviet system as a whole—all called for a (primarily domestically) credible military strategy. It is not by accident that the 1982 Defense Guidance calls for the United States to acquire forces that would make it possible to prevail in a prolonged nuclear war. In order to achieve this objective, a comprehensive effort was initiated:

> The Reagan administration . . . recognized several deficiencies in our force structure that hampered its [the policy of flexible nuclear options] implementation. Among the shortcomings were a vulnerable command and control structure, an increasingly vulnerable ICBM force, U.S. inferiority in prompt hard-target-kill capability, and an aging bomber force. In response, the president approved a comprehensive program to modernize our strategic forces. . . .[7]

Taking an overview of the strategic debate over the past thirty years in the United States, the following main traits can be discerned. First, in a world in which both the United States and the Soviet Union can inflict assured destruction upon one another, a defense policy based on MAD makes neither military nor political sense. It is both militarily and politically incredible. Second, to base defense policy upon flexible or selective nuclear options adds little military credibility. Since the fact of MAD exists, the possibility of uncontrollable escalation remains inescapable. Third, for domestic political reasons and as a definitive element of U.S.-Soviet relations, a policy of flexible nuclear options is nevertheless desirable, perhaps even necessary. In other words, at the political level (U.S. domestic and foreign), there are different identifiable levels of deterrence credibility despite the fact that there are no credible military options. Thus the search for nuclear options will continue out of political necessity. Options will be created to score

---

7. Nitze, "U.S. Strategic Force Structures," p. 1

political points or, if created by the Soviet Union, they will be matched in order to deny the Soviets the political benefits that are believed to derive from them.

Yet, as suggested earlier, at precisely the time when politically credible options were most needed, existing options had become highly questionable. The aforementioned threat to the survivability of the U.S. land-based intercontinental ballistic-missile force (ICBMs) became the single most important debating point of the U.S. defense community in the early 1980s.[8] For many analysts, ICBM vulnerability was said to undermine strategic stability. There are solid technical reasons for taking ICBM vulnerability seriously. Conventional wisdom holds that a strategic triad provides greater stability than a dyad. A triad complicates a possible Soviet decision to launch a surprise attack by a factor of three. In addition, a triad is a better hedge against Soviet technological breakthroughs in anti-submarine warfare. Yet the driving force behind ICBM vulnerability concerns was and is political. The president's Scowcroft Commission on Strategic Forces specifically addressed this problem in its April 1983 report:

> The overall military balance, including the nuclear balance, provides the backdrop for Soviet decisions about the manner in which they will try to advance their interests. This is central to our understanding of how to deter war, how to frustrate Soviet efforts at blackmail and how to deal with the Soviets' day-to-day conduct of international affairs.[9]

In support of the assessment, the Commission highlighted the fact that "more than half of the Soviet ICBMs—the SS-17, SS-18 and SS-19 missiles—have been deployed since the last U.S. ICBM was deployed."[10] And,

> the *overall perception* of strategic imbalance caused by the Soviets' ability to destroy hardened land-based targets—with more than 600 newly deployed SS-18 and SS-19 ICBMs—while the U.S. is clearly

---

8. Barry R. Schneider, Colin S. Gray and Keith B. Payne, eds., *Missiles for the Nineties* (Boulder: Westview Press, 1984); Jake Garn, J. I. Coffey, Lord Chalfont, Ellery B. Block, *The Future of U.S. Land-Based Strategic Forces* (Cambridge: Institute for Foreign Policy Analysis, 1980); *MX Missile Basing*, Congress of the United States, Office of Technology Assessment, September 1981.

9. *Report of the President's Commission on Strategic Forces*, Department of Defense, April 1983, p. 3.

10. Ibid., p. 4.

not able to do so with its existing ballistic missile force, has been reasonably regarded as destabilizing and as *a weakness in the overall fabric of deterrence.*[11]

Given the Commission's perception about the relationship between Soviet conduct and military power, the political need was imperative to redress the mainly political advantages that seemingly had accrued to the Soviet Union through its own increased military capability and the lack of a timely U.S. response.

The Commission's final report supported the deployment of a limited number of MX missiles in specially hardened Minuteman III silos as an interim measure but suggested a move towards a small, single-warhead ICBM the mobile-basing mode of which would go a long way towards reducing U.S. ICBM vulnerability. More generally, however, the Scowcroft Commission report was an affirmation of existing nuclear strategy and force posture. Its task had been to provide a comprehensive assessment of how existing nuclear options were to be maintained in light of advanced Soviet capabilities. Apart from its specific force-structure improvement proposals, the report's overriding political significance derives from the fact that the United States was seen to address the large-scale Soviet military buildup of the 1970s at the highest political level, sending an unambiguous signal of political resolve to the Soviet Union.

To a number of defense analysts, neither the Scowcroft report nor previous efforts to improve ICBM survivability and with it the maintenance of U.S. nuclear options appeared to achieve their objectives. Beginning in the late 1970s, parts of the U.S. defense community revived the concept of active defenses at the strategic level.[12] The reasons for this revival were as varied in background as were the participants in the debate. One can identify at least five distinct groups of defense analysts.

First, there were those whose interest in active defense stemmed from a profound dissatisfaction with the reality of mutual assured destruction. To them, nuclear weapons had fundamentally changed the nature and use of force in relations between states. The pursuit

---

11. Ibid., p. 13 (emphasis added).

12. William Schneider, Jr., Donald G. Brennan, William A. Davis, Jr. and Hans Ruhle, *U.S. Strategic Nuclear Policy and Ballistic Missile Defense: The 1980s and Beyond* (Cambridge: Institute for Foreign Policy Analysis, 1980).

of national security policy on the basis of and with vast arsenals of nuclear weapons was at best dangerous and at worst disastrous. The moral dilemma of threatening the destruction of an opponent's society could not be permanently accepted. An active defense against nuclear weapons would achieve two things. One, it would afford the protection of one's own society from nuclear attack, or at least make some form of damage limitation appear feasible; two, it would alleviate the moral burden of threatening the use of nuclear weapons. This dual appeal of active defenses as opposed to the mechanistic, no-choice prescriptions of MAD suggested a more responsible and morally more acceptable basis for national security planning.

Second, there were those primarily concerned with the issue of ICBM vulnerability. Without some form of ICBM protection, the rationale for land-based systems would very quickly erode, given Soviet advances in targeting accuracy. Moreover, this group was very concerned with the threat to crisis stability posed by vulnerable nuclear forces. If U.S. land-based systems could be targeted by the Soviets with a relatively minor part of their heavy ICBM arsenal, a U.S. president in time of crisis might be tempted to launch vulnerable ICBMs merely to avoid losing them. To this group, ICBM protection would afford both crisis stability and ICBM survivability for selective retaliation.

Third, another group showed interest in a revival of the ballistic missile defense debate primarily in order to maintain flexible nuclear options. While they were not unconcerned about crisis stability, the basic incentive for protecting ICBMs stemmed from a strong belief in deterrence credibility on the basis of options below an all-out strategic exchange. ICBM protection appeared to offer an ability to fine-tune existing options and a range of new targeting options.

Fourth, there were those who believed that active defenses could restore at least a degree of strategic superiority to the United States. Proponents of superiority do not subscribe to the cooperative element inherent in the reality of mutual assured destruction. Without defenses against nuclear weapons, the survival of the United States is dependent upon the rationality of Soviet leaders. In other words, U.S. security requires the cooperation of the Soviet Union. Active defenses could allow the United States to replace cooperative with unilateral security measures. Defense superiority would allow the United States to threaten the Soviet Union more credibly and in turn provide a greater degree of political maneuverability.

Fifth, active defenses appealed to those who have always felt that U.S. superiority is a prerequisite for extended deterrence. The vulnerability of the continental United States severely undermines the credibility of defense commitments abroad. To this group, strategic parity with the Soviet Union is no basis upon which credible alliance commitments should be made. Rather than continuing an arms race with offensive nuclear weapons, protection of at least U.S. retaliatory forces could make extended deterrence much more feasible.

To all these groups, a revival of the strategic defense debate was desirable, to some even imperative. Ballistic missile defenses offer distinct opportunities to each group. But the groups share a profound unilateralism in their approach to nuclear weapons, deterrence and security planning. Moreover, the arguments put forth by each group are dangerously one-sided, displaying an equally profound disregard for one another and possible Soviet responses.

Until the president's SDI speech in March 1983, the debate over active defenses was carried on mainly in professional journals, although it can be assumed that this debate stimulated attention and interest in BMD beyond scholarly circles. What is important to note is the fact that the BMD debate of the late 1970s was one of conceptual revival. There is little in the literature of that period which would suggest detailed analysis of BMD systems and their technical and operational requirements. Most analysts were concerned with making the case for active defenses as part of U.S. deterrence strategy rather than proposing feasible systems or political strategies for transition periods.[13] Retrospectively, it can be argued that this debate served to prepare the conceptual and intellectual grounds for the Strategic Defense Initiative of 1983.

Looking at the Strategic Defense Initiative within the context of an ongoing strategic debate, it is not surprising to discover that the concept of active defense is neither new, nor revolutionary nor particularly alien. The observation that it is not new goes beyond the obvious

---

13. General David Graham, *High Frontier: A Strategy for National Survival* (New York: Tom Doherty Associates, 1983). For a much more cautious approach to the conceptual and practical problems of BMD, see Ashton B. Carter and David N. Schwartz, eds., *Ballistic Missile Defense* (Washington, DC: The Brookings Institution, 1984). In the introduction, Ashton Carter explains the purpose of the study: "This volume aims to provide a comprehensive and unified treatment of the technical, strategic, and political aspects of ballistic missile defense, with an eye to offering the public and policy-makers a basis for discussion and analysis. It can serve as a guide or reference to a renewed national discussion of BMD. The book is not intended to promote any particular BMD policy and makes no recommendations."

similarities and parallels SDI has with the 1960s' ABM debate. Indeed, close examinations of the earlier ABM debate and the strategic environment within which it took place does not support the view that the 1972 ABM Treaty conclusively settled the question of BMD. The limits that defined the scope of the BMD debate then and throughout the 1970s were those of technology, not strategic wisdom. Neither is the Strategic Defense Initiative a revolutionary concept. While SDI has been severely criticized for strategic political and military reasons, this criticism alone does not testify to SDI's revolutionary implications. Whatever the different persuasions of SDI/BMD proponents, active strategic defenses are part and parcel of the strategic debate; the president merely increased their prominence within that debate.

Given the above-surveyed history of the strategic debate, it stands to reason that SDI has become but an important aspect of this broader debate. There is no substantial evidence in support of the strategic debate entering a relationship subordinate to SDI. Moreover, students of American government organization are fully conversant with the limitations of even the presidential office. The president can launch political initiatives, promise funds for their realization and canvass congressional and public support. It would be foolish to assume, however, that without support or even against outright opposition within the administration or Congress, presidential initiatives would flourish nonetheless. Quite the contrary. Presidential effectiveness crucially depends upon the president's ability to (1) make use of existing perceptions, (2) shape ongoing discussions, and (3) direct the future course of debate. For the purposes of this analysis, it is certain that the president's SDI speech found a fertile environment in Congress, the military and large sections of the defense industry, the strategic community and, of course, within his own administration.

Since the March 1983 speech, the president has been seen to successfully shape the SDI discussion. As previously discussed, by the early 1980s strategic deterrence based on offensive forces had drawn vociferous critics. Over thirty years of strategic debate had been unable to resolve the deterrence credibility dilemma and the inherent uncertainties pertaining to the controlled use of nuclear weapons. The Strategic Defense Initiative has drawn upon existing dissatisfactions; its technological promise has raised many different hopes among as many different intellectual communities. SDI's long-term objective of a perfect defense against ballistic missiles has forged a pro-SDI consensus across a wide political spectrum. Moreover, long-term objectives do not preclude short- and medium-term achievements, therefore increasing the possibility for the SDI consensus to remain stable over time. At present, with the research initiative being only vaguely defined regarding scope, technical requirements, and military capability, and even more vaguely spelled out as regards Soviet interests and countermeasures, SDI is able to accommodate and harmonize different strategic views.

Despite the shared dissatisfaction with deterrence among SDI proponents, dissatisfaction alone as the basis for a consensus on SDI is not likely to endure. Indeed, this consensus is likely to be broken apart by the very forces that originally forged it. SDI-related technology research will yield data that will determine the direction and scope of the initiative. What the initiative gains in definition, it is bound to lose in support. In order to maintain political support for as long as possible, the administration has focused on the 'less-than-perfect' defense objectives. These allow the administration to publicly continue with its stated goal of perfect defenses while meeting the far more specific requirements of its diverse groups of supporters.

The less-than-perfect defense objective is that of bolstering strategic deterrence. In his 1985 report to Congress, Secretary of Defense Caspar Weinberger stated that

> . . . advanced defensive technologies could offer the potential to enhance deterrence and to help prevent nuclear war by reducing significantly the military utility of Soviet preemptive attacks. . . . [14]

Similarly, in his 1986 *Annual Report,* he emphasized,

> Defenses that could deny to Soviet missiles the objectives of an attack, or deny to the Soviets confidence in the achievement of those objectives, would discourage them from even considering such an attack, and thus be a highly effective deterrent. [15]

And again, in the DOD 1987 *Annual Report:*

> . . . strategic defense represents a natural extension, the capstone of an array of changes in our strategic nuclear forces, motivated by the search for a more secure deterrent. [16]

---

14. Caspar W. Weinberger, Secretary of Defense, *Annual Report to the Congress, Fiscal Year 1985,* Department of Defense, February 1, 1984, p. 58.

15. Caspar W. Weinberger, Secretary of Defense, *Annual Report to the Congress, Fiscal Year 1986,* Department of Defense, February 4, 1985, p. 54.

16. Caspar W. Weinberger, Secretary of Defense, *Annual Report to the Congress, Fiscal Year 1987,* Department of Defense, February 5, 1986, p. 74.

The 1985 report to Congress by the Strategic Defense Initiative Organization (SDIO) office speaks of a "broader-based deterrence by turning to a greater reliance on defensive systems."[17] Former presidential science advisor George Keyworth, writing in April 1985, spelled out the medium-term SDI objectives:

> These would not necessarily be "leakproof" defenses, especially during early transition phases. But they do not have to be. In its initial implementation, it has only to negate the first-strike option to achieve a great leap in stability.[18]

On the surface, a comparison between SDI's lesser objectives with the original (and still ultimate) goal of an impenetrable shield appears to be reassuring to those who, given the choice, would opt for less rather than more defensive capability. The problem with the SDI-for-deterrence approach is not one of small defensive capability versus more comprehensive capability. Even a limited defensive capability pursued ostensibly for deterrence reasons could destabilize the U.S.-Soviet security relationship.

A limited capability against ballistic missiles is not well defined in the professional literature or in government documents. It can mean anything from a thin area defense to point defense or a combination of both. Most certainly, a limited defense capability would mean a mixed offense-defense force structure. No military planner would renege on his offensive forces for a less-than-perfect defensive system. At present, the administration's aim is to deter a preemptive Soviet missile attack through a layered defensive system. It is interesting to note that a layered defensive system, apart from its technical appeal, does not need to be explained in terms of U.S. ICBM defense. Destruction of missiles in their boost, post-boost and mid-course phases, that is, before their ultimate targets are known, does not require the administration to define SDI in terms of a point (ICBM) defense capability, a political asset that will undoubtedly help maintain a political SDI consensus for some time. Nevertheless, given the perceived vulnerability of U.S. ICBMs, the existing strategic debate and the medium-

---

17. Strategic Defense Initiative Organization, *Report to the Congress on the Strategic Defense Initiative*, Department of Defense, 1985, p. 7.

18. George A. Keyworth, "The Case for Arms Control and the Strategic Defense Initiative, *Arms Control Today* 15, No. 3 (April 1985), p. 2.

term aim to employ SDI technology to bolster deterrence, ICBM protection is a likely course of action.

The effectiveness of even a limited defensive system does not need to be high. For political reasons, however, it appears improbable to aim for an effectiveness of, say, 10 percent. Expenditures of $26 billion over five years, adding a mere 10 percent to Soviet preemptive-strike risk calculations, hardly seem worth the effort. Also, the Soviets would be able to overcome such a defense relatively easily. Thus, in order to maintain political support and to impact upon Soviet risk-taking assumptions, a defensive capability requires at least a 50-percent effectiveness, preferably more. Speaking for many SDI proponents, George Keyworth envisages a defense system 80-percent effective against Soviet countermeasures:

> For the sake of argument, even an 80-percent effective boost-phase defense would require an enormous—and enormously expensive—increase in the Soviet fleet. They would have to increase their booster fleet by a factor of five just to achieve the same number of warheads passing through merely the first layer of the defense. But added to that problem would be that they still would have no assurance of which warheads would get through—which means no assurance of which targets could be attacked. The Soviet's traditional preemptive strategy would simply be incompatible with such a boost-phase-dominated defense.[19]

Achieving 80-percent effectiveness is a tall order. Apart from the well-known technical problems associated with a layered defense system, how does one measure effectiveness of any degree? If deterrence fails, a 20-percent damage rate would still mean large-scale destruction and millions of casualties.

Yet the most serious problem of Keyworth's argument is that

> a mixed offense-defense posture designed to deprive the opponent of a first-strike capability is itself likely to look—in motivation and in capability—uncomfortably like a first-strike posture. This would be true, particularly, of a space-based ABM system, where the fragility and vulnerability of the space-based components would make them a poor reliance except in support of a preemptive strike.[20]

---

19. Ibid.

20. Sidney D. Drell, Philip J. Farley and David Holloway, *The Reagan Strategic Defense Initiative: A Technical, Political and Arms Control Assessment* (Stanford: Stanford University, July 1984), p. 69.

One may also want to add that the inherent instabilities of such a posture would probably be compounded by Soviet incentives to launch a preventive first strike. Placing the Soviets in a position in which they have to fear the loss of their retaliatory forces through a U.S. preemptive strike might make it imperative for them to act preventively. Rather than bolstering deterrence, such a posture would seriously undermine it. Moreover, a defense-based posture by the United States would be destabilizing long before a defense system would be judged effective by its planners. The Soviets have 75 percent of their nuclear forces based on land. That plus the conservative nature of military planning (which tends to attribute greater capability to the opponent's system than to one's own) makes a U.S. defense posture in the eyes of the Soviets much more threatening, irrespective of the actual defensive U.S. capability. While an offense-defense mix increases uncertainty in the minds of the Soviets as to the effectiveness of their forces, and the attainability of military objectives through the use of force is a classical argument of deterrence theory, the paramount objective of political and military planners must be that of nuclear war avoidance through the maintenance of strategic stability. No offense-defense mix that has thus far been proposed by SDI proponents promises more stability and therefore greater security than the existing deterrence system of offensive nuclear forces.

Another no less important problem arises from the basing mode of even a limited point defense. SDI limited to ICBM protection could still be space-based as far as some components such as sensors and mirrors are concerned. These are vulnerable unless they themselves are defended. Three problems arise. First, vulnerable space-based components are attractive targets and their vulnerability would be the same as that of the vulnerable ICBMs they are meant to protect. From a Soviet point of view, their only purpose would be one of supporting a first strike. Second, if space components are defended, the same system that defends them could most probably be used to disable Soviet early-warning and communication satellites. Again, the Soviets would be forced to use their nuclear forces early on, while they could still control and communicate with them. Third, what kind of BMD is it going to be? Could the technology used for point defense conceivably be upgraded for larger area defense? If the Soviets could not be assured of the limited capability of a U.S. defensive system, crisis stability would be threatened. As regards Soviet countermeasures to a U.S. BMD capability, they could probably offset some of these instabilities, but because each side would continue to regard the other's system as more capable than its own, instabilities would remain and could lead to an offense-defense arms race.

Technological and military strategic obstacles and uncertainties aside, the past four years have shown SDI to be an exercise in strategic unilateralism. Of course, it is true that the uncertainties surrounding SDI are directly related to the largely unknown technology that is being investigated. Yet unknown technology should not obscure the fact that an equal number of SDI uncertainties concern the political relationship between the United States and the Soviet Union. In the nuclear age generally and since a condition of strategic parity has emerged, U.S. security is not only relative with regard to the Soviet Union but directly dependent upon Soviet cooperation. SDI, however, was launched and has proceeded as though the Soviet Union did not exist. Although Soviet defensive activities have, since 1983, become a prominent rationale for pursuing a vigorous SDI program in the United States, little thought has been given to what SDI means from the Soviet point of view. Many scholars on the Soviet Union would agree with Stephen Meyer, who recently concluded an analysis of Soviet perceptions of SDI stating that

> an off-setting response to SDI is not sufficient; an emulating response
> is required as well. . . . Soviet military and political leaders do not
> see SDI as simply another military challenge or another spiral in the
> continuing nuclear arms competition where off-setting measures
> would suffice. Rather, SDI is seen as a profound technological chal-
> lenge.[21]

Since SDI has remained non-negotiable, there is presently no common understanding between the two superpowers on how to approach emerging defensive technology in the strategic field; how to introduce defense systems into an offense-dominated security framework without sacrificing stability; how to forestall an offense-defense arms race; how to amend the ABM Treaty; how to reduce offensive weapons on either side; and how to obtain a political framework within which these and other questions can be addressed.

After four years of SDI research, it is unlikely that defensive systems, whatever their degree of effectiveness short of total protection, will buy the United States more security from nuclear ballistic-missile attack than it enjoys today. This author agrees with the observation made by the Stanford Arms Control Group and many others that

---

21. Stephen M. Meyer, "Soviet Strategic Programmes and the U.S. SDI," *Survival* 27, No. 6 (November/December 1985), p. 275.

the only way to save lives from a nuclear exchange is to avoid nuclear war, by deterrence and other political and arms control measures to enhance stability and preserve peace. The prime test of ABM is how it supports such efforts—and that test is not favorable to ABM.[22]

It was argued in the introductory section that the past four years have given us a glimpse of the world beyond the ABM Treaty. The subsequent discussion of the evolution of U.S. strategic thinking showed that contrary to perceptions held by the general public, and even more informed politicians, a debate about the paradigms of deterrence has been going on for as long as nuclear weapons have existed. The issue of defense against nuclear weapons and, more specifically, against ballistic missile attack as a challenge to offensive deterrence strategies had not been resolved decisively at the conceptual level. In the late 1960s, that debate was merely shelved. Technology itself imposed limitations of feasibility and exposed conceptual pitfalls. The Strategic Defense Initiative suggests that both feasibility and conceptual developments warrant a reopening of the ABM case; the prospect of the 'ultimate technological fix' seems just over the horizon. In the late 1960s, however, the debate was also shelved because the possibility of MIRVing ballistic missiles so overwhelmingly negated opportunities provided by state-of-the-art defensive technologies. Now that MIRV technology is in place and has become sophisticated over the past ten years, the case for acquiring defensive capabilities appears more imperative, while, at the same time, there is no new offensive capability that could once again and unambiguously decide the case in favor of continued reliance on offensive nuclear weapons. Of course, there are various countermeasures the Soviet Union could employ to defeat an operational ABM system. But that will most likely not factor decisively in the American defense debate. The decisive fact is that the debate over defensive systems itself will remain open-ended and with us for the foreseeable future. What we are experiencing now is the debate we could not have in the late 1960s. This debate will reinforce existing uncertainties as to what role nuclear weapons play, should play and can play in our thinking about international security. SDI and the BMD issue epitomize the inherent conceptual tensions of the nuclear age. What is deterrence? How does it work? Perhaps even more important for future considerations, SDI and BMD challenge the cooperative logic

---

22. Drell, Farley and Holloway, *The Reagan Strategic Defense Initiative*, p. 69.

of the nuclear age, which postulates security *interdependence* with the adversary, irrespective of unilateral additions to existing force stockpiles.

The world beyond the ABM Treaty, then, is one of profound conceptual uncertainty, able to give only little guidance to policy-makers. It is unlikely that technology will resolve this debate, either through its success or failure. The only opportunity to address and perhaps resolve the uncertainties of the defense debate is in the political field. The cooperative logic of nuclear weapons demands a cooperative relationship between the United States and the Soviet Union. Nuclear parity has established a cooperative relationship in the military field. Mutual vulnerability has made the security of one dependent upon the rational cooperation of the other. The BMD issue challenges both mutual vulnerability and the cooperative implications of nuclear parity. What is required is a cooperative relationship at the political level that takes account of the military reality and reinforces it through policy. Both the United States and the Soviet Union are a considerable way away from working towards such an understanding.

The Reykjavik summit could have provided an opportunity for both superpowers to clarify their conceptual concerns about the future of the deterrence relationship and to explore policy options for nuclear arms control. In the event, the meeting at Reykjavik was concluded with none of the issues sufficiently resolved to serve as a stepping-stone for the arms control teams at Geneva. While no one really expected any major breakthroughs from the Reagan-Gorbachev exchange, it was nevertheless widely assumed that a meeting between the two leaders would yield an accord based on mutually desirable progress in the talks on strategic and intermediate nuclear weapons. What emerged after Reykjavik was that far-reaching and comprehensive arms control proposals had indeed been discussed, only to founder on disagreements over what kinds of SDI-related testing the United States would be allowed to undertake during a ten-year SDI deployment postponement offered by the president.

At first sight, it seemed that SDI had once again been the stumbling block for agreeing on decisive cuts in offensive nuclear forces. A closer look, however, reveals that the SDI issue prevented nothing short of the abandonment of nuclear deterrence as we know it. At Reykjavik, the president proposed the elimination of all ballistic missiles within ten years. Gorbachev went one step further and suggested the elimination of all strategic forces. Given the Soviet nuclear force structure, elimination of ballistic missiles alone would have left the increasingly formidable U.S. bomber and cruise missile forces untouched. In suggesting total elimination of strategic forces, Gorbachev wanted to offset possible U.S. advantages. Gorbachev also proposed a withdrawal of all Soviet SS-20s for the removal of all U.S. European-based Pershing IIs and cruise missiles. Everything Gorbachev offered, however, hinged upon an agreement on SDI acceptable to the Soviets. The president refused.[23] After claims and counterclaims by both sides as to what had and had not been achieved at Reykjavik subsided, it appeared that President Reagan had been ready at Reykjavik to accept Gorbachev's nuclear arms elimination proposals and that SDI had been the only major obstacle to agreement.

Ballistic missiles and other strategic nuclear forces have been the bedrock of U.S. and NATO deterrence strategy for a number of decades. As was previously discussed, nuclear weapons as part of one's military strategy raise questions about military and political credibility. Yet both the massive retaliation *and* the nuclear options proponents rely upon ballistic missiles to carry out retaliatory missions, be they on a massive scale or limited to selective strikes. Elimination of ballistic missiles would shift the burden of deterrence to nuclear bombers and cruise missiles. Although technological advances in both fields have been made, neither bombers nor cruise missiles match the combined effectiveness of speed, accuracy and penetration available only with ballistic missiles. Technical problems of weapons systems aside, getting rid of ballistic missiles would severely limit the ability of the United States to extend a security guarantee to its European allies. Thus far, questions about the credibility of extended deterrence have revolved around the problem of the U.S. political commitment to the alliance's principle of risk-sharing. In the absence of ballistic missiles, the United States would be unable, not unwilling, to provide an alliance with a security embrace. Should the elimination of ballistic missiles go hand in hand with the withdrawal of INF forces from Europe, as envisaged at Reykjavik, Europe's decoupling from the United States would be complete. NATO Europe would be faced with the Warsaw Pact's conventional threat.[24] Under such circumstances,

---

23. "New U.S. Orders For Arms Talks: Focus on Missiles," *The International Herald Tribune*, October 29, 1986, pp. 1–2; "Reagan Shifts on Missiles," *The International Herald Tribune*, November 11, 1986, pp. 1, 7.

24. "After Reykjavik, Transatlantic Strains Will Grow," *International Herald Tribune*, November 4, 1986, p. 4.

it would also be difficult to argue that the American public would continue to allow the stationing of U.S. troops in Europe. Currently U.S. troops in Europe, particularly in Germany, are the visible symbol of the U.S. defense commitment. Elimination of ballistic missiles could very quickly redefine their role from symbolic to that of sitting ducks.

Abandonment of ballistic missiles also raises the problem of persuading third countries of the wisdom of this action. China, Britain and France rely heavily on ballistic missiles for their national deterrent forces. Since the United States has not been able to persuade Britain and France to relinquish their nuclear forces while the U.S. nuclear umbrella is still in place, it seems unlikely that the United States would be more successful once the United States itself has eliminated its own ballistic missiles. Britain and France would more than ever feel the need to maintain their national deterrents.

If little else, Reykjavik showed the vulnerability of deterrence in both the offensive and defensive area. If active defense against nuclear attack leads to an offense-defense arms race, crisis instability, preemption and the militarization of space, elimination of ballistic missiles raises the equally undesirable specters of European decoupling and the assured incredibility of NATO strategy. Also, the SDI issue prevented, for the time being, the latter from becoming fact. As Charles Krauthammer of *The Washington Post* observed, "lucky nothing was signed."[25]

At present, U.S. and Soviet negotiating teams at Geneva are discussing a 50-percent cut in strategic forces over a five-year period. There are still grave differences over sublimits, particularly with respect to the number of warheads carried by Soviet heavy strategic missiles. It has, however, become apparent that the United States has modified its arms control position since Reykjavik. When the British prime minister visited Washington in November 1986, President Reagan did not mention an abandonment of ballistic missiles within ten years. Instead, he emphasized the 50-percent cut in strategic forces, spoke of "sweeping" reductions in INF and of "addressing" the conventional force imbalances.[26] At the same time, however, the United States has maintained that its Reykjavik proposals are still on the table at Geneva,

25. "Poker Game at Reykjavik: Lucky Nothing Was Signed," *International Herald Tribune*, October 18/19, 1986, p. 5.

26. *International Herald Tribune*, November 11, 1986.

this despite strong European, congressional and military concerns, especially by European NATO commanders and the U.S. Joint Chiefs of Staff. Not surprisingly, this "dual track" approach by the U.S. administration has caused some confusion as to what the ultimate objective of U.S. arms control policy really is.

This confusion is exacerbated by renewed pressure from the Pentagon towards an early presidential decision on SDI deployment. Perhaps fearing a perpetual SDI research phase limbo, Secretary Weinberger has been actively campaigning for a positive decision on first-phase SDI deployment. It is unclear how this effort relates to the president's Reykjavik offer of a ten-year SDI deployment deferral and concomitant adherence to the ABM Treaty; there are obvious conflicts between the two objectives.[27]

In retrospect, the Reykjavik experience epitomizes the profound lack of political purpose that has characterized so much of this administration's approach to the Soviet Union, arms control and the NATO alliance. Nuclear strategy poses serious intellectual and practical problems that require careful deliberation and policy planning. An unimpeded arms race can be as dangerous as a hasty decision to abandon nuclear ballistic missiles. Security should not be likened to a game of poker where the stakes of more arms or fewer arms are raised according to short-term political benefits. Reykjavik will undoubtedly provide food for thought to both nuclear disarmers and nuclear strategists.

Part II: The European Context

The issues pertaining to SDI and ballistic missile defense could also provide an opportunity for the NATO alliance to integrate the defense debates on both sides of the Atlantic. The U.S. strategic debate generally has taken little account of West European security perceptions and their development. The conceptual problems of extended deterrence derive from the more general uncertainties of deterrence credibility; little conceptual attention has been given to the European security environment and the way extended deterrence has shaped European

---

27. "What Is SDI Policy?" *The Washington Post*, reprinted in *International Herald Tribune*, January 19, 1987, p. 8; "Reagan Aides Split Over Star Wars Deployment," *The Guardian*, January 24, 1987, p. 5; "U.S. May Decide Soon When to Deploy SDI," *International Herald Tribune*, January 24/25, 1987, p. 2.

perceptions about war, deterrence credibility and political relations with the Soviet Union and Eastern Europe. SDI and BMD go to the heart of extended deterrence and the political-military framework it has created.

It was argued in the previous section that the U.S. quest for a credible nuclear strategy has failed while the political reasons and motives for continuing this quest have persisted and seemingly gained in importance, particularly in light of strategic nuclear parity between the United States and the Soviet Union. In the context of that discussion, SDI and BMD generally were explained as an attempt on the part of the United States to enforce the credibility of the existing nuclear strategy. At the political level, SDI deals with the moral dilemmas of nuclear retaliation and invokes visions of obsolescent nuclear forces. At the military level, SDI is an evolutionary step in U.S. thinking about nuclear weapons and deterrence credibility. SDI is meant to preserve the orthodoxy of nuclear thinking, not to transform it. Most important, however, the above discussion showed that the existing orthodoxy is beset with serious flaws. Despite the fact that they are largely recognized by those who uphold orthodox thinking, it seems almost impossible to rectify these flaws. Whether one big bluff or a succession of smaller ones, a strategy that includes the ultimate use of nuclear weapons in whatever shape or form is destined to be flawed. Despite the persuasive logic of nuclear deterrence theory, the reality of mutual assured destruction has turned the logic of theory into real-life mockery.

If a theory is flawed in its basic assumptions about the framework within which it is meant to guide policy and predict policy responses, it is reasonable to deduce that theoretical concepts derived from it are similarly questionable. If such is the case, an analysis of the relevance to European security of the characteristics of the nuclear age and of orthodox deterrence thinking raises two very important questions. One, are the basic flaws of nuclear strategy inherent also in the concept of extended deterrence? And, if this is the case, what military and political measures (if any) have been taken in order to reduce or offset the conceptual and practical problems of extended deterrence?

It is well known that the purpose of extended deterrence is to apply the same criteria of assessment to the security of West European territory as apply to the continental United States. Since there have been shown to exist profound problems with integrating nuclear weapons into military strategy per se, irrespective of the extension of territory such a strategy intends to safeguard, the concept of extended deterrence does not lose credibility on grounds of territorial size. In this sense, the security of Western Europe is not threatened or undermined by the physical separation of the United States from its NATO allies. Rather, it is the nuclear part of NATO strategy that continues to raise doubts as to the wisdom of an ultimately nuclear response to Warsaw Pact aggression. This interpretation of extended-deterrence credibility differs in important respects from conventional wisdom. The latter maintains that the credibility of extended deterrence rests primarily with the political commitment on the part of the United States to defend Western Europe with nuclear weapons and that it is first and foremost the uncertainty of this commitment which raises questions of deterrence credibility. It is argued here, however, that the problem of deterrence credibility is of a different nature and in the longer term perhaps an even more durable one.

The defense of Western Europe with nuclear weapons or the threat of nuclear retaliation makes as little sense in a European theater as it does in a purely U.S.-Soviet strategic context. It suffers from the same pitfalls as the deterrence theory that informs it. Extended deterrence policy is therefore not less credible than central or primary deterrence but equally incredible. Repeated political commitments to the nuclear defense of Europe both attest to a persistent unease about the ultimate implication of policy implementation and obfuscate the fact that the military logic of extended deterrence is not negated through political pronouncements.

If a strategy of extended deterrence is as much a myth as nuclear strategy itself, why is so much intellectual and political energy spent to make it appear less so?

From a U.S. point of view, Western Europe presents as much a testing ground for the validity of strategic theory as a constant reminder of the imperfectibility of that theory. In the former case, Western Europe is part of the U.S. desire to rationalize and legitimize the theory of military options. Compared to an attack on the continental United States, Europe *is* the lesser contingency. Moreover, the structure of NATO forces in Europe is composed of nuclear *and* conventional elements providing a greatly more differentiated spectrum of options. Indeed, it can be argued that since the inception of NATO, conventional forces have had the function of dealing and coping with the flaws of a primarily nuclear-based strategy. Thus, conventional forces fulfill two roles. On the one hand, they are part and parcel of a spectrum of military options. On the other hand, and most important, conventional forces lend legitimacy to what might otherwise appear a strategy of little credibility. Conventional forces, then, also have a demonstrative function. They need to display operational readiness and combat effectiveness. If that can be achieved, a demonstrable ability to fight at the conventional level is believed to enhance the credibility of the nuclear threat. Witness, for example, the recurring debates over nuclear first use, the nuclear threshold, the 1960s debate over flexible response and the present one over emerging technologies. In each instance, the debate has been about doubts regarding the nuclear part of NATO strategy and in each case these doubts are addressed through measures in the conventional field. Since these debates are usually resolved with calls for an increase in NATO's conventional capabilities, this also suggests that with an increasing loss of confidence in nuclear strategy, conventional forces will more and more come to be seen not as the avant garde but as the main keepers of alliance defense strategy. Indeed, recent years have seen an emerging trend towards increasing conventional options. From what used to be a simple holding pattern along the intra-German border, NATO's conventional strategy has begun to emphasize mobility and maneuverability, long-range interdiction and offensive counter-air operations. Should this trend continue, and it may well do so, conventional forces could, instead of enhancing the nuclear threat, enhance themselves.

Eventually, developments of this kind are likely to jeopardize the very connection between nuclear and conventional responses to attack they are meant to preserve. At some point in the future, conventional forces, because of their own increased capability, will lose their ability to enforce the nuclear threat; instead, they will make the nuclear threat less probable. Should this possibility concern politicians and military planners? The answer to this question is entirely dependent upon one's assessment of the need for a nuclear/conventional force mix and the level of credibility one wants to achieve. Without necessarily supporting the view that there is a direct relationship between conventional force increases and a doctrinal shift towards acquiring a conventional warfighting capability, the possibility that such a relationship exists demands careful observation of the implications of more capable conventional forces for NATO strategy.

What emerges from the above considerations is the vital role of conventional forces in maintaining at least a semblance of nuclear credibility. If NATO were a purely military alliance, relying entirely upon the military credibility of its defense strategy, it is doubtful whether the alliance would have lived as long as it has. NATO's military strategy is flawed for the same reasons that have plagued U.S. defense planners for many years: if deterrence fails and war breaks out, NATO is faced with implementing a primarily nuclear strategy. What has held the alliance together despite the problems of strategy is an orthodoxy of deterrence thinking that is entirely different on either side of the Atlantic. Although extended deterrence for Europe is as flawed as central deterrence is for the United States, West Europeans have interpreted the relevance of these flaws to their security very differently than has the United States. In other words, the flaws of nuclear strategy matter differently on different sides of the Atlantic. Threatening the use of nuclear weapons to deter the outbreak of war in Europe is a mere option to the United States but is, to most West Europeans, the mainstay of their security. What the history of NATO has borne witness to is a tug-of-war between the United States and Western Europe over what each believes best serves its own security interests. When West Europeans emphasize the risk of nuclear escalation, they are in fact subscribing to the threat of massive retaliation. In other words, Western Europe threatens the ultimate response for the smallest contingency—a concept the United States has been trying to improve on, if not abandon, since the late 1950s. How can this threat by NATO be credible? The answer is quite simple: since no one knows how to fight a nuclear war, inadvertent, if not deliberate (although NATO threatens that, too) nuclear escalation is always a possible outcome once war has been initiated. As long as Europe remains a peacetime strategem and a wartime spoil for the superpowers, its security rests on the same stable (or unstable) ground as that of the United States or the Soviet Union. Measures taken by NATO in the doctrinal field or that of weapons acquisition serve mainly two political purposes: one, to maintain alliance political cohesiveness, and, two, to counter increasing Warsaw Pact capabilities in Europe. Both have as their ultimate objective the prevention of the Soviet intimidation of Western Europe. In pursuit of this dual objective, NATO has not been consistently successful. An appreciation of the obstacles to alliance cohesion vis-à-vis the Warsaw Pact requires a brief historical review.

Despite the countless political and military problems that NATO has encountered over the course of its thirty-seven-year history, the alliance has shown itself remarkably resilient to even minor challenges. Considering NATO's structural framework, it has remained essentially unchanged. Although Britain and France have acquired a nuclear capability of their own, neither has had reasons compelling enough to seriously consider leaving the alliance. The country other NATO members were most anxious to contain was West Germany. The Federal Republic has developed from a minor political actor to NATO's most important European member, militarily the most powerful U.S.

ally in Europe. West Germany has not acquired nuclear weapons but has rather used the political-military strength of the alliance as a whole to develop a consistent policy towards the West and, more recently, towards the East. NATO strategy has remained defensive both in posture and force structure. The United States has maintained its control over nuclear weapons stationed in Europe as part of NATO's deterrence strategy. Non-nuclear European members have desisted from reforming the nuclear control arrangement and release procedures.

Maintaining NATO's static structure yet adapting NATO policy that derives from it to a dynamic security environment has not been an easy task for West Europeans. Yet it is reasonable to argue that from a West European point of view most major and minor challenges have been those that have emerged from an intra-alliance context. The 1970s have shown that Western Europe has emerged from the postwar era of economic recovery and lack of political self-confidence as an economically and politically important and influential actor in international affairs. The fact that West European countries do not always manage to act in unison should not be misunderstood as a sign of collective weakness but as a factor of individual strength. Indeed, they have rediscovered 'the national interest' as an indispensable component of foreign and domestic policy-making. While Western Europe has gained political and economic strength, its lack of an indigenous European security policy has been perpetuated. What is different now from the situation in the late 1960s and early 1970s is the fact that security dependence upon the United States is more pronounced, precisely because security is the only field in which Western Europe has remained in, and is constantly reminded of, its junior position in the alliance. Despite this, however, economic and political strength has given Western Europe as a whole and individual countries a degree of political room of maneuver they did not previously possess. Not only are West Europeans now much more able to distinguish between alliance interests and individual national interests, they are also much more ready to do so. Without doubt, European recovery has changed the power relationship within the alliance in favor of Europe. West Europeans, governments and publics alike, are far more critical of the alliance and its leading member than they used to be; they have also developed a more differentiated attitude to the global aspects of U.S. power and their own limited regional security concerns.

West Europeans and Americans have not found it easy to come to terms with their evolving positions vis-à-vis each other. Americans find it difficult to recognize the emerging limitations to their influences within the alliance and West Europeans are plagued by uncertainties as to the nature of political responsibility that accompanies their increased status inside and outside the alliance. Because of this, recent years have witnessed seemingly unnecessary policy divergences between the United States and its European allies. They might have been unnecessary but certainly not without import. Students of Atlantic relations are familiar with the different assessments on either side of the Atlantic of such events as the crisis in Poland, or the European-Soviet gas-pipeline deal, U.S. policy towards Central America and West European reluctance to impose economic sanctions in support of U.S. foreign policy generally. Each case—and there are many other such instances—warrants close analysis in its own right. What is important here, though, is the recognition of an emerging political trend in Europe toward the Europeanization of the Atlantic alliance.

During the early years of the alliance, when Atlanticism carried the day in so many European-American debates, a West European point of view was seen by the West Europeans themselves as harmful to the cohesion of the alliance. France's partial withdrawal from NATO provided the proverbial exception to the rule. Now, with West European political commitment to the alliance well established and particularly with successful West German integration into Western Europe, membership alone is no longer the all-informing basis of foreign policy. West Europeans want to make the alliance serve their individual national and collective European interests as well. They have begun to understand that a passive security dependence upon the United States may not serve their interests as well as a more active involvement in the formulation of alliance policy.

Ongoing disagreements in the alliance are signs of Western Europe and the United States trying to find a new balance of power within their relationships. Debates are heated and often divisive but the majority of elite- and public-opinion polls display a strong commitment to the alliance. West Europeans have made a number of attempts to give expression to their increasing desire for greater political input in the alliance. The revival of the Western European Union, the closeness of Franco-German military relations and European multilateral defense cooperation serve as examples. Yet in attempting to redefine Western Europe's role in the alliance, Europeans face two challenges. One, while increasing their own influence, they only want to reduce the scope of U.S. influence, not its effect on the maintenance of European security. Two, they do not want to increase Soviet political leverage towards Western Europe by exploiting political disagreement in the alliance. Both are formidable tasks and their political management by the West Europeans will reveal whether Europeanization of the alliance can be more than a zero-sum game.

In their endeavor to shape U.S. policy in the alliance towards European interests, West Europeans are not only tasked to cope with an uncertain future but also with their own past ignorance of security matters. This ignorance is only partially self-inflicted. Europe has had little incentive to engage in discussions of strategic policy, the military role of nuclear weapons and military responses should deterrence fail. At the conceptual level, deterrence has always been understood in Western Europe as an absolute concept. It either works or it does not. There is no room for a degree or a measure of deterrence. Deterrence cannot fail partially—only totally. Such European thinking has remained unchanged since the 1950s. War avoidance of any kind through the threat of escalation to the strategic nuclear level has been the key to West European understanding of deterrence.

West Europeans do not share U.S. credibility concerns over nuclear strategy. They do not believe in the need for nuclear options for political or military reasons. If they did, they would undermine their own understanding of deterrence. First, subscribing to the view that nuclear options are essential for maintaining central deterrence *and* extended deterrence would raise the specter of limited nuclear war, possibly fought in Europe. Second, anything that diverts from the horrors of nuclear war could make the fighting of war appear a plausible military option.

West Europeans have not, however, been insensitive to U.S. concerns over deterrence credibility, a fact that is best illustrated by their acceptance of the flexible response strategy in 1967. Moreover, it was the West Europeans who in the late 1950s and early 1960s asked for the stationing of U.S. nuclear weapons in Europe as a visible symbol of U.S. commitment. Similar reasoning was behind former West German Chancellor Helmut Schmidt's address to the London International Institute for Strategic Studies in 1977. Yet fundamental differences in the understanding of how deterrence works have remained and are unlikely to change. For deterrence purposes, West Europeans rely on the uncertainties pertaining to the use of force in the nuclear age. Deterrence is maintained not because of elaborate theories of nuclear options, escalation control and targeting accuracy but because of the inherent uncertainties nuclear weapons have created in a potential aggressor's risk assessment. The earlier discussion of MAD, however, has shown that the responsibility of possessing nuclear weapons coupled with a competitive relationship with the Soviet Union gave rise to grave concern among many as to how both nuclear weapons and the Soviet Union should be handled. MAD alone seemed to take account of the destructive power of nuclear weapons but did little to inform the U.S.-Soviet competition. Nuclear options, on the other hand, reflect this competition much more accurately—with nuclear weapons the units of political exchange. Yet strategic nuclear flexibility denies the reality of MAD by seemingly reintroducing the classical, pre-nuclear concepts of warfighting, making nuclear weapons appear usable.

There is a certain irony in this. For forty years the United States has been searching for a militarily credible nuclear strategy. What it has come up with is a strategy that is militarily incredible but politically necessary in order to counter Soviet capabilities which are believed to provide the Soviets with opportunities for nuclear blackmail in times of crisis and instruments of intimidation in times of peace. To the United States, this understanding of deterrence and nuclear strategy is imperative *despite and because of* the MAD reality and nuclear parity. In the former case, taking account of the MAD and nuclear parity implications would spell the end of nuclear strategy and imply unilateral disarmament. Yet the realities of MAD and nuclear parity do exist. In the latter case, therefore, the concept of nuclear options does take account of the enormity of the mutual threat. In other words, because the reality of MAD is recognized and solutions to it at either end of the spectrum (unilateral disarmament/assured destruction) are not feasible, the strategy of nuclear options needs to be maintained to salvage at least the political benefits and opportunities that accrue from a nuclear options strategy. Indeed, SDI is meant to achieve precisely that. If Americans are the strategic pragmatists who grapple with the challenges of the nuclear age, their competitive relationship with the Soviet Union, a flawed strategic doctrine and defense commitments abroad, West Europeans are the theoretical purists. With their emphasis on inadvertent nuclear escalation as the all-informing principle of deterrence, they adhere more closely to the dictates of nuclear reality than do Americans. Where Americans want to introduce certainty of response to attack into the minds of the Soviets, West Europeans are less ambitious, relying on the inherent uncertainties of nuclear use.

These seemingly divergent approaches have caused friction within the alliance but, as discussed earlier, the acquisition of a range of conventional and nuclear capabilities has allowed NATO to patch up strategy whenever nuclear orthodoxy on either side of the Atlantic became subject to criticism. In other words, the alliance was able to compromise between divergent views on force levels and the conventional/nuclear mix. The Strategic Defense Initiative has the potential to challenge both the West European deterrence orthodoxy and in turn NATO's ability to innovate the alliance through a redefinition of the compromise. Moreover, SDI could bring about the first real test of extended deterrence because, unlike previous force adjustments, SDI would expose the flaws of NATO orthodoxy beyond repair.

Since the reintroduction of the ballistic missile defense issue into alliance affairs, West Europeans have been at odds with one another and with the U.S. government as to what SDI is, how it would affect Europe and what role Europe should play in this initiative. The way SDI has been approached and discussed in Europe clearly illustrates a less than full appreciation of the U.S. strategic debate, a misreading of the reasons that have led to the emergence of SDI, and a consequent underestimation of the issue's staying power.

In 1983-1984, SDI seemed to many West Europeans a mere replay of the earlier ABM debate in the late 1960s. Once again they were concerned about the linkages between U.S. and West European deterrence and the maintenance of the flexible response strategy. Despite apparent similarities, there were, however, important differences that began to emerge in early 1985. As discussed above, over the past fifteen years the alliance has matured, although its structure has remained essentially unchanged. European interest in East-West relations has increased and some countries, notably West Germany, have developed sizable stakes in an improved European East-West dialogue. Arms control, too, has expanded its scope to include nuclear weapons stationed in Europe, previously referred to as grey-area weapons since arms control negotiations between the United States and the Soviet Union did not address them. When NATO took the decision in December 1979 to deploy intermediate-range nuclear weapons and to pursue arms control negotiations with the Soviet Union in the hope of making INF deployments unnecessary, a large arms control constituency had already developed in Western Europe. It was important to Europeans to implement the prescriptions of the 1969 Harmel Report on defense and detente. The reasoning of the Harmel Report is truly European. It accepts the Soviet military challenge, is willing to respond to it by military means (i.e., force modernization, rearmament), but it also highlights the political context within which military activity must take place. The arms control part of the 1979 decision was meant to provide this political environment. The fact that it fell victim to the general deterioration of East-West relations should not detract from the deeply held European view that military measures alone will not improve East-West relations.

To both the United States and its West European allies, INF proved a painful and divisive experience. The old and trusted bargain of stationing U.S. missiles in Europe as a visible sign of U.S. defense commitment lost a great deal of popular support within and outside of West European governments. Nuclear weapons and particularly additions to existing stockpiles came to be seen as obstacles to halting the arms race and improving East-West relations, particularly at a time when the military relationship with the Soviet Union appeared to take a dominant role in U.S. assessments of the strategic balance. In order to maintain extended deterrence, the West Europeans had asked for INF but subsequent developments made INF deployments seem a high price to pay.

Beyond the immediate political INF experience, thoroughly analyzed elsewhere,[28] INF was an educational experience for Western Europe. It highlighted Western Europe's security dependence on the United States not only in the traditional military form but also in the political field. If there is no political relationship between the two superpowers, European security dependence becomes more pronounced and European foreign policies can improve East-West conduct only at the margins. Neither situation is satisfactory to Europeans; both command little public support.

Retrospectively, however, the European INF debate sparked off a sustained process of self-education in strategic affairs. What used to be a mere handful of European defense experts has increased substantially. Particularly in West Germany, where for historical reasons defense studies had resembled an intellectual taboo, the number of people inside and outside government concerning themselves professionally with defense issues has grown. Without question, this is a long-term process.

The present European SDI debate reflects this. It comes as no surprise that only recently West Europeans have begun to understand that SDI is a defense program, not a technology program, and that the concept of a population-protecting shield has undergone a major transformation.[29] Prior to this, the technological aspects of SDI had

---

28. For a cogent summary of the post-INF political atmosphere in Europe see Stephen F. Szabo, "European Opinion after the Missiles," *Survival* 27, No. 6 (November/December 1985), pp. 265–273.

29. Robert Held, "SDI bereits im Wandel," *Frankfurter Allgemeine Zeitung*, March 8, 1986, p. 12.

more often than not dominated the debate. This in turn was also due to an overly formal invitation extended to the Europeans for industrial participation in SDI. The invitation gave SDI a far greater political profile than many European politicians were willing to concede. In early 1985 British Foreign Secretary Geoffrey Howe and German Foreign Minister Hans-Dietrich Genscher voiced strong reservations as to the political wisdom of an accelerated ballistic missile defense effort and cautioned against the immediate attraction of technological spinoffs.[30] Since then, both countries have agreed to industrial participation in SDI and regulations on the transfer of technology. Both countries are also aware that despite their emphasis on industrial SDI issues, their signature in an SDI-related agreement can only be seen as an implied if not outright endorsement of the Strategic Defense Initiative. The fact that then Defense Secretary Michael Heseltine for the United Kingdom and Minister for Economics Martin Bangemann for West Germany signed the agreements was a weak excuse for a political signal intended to indicate less than full political support.

Unlike the INF debate, which spurred mass demonstrations in European capitals, the SDI debate has remained a debate among experts. For the time being, the peace movement, like other mass movements before it, has run out of steam. Time will tell if SDI has as great a potential for public mobilization as did INF. While SDI remains as vaguely defined as it is at present, leaders of the peace movement will find it difficult to sustain an anti-SDI momentum. A possible relationship between a narrowing of the U.S. SDI purpose and popular response in Europe will, however, be interesting to observe.

Putting the West European SDI debate in perspective, the following main traits can be discerned. First, given the divisive experience of INF, West European leaders have been reluctant to permit SDI to become the next controversial alliance issue. Rather than repeating the INF debate, West European governments, particularly Britain and West Germany, are interested in reestablishing alliance consensus rather than nurturing old wounds. Second, governement criticism has focused on the uncertainty that SDI might introduce into the strategic relationship and its impact on European East-West relations. Third, they have been hesitant to engage in speculation as to what their position would be should the research initiative lead the United

---

30. British Information Service, *Policy Statements*, 6/85 (March 15, 1985); German Information Center, *Statements and Speeches*, VII, No. 12 (April 22, 1985). (See Appendix.)

States to development and perhaps even deployment consideration. They have repeatedly emphasized that they regard BMD research as a prudent hedge against a possible Soviet creep-out or breakout of the ABM Treaty, but have equally strongly called for cooperative U.S.-Soviet measures to prevent an arms race in space. Fourth, while there are substantial misgivings about strategic defenses, it does appear that for the time being the desire to maintain alliance consensus has been Europe's first priority.

Much has been written on a large variety of European security scenarios. All are highly speculative. No one knows for certain why Europe has been at peace since 1945 and why there has not been a conventional or nuclear war. Perhaps the awesomeness of nuclear power has imposed the kinds of constraints upon state behavior many people think it has; perhaps the Soviet Union or the United States has not had a sufficiently persuasive reason to override these constraints and go to war nonetheless. Whichever applies, and the truth probably lies somewhere in between, the flaws in NATO orthodoxy have not undermined the very precisely defined 'security essentials' of the Europeans. Again it must be stressed that these 'security essentials' have the primarily political functions of reminding the Soviet Union of the risks of aggression, the U.S. defense commitment to Europe and NATO's peacetime cohesiveness. These 'security essentials'[31] are:

1. The principle of equal risk: the alliance cannot tolerate different regions of vulnerability.

2. The principle of forward defense, that is, the defense of West European territory at the intra-German border. Defense in depth is neither geographically possible nor militarily sustainable.

3. The principle of nuclear first use, that is, the threat to use nuclear weapons first, both to offset possible conventional defeat and to enhance deterrence.

4. The principle of nuclear escalation to the strategic level, that is, the commitment by the United States to translate the strategic relationship between itself and the Soviet Union into a regional European security concept.

---

31. These "security essentials" are more fully discussed in K.-Peter Stratmann, "Strengthening NATO's Deterrence in the 1980s," in Uwe Nerlich and James A. Thompson, eds., *The Soviet Problem in American-German Relations* (New York: Crane Russak, 1985), pp. 273–305, especially pp. 295–298.

Since there is a strong linkage between these principles, by undermining one, BMD would automatically threaten the viability of the other three. The likely introduction of defensive systems into the strategic offense-dominated deterrence structure must be very carefully considered if instabilities are to be avoided.

Strategic instabilities, whether caused by offensive or defensive deployment, affect Europe. Of more immediate concern at present are the consequences of U.S. BMD deployment for those parts of NATO strategy that apply to Europe. If pursued unilaterally by the United States, that is, without an agreed U.S.-Soviet framework on whether and how BMD could be introduced, different zones of alliance security would be created. NATO's nuclear first-use option, without the threat of escalation, would not be credible and might mean a limited nuclear war in Europe. Moreover, Western Europe would then have to rely much more on real conventional deterrence, a concept questioned by many, given NATO's conventional inferiority. Increasing NATO's conventional capability is even now difficult to achieve. But even if NATO were able to afford conventional forces that could defeat a Warsaw Pact attack, this capability would fundamentally alter NATO's defensive posture. NATO would need to acquire a conventional warfighting strategy and the clock would be turned back to where it was in the pre-nuclear 1930s. Generally speaking, West Europeans have approached the issue of ballistic missile defense in exactly the same way they have dealt with challenges to their deterrence orthodoxy in the past. Then, recourse was taken in the conventional and nuclear fields either through increased numbers of U.S. nuclear weapons stationed in Europe or expanded conventional capabilities. Consequently, U.S. military options were maintained or even improved while additional military capability did not reduce the risks of nuclear escalation. In other words, both orthodoxies were harmonized successfully. The challenge of BMD is that it allows the United States to maintain its traditional deterrence orthodoxy while it undermines European efforts to maintain theirs. Military options based on retaliation do not threaten European deterrence when their number increases. Military options based on denial, on the other hand, reduce the risk of escalation.

It is difficult to ascertain definite reasons that might conclusively explain European behavior over the SDI/BMD issue. The technological challenge from the United States certainly plays a role; so do the memory of the INF debate, the stakes in *Ostpolitik* and European detente generally, shifting power relations within the alliance and the periodic doubts about alliance orthodoxy. These problems notwithstanding, it is argued here that West Europeans still perceive SDI as a traditional challenge to be met by traditional means rather than as one of a decisively different nature. It is therefore not surprising to see West Europeans, and particularly West Germans, responding to SDI with efforts to strengthen NATO's conventional capabilities. West European interest in defenses against anti-tactical ballistic missiles (ATBMs) serves as an example of orthodoxy at odds with the means employed in its defense.

On the surface, pro-ATBM arguments appear plausible. ATBM proponents argue that unless NATO deploys its own ATBM system, the USSR will soon acquire the capability to target vital NATO installations with conventional and chemical ballistic missiles.[32] At present, the Soviet Union can effectively destroy these facilities—command and control facilities, storage sites and ports and, most important, Pershing II and cruise missile peacetime deployment bases—only with its nuclear weapons. A conventional/chemical missile force would allow the Soviets to destroy such key wartime objectives with non-nuclear means without sacrificing speed or accuracy. The increasing conventionalization of the Warsaw Pact's military doctrine and capabilities strongly suggests that the USSR will increasingly incorporate non-nuclear missiles into its force posture, particularly if conventional technology makes warhead substitution an attractive alternative. The USSR will not want to fight a nuclear war in Europe and risk escalation if other means of assuring victory become available.

The most worrisome aspect of a conventional/chemical Soviet missile force would be its ability to deny NATO its nuclear options. If a Soviet conventional/chemical missile force were able to destroy Pershing II missiles before they could disperse, NATO's first-use option, crucial for the credibility of flexible response, would disappear. Alternatively, NATO might be forced to use the Pershing IIs preventively in order to escape the new conventional threat. Such an alternative—which would heighten preemptive instabilities on both sides in a crisis—would not find much public support in Europe.

ATBM proponents also highlight the increasing sophistication of Soviet air-defense systems. A Soviet conventional/chemical missile force would free large parts of Warsaw Pact tactical fighter forces to engage other NATO targets, thereby jeopardizing NATO's chances to achieve air superiority. In addition, future Soviet air-defense sys-

---

32. Manfred Woerner, "A Missile Defense for NATO Europe," *Strategic Review* 14, No. 1 (Winter 1986), pp. 13–20.

tems could intercept NATO nuclear missiles that escape the conventional missile attack. NATO planners are particularly worried about the SA-10 surface-to-air missile and the still experimental SA-12. Some future combination of Soviet conventional missile capabilities and highly effective air defenses would incapacitate NATO to an intolerable degree. At present the Soviets are believed to have over 700 SS-21s and some 350 SS-23s plus about 100 SS-22s targeted on Europe; the SA-10 is deployed in some 800 launchers.[33]

An ATBM system, some have argued, would in fact restore credibility to flexible response. An ATBM system, in this view, would enhance deterrence by increasing uncertainty in the minds of Soviet planners as to the success of a conventional missile attack. Thus far no specific defense system has been proposed by ATBM advocates. In a recent Wehrkunde address, West German Defense Minister Manfred Woerner suggested a non-space-based, non-nuclear terminal defense system based on the Patriot air-defense system and the improved Hawk missile. Neither system, however, constitutes a very satisfactory technical solution. A great deal of further research is required before NATO can even begin to consider such systems in an anti-tactical mode. Other concepts worth considering include some of the less exotic SDI-related technologies currently under research in the United States, such as ground- and space-based ATBM components as required for eximer and free-electron lasers.

The central problem with ATBM defenses, which has been underplayed by ATBM proponents, is the possible Soviet reaction to a West European ATBM system. With their existing air-defense system designed to cope with existing NATO forces, a concerted NATO effort to develop and deploy an extensive ATBM system would provide the Soviets with a strong incentive to upgrade their present air-defense system. It is furthermore very probable that the Soviets would in that case expand their offensive conventional/chemical missile force so as to saturate any defenses NATO might deploy.

If NATO were to engage in developing ATBMs, it would be difficult for the West Europeans to maintain that they were merely assuring the viability of the flexible response strategy. Moscow would almost certainly view large-scale deployment of ATBM systems as part of the U.S. SDI effort.

33. Manfred Woerner, "Europe braucht eine Raketenabwehr," *Die Zeit*, No. 10, February 28, 1986, p. 45.

The size of any future ATBM systems could therefore be crucial in persuading the Soviets of the non-threatening nature of NATO ATBMs. In order to forestall an offense-defense arms race in Europe, NATO should not attempt, if at all, to develop more than a limited point defense for such hard targets as command and control centers, aircraft shelters and key military installations. Such limited defenses should assure the feasibility of NATO's nuclear options and in turn enhance European deterrence. Protection of such a small number of sites would also reassure the Soviets that NATO is not aiming at threatening Soviet retaliatory forces, even if European ATBMs were to be linked to a far more capable SDI at some future point.

The case for a small ATBM capability could be strengthened through additional measures that would enhance the survivability and penetration capability of NATO's remaining ballistic missile forces. Surveillance and reconnaissance could be improved in order to obtain real-time intelligence on Soviet military moves. The more time available, the more time NATO has to disperse its missile force and the harder it will be for the Soviets to target them. NATO could also make extensive use of standoff weapons that could disrupt Soviet air defenses. In other words, there are a variety of passive means that NATO should explore.

The ATBM issue in Europe makes two things very clear. One, ATBMs are discussed in order to maintain flexible response. Two, ATBMs will not help Europe solve the larger SDI/BMD problems. Indeed, it has the potential to cause a conventional arms race in Europe. Moreover, the synergism that exists between conventional and nuclear forces would be threatened by the synergism that informs the SDI-ATBM relationship as long as the Europeans shy away from recognizing that ATBMs are part of the BMD debate.

West Europeans should also remind themselves of the mechanisms that set the INF issue in motion a few years ago. At that time, West Europeans created the issue and sparked off a political momentum for INF deployment in the United States that developed far beyond what Europeans initially desired and quickly went beyond their control. The political momentum for SDI already exists in the United States and a West European interest in their own version of SDI could once again create a political constituency in the United States, this time for ATBMs, which could quickly acquire a pace and take a direction that might not serve West European interests.

If the INF debate threatened alliance cohesion, it is very questionable whether West European support for SDI is the right instrument with which to demonstrate cohesion. Earlier, reference was made to West European uncertainty as to its future role in the alliance. The course of the West European SDI debate shows the extent to which this uncertainty pervades West European politics.

Thus far, alliance political and military doctrines have been able to accommodate doctrinal developments that have taken place in the United States. Similarly, the alliance has not been affected by military technological changes to an extent that would have threatened European 'security essentials' and demanded a change in NATO's strategy or posture. Flexible response is a unique example of the alliance successfully harmonizing differently developing defensive orthodoxies. Advancing technology such as MIRVs and the increasing accuracy of warheads allowed the United States to increase its counterforce options. At the same time, an increase in options did not preclude the possibility of escalation to a massive nuclear exchange. This interpretation was and is favored by Europeans.

SDI and the BMD debate generally have the potential to seriously undermine NATO's ability to harmonize diverging intra-alliance security interests. For the past thirty years, the alliance has based its security policy on diversity rather than uniformity of perceptions. This was primarily possible because the concept of deterrence based on offensive nuclear forces is itself flexible. Extended deterrence, despite periodic doubts about its conceptual logic and the U.S. political commitment to the defense of Europe and despite the condition of strategic parity, is still credible: no one knows how to fight with nuclear weapons. Doctrinal flexibility has allowed diversity of perceptions to be contained in a single alliance security policy. The SDI/BMD technologies and debate potentially threaten this continued diversity and may no longer permit a single alliance approach to security.

The flawed defense orthodoxies on both sides of the Atlantic have created policy-making frameworks within which a variety of non-defense policy priorities are being formulated. For the United States, deterrence through limited nuclear options also deals with Soviet political challenges. For the West Europeans, deterrence through escalation provides enough security to live in free democratic societies next to the Soviet Union. Flaws in orthodox thinking will continue to puzzle and concern policy-makers and scholars alike. SDI/BMD is unlikely to solve the puzzle of nuclear strategy; neither will it alleviate the Western policy-makers' burden of defending an essentially flawed orthodoxy to their publics.

The Reykjavik formula that emerged after the U.S.-Soviet meeting in October 1986 did little to dispel West European fears that developments in the security field were moving decidedly against their traditional interests. It was suggested earlier that U.S. concern about strategic options could be reconciled with Europe's understanding of the workings of deterrence. The 1979 decision to deploy intermediate-range nuclear forces in Europe was based upon West European fears of relative Soviet invulnerability in a European contingency; the link between INF and the SS-20 was a political afterthought. The Reykjavik proposal to eliminate both INF and SS-20s in Europe, even if some INF were permitted to be retained in the United States, would be in contradiction to the 1979 security rationale.

The elimination of ballistic missiles, or any other move toward minimal deterrence, leaves Europe facing short-range Soviet nuclear missiles and Warsaw Pact conventional forces without the threat of nuclear escalation. It seems that a future combination of SDI and no strategic ballistic missiles (although it is doubtful why strategic defenses should be put in place in the absence of ballistic missiles) is tantamount to a cancellation of the Atlantic alliance. West European leaders and NATO generals and defense ministers have repeatedly impressed upon the U.S. administration that nuclear cutbacks and particularly the elimination of whole weapons categories must go hand in hand with conventional arms control efforts. At their December 1986 meeting in Brussels, NATO foreign ministers issued a proposal for conventional troop cuts in Europe that would embrace all territory from the Atlantic to the Urals.[34] It appears evident to West Europeans that an effective agreement on conventional force reduction may be as vital to their security as developments in the nuclear arms control arena.

Reykjavik has shaken West European leaders although public criticism of the U.S. stance has remained muted. Yet Chancellor Helmut Kohl's and Prime Minister Margaret Thatcher's visits to Washington in the immediate aftermath of the Reagan-Gorbachev meeting provide ample evidence of West European fears about their security having almost been bargained away.

Concerns over American arms control wisdom should tell the West Europeans something else, too. First, unqualified reliance upon the United States to represent its own *and* West European security interests when speaking to the Soviet Union cannot and should not be automatically assumed. Second, if West Europeans recognize this, they have to become more articulate about their own security position. They should either jointly or on a bilateral basis undertake a more concerted effort to strengthen West European understanding in Washington, both at the executive and congressional levels. West Europeans should

---

34. "NATO Proposes New Talks on Conventional Troop Cuts," *International Herald Tribune*, December 12, 1986, pp. 1, 8.

not rely on the modest achievements of most past arms control negotiations where the disarmament rhetoric tended to exceed the practical
arms control results. West European influence upon U.S. policy-making is, of course, limited. This limitation should not, however, lead
to West European complacency. Not despite but because of West
European security dependence upon the United States, West European leaders must apply themselves to explore and effectively use all
avenues open to them. The political and military strength of the alliance may depend upon it and with it the future of East-West relations.

Conclusion

INF posed a profound challenge to the NATO alliance from 1979
to 1983. NATO governments had to defend a flawed strategic orthodoxy to their respective publics. SDI and BMD threatened Western
Europe's ability to continue defending NATO strategy. The difference
between INF and SDI/BMD is that the former was the last in a series
of challenges to the flaws in NATO strategy, while the latter only
indirectly exposes these flaws but directly threatens the mechanism
of doctrinal compromise which in the past made it possible for Europeans to find security within the confines of the alliance.

The Strategic Defense Initiative Office (SDIO) is aiming to make a
decision on SDI development programs in the early 1990s. At present,
it seems unlikely that either technological breakthroughs will allow a
comprehensive defense shield to be developed or that no positive
development decision will be taken. On the contrary, it appears entirely possible for some defense systems to be developed. As previously suggested, the development of strategic doctrine, the vulnerability of land-based nuclear systems and SDIO's own time scale favor
a positive development decision less than ten years from today. If
such is probable, and not even SDI's most determined critics can
permit themselves to discount this probability, what are the implications for the future of the Atlantic alliance and East-West relations?

European options are few and time is not on Europe's side. What
West European governments must understand first of all and as a
prerequisite to an active policy is that the SDI/BMD issue is not one
of alliance cohesion, to be best handled by downplaying it and placing
political emphasis on SDI's research phase. Europe should be asking
itself the question that if strategic defenses are going to be developed,
what kind of defenses should one be considering?

Despite the previously identified weaknesses in the argument on
defenses for the enhancement of deterrence, West Europeans may

want to focus on that in order to see most of their own interests maintained. For the United States and Western Europe to remain in one and the same alliance, strategic defenses must meet both U.S. and European interests. In other words, the strategic defense effort must be tailored in such a way that it addresses the U.S.-Soviet competition *and* the security requirements of Europe. The primarily political concern in the United States over a Soviet first-strike capability against U.S. ICBMs cannot be given priority over West European nuclear escalation thinking. With regard to SDI, the only feasible way to balance both objectives is to keep strategic defenses at the lowest possible level. It is certain, however, that if the U.S.-Soviet competition is permitted to remain concentrated on the strategic environment alone, the chances for a very limited defensive capability are slim. Yet only a small strategic defensive capability will in turn allow the Europeans to maintain the nuclear escalation orthodoxy and, equally important, spare them the political fallout of a strategic offense-defense arms race, part of which is likely to happen in space. How small a defensive capability should be must be negotiated with the Soviet Union.

What Europeans should do is to convince the United States to decide on a very limited capability in the first place. Some of the political pressure in favor of strategic defenses might also be reduced through arms control measures and responsible military procurement planning. There are some who would argue that a negotiated environment, such as that provided by arms control, would make defenses more effective and therefore more likely to be deployed. Consider, however, that in the absence of an arms control agreement on offensive systems, the currently alleged Soviet first-strike capability would in all likelihood increase, while the original problem of U.S. ICBM vulnerability would get worse. Of course, it is unlikely that an understanding with the Soviet Union could be attained on the basis of large offensive reductions in exchange for large-scale BMD deployments. It appears far more reasonable to argue for limited BMD and large reductions in strategic forces on both sides. Both sides should be urged to reconsider their understanding of strategic flexibility. To increase the uncertainty in the mind of one's opponent as to the success of his action does not require large-scale BMD. Neither does it have to be space-based.

The suggestion of limited BMD deployment is certain to raise formidable criticism from SDI proponents still expecting imminent technological breakthroughs and advocating a comprehensive defense shield. A limited BMD proposal would drastically focus the defensive programs, most likely reduce SDI budgets even further than Congress has done already, and make SDI negotiable.

Thus far, no convincing argument has been advanced for large-scale defenses that would enhance strategic stability between the United States and the Soviet Union. The fear of a nuclear first strike exists on both sides. The contribution of strategic defenses to alleviate these fears should be explored jointly. West Europeans have a vested interest in containing both the size of strategic defenses and persuading the United States of the necessity of a joint approach to BMD. This is no easy task by any means. Thus far, West Europeans have tended to treat SDI as one more traditional challenge. In order to represent effectively their security interest towards the United States, their very own first task is to understand that *the* strategic debate has begun and that if they fail in this, the debate and its consequences will be experienced rather than influenced.

2

Space Defense and East-West Relations

PETER RAJCSANYI

Introduction

The commitment of the Soviet Union and the United States of America to negotiate the reduction of strategic offensive and defensive nuclear forces as well as medium-range nuclear forces was reaffirmed and strengthened at the first summit meeting between U.S. President Ronald Reagan and Soviet General Secretary Mikhail Gorbachev in November 1985. The two sides confirmed the importance of the ongoing dialogue and expressed "their strong desire" to seek common ground on the problems of arms reduction. Reflecting the contradiction between the commitment to negotiate arms reductions and the continuing arms race, the negotiating partners in their joint statement agreed "to accelerate the work" at the Geneva negotiations on nuclear and space arms "to prevent an arms race in space and to terminate it on earth, to limit and reduce nuclear arms and enhance strategic stability."

The first Soviet-American summit meeting after an interval of more than six years obviously could not eliminate the deeply rooted mistrust and differences between the parties. It was only the first step in, hopefully, a steady process leading to compromises, perhaps agreements, on the most burning issue: how to avoid a nuclear war.

At the Reykjavik meeting in October 1986, another important shift occurred when General Secretary Gorbachev and President Reagan displayed similar approaches to the general idea of deep cuts in strategic offensive nuclear weapons. The two parties narrowed their differences, in principle, on the elimination of all ballistic missiles and that of medium-range nuclear forces in Europe. Extensive discussion was also held on banning nuclear tests as well as on verification.

General Secretary Gorbachev and President Reagan could not, however, reconcile their views on the issues of strategic defense and space arms. After President Reagan's speech in March 1983* launching the Strategic Defense Initiative, the issues of strategic defense reemerged in the context of negotiations to limit strategic offensive forces. The key point is that the American president does not regard his proposal to build a comprehensive strategic defense system merely as a somewhat expanded research program, but as a total change in policy. What is contemplated is not only his dream but a policy decision to set in motion driving forces in the military, the economy and foreign policy that will acquire ever-increasing momentum. This momentum may, however, trigger the resumption of an offense-defense arms competition rather than bring about a new type of security; it may open the door for unlimited nuclear escalation by compelling the Soviet Union to compete pugnaciously in maintaining parity.

In principle, there is nothing new about the idea of developing an anti-ballistic missile defense. Such proposals have been examined, debated and rejected several times in the last twenty-five years. The present international climate and, above all, the vigor with which the Reagan administration has pushed the issue warrant a very careful examination of SDI. Moreover, it is a widely held view that the allies of the two great powers in Western and Eastern Europe as well as other countries (such as Japan) cannot escape the consequences of this situation and its possible implications for their own security and foreign policies.

While a large part of the public discussion has centered on technical arguments and speculation, this study will consider the strategic and international political aspects of space defense. In order to emphasize the main points, I have avoided detailed discussion of technicalities, budgetary and legal issues and tried to synthesize rather than describe and dissect.

The Role of Strategic Defense
in Military Policies

What has become evident from official presentations subsequent to President Reagan's March 23, 1983, speech is the uncertainty regarding SDI. This has manifested itself in animated discussion of the feasibility, desirability, cost, scope and purposes of strategic defense. The pres-

* See Appendix.

ident's original moral vision of "rendering nuclear weapons impotent and obsolete" soon became less and less frequently cited as the main goal of his initiative. Even the official White House pamphlet which was issued to explain SDI to the public openly admitted that "the Strategic Defense Initiative, by itself, cannot fully realize this vision or solve all the security challenges we and our allies will face in the future."[1] As it has become obvious that a leak-proof, cost-effective population defense covering the United States and its allies is impossible, the ongoing debate about strategic defense deserves evaluation from a rather different angle—that of military strategy and international politics. While the question of technical feasibility, cost and efficacy[2] of a strategic (and tactical) defense may be of paramount importance to whomever is working on its design and installation, the key issues lie elsewhere.

In the military realm the most important issues are: 1) how strategic and tactical defense fit into the overall military policies of the United States and the Soviet Union; 2) which goals of military policy may be particularly strengthened by deploying a defense system; 3) whether recent changes in U.S. military doctrine and the domestic political atmosphere can sustain a radical change towards a greater reliance on defense (with or without reducing offensive forces); and 4) whether and how this can be sustained in the future. As far as international politics are concerned, the key issues are related to the Soviet-American relationship, the role of strategic parity between the two great powers and the impact on the superpowers' allies of reintroducing defense with a new emphasis on the strategic and European military equation. An additional problem is the effect of reintroducing greater reliance on defenses on the entire international system and general political climate.

The United States and the Soviet Union have been conducting research on several elements of strategic defense for decades. While the quest for strategic defense started many years before the negotiations on the ABM Treaty, during the 1970s both countries decided and agreed that such systems were unreliable, costly to deploy nationwide,

---

1. Excerpts from the White House pamphlet, "The President's Strategic Defense Initiative," reprinted in part in *The New York Times*, January 4, 1985.

2. The majority of the published articles and official speeches in the United States focused on these aspects of the question. In the debate about such issues, often insupportable data or highly hypothetical assumptions were used to argue for implementing strategic defense. Some articles arguing against strategic defense were not devoid of similar features.

destabilizing militarily and undesirable politically. The ABM Treaty concluded in 1972 and the ABM Treaty Protocol signed in 1974 (which came into force in 1976) severely limited the deployment and testing of defense systems, although permitting that the "modernization and replacement of ABM systems or their components may be carried out."[3] The overwhelming majority of experts who support the preservation of the ABM Treaty maintain that these principles and the understanding which prevailed in the early 1970s are still valid and continue to argue against any plan to deploy a defense system which is not comprehensive.[4] The main arguments used by these experts are that large-scale efforts to reintroduce defense into the strategic equation will directly stimulate an all-out arms race in offensive and defensive systems, respectively; darken or abolish the prospect for a noticeable improvement in Soviet-American relations; and destroy the single most important arms control accord (the ABM Treaty) agreed upon by the two superpowers to date. Regarding other likely consequences of a policy directed towards the deployment of strategic defense, their evaluation concludes that the probability of nuclear war (or large-scale conventional war) would be higher and crisis stability would be diminished in the case of a new mix of defensive and offensive systems—the likely outcome of the Reagan administration's initiative.

Notwithstanding the thoroughness of these arguments, one cannot ignore the fact that the contemporary international climate significantly differs from that of the early 1970s, that confidence between the United States and the Soviet Union has been at rock bottom and that changes have been occurring in defense-related technologies. The question of whether these technological developments justify and, even more importantly, create a solid basis for deploying some kind of strategic defense needs to be addressed briefly in order to ascertain the actual role assigned to strategic defense in American and Soviet strategy.

---

3. "Treaty between the United States of America and the Union of Soviet Socialist Republics on the Limitation of Anti-Ballistic Missile Systems," in *Arms Control and Disarmament Agreements: Texts and Histories of Negotiations* (Washington, DC: U.S. Arms Control and Disarmament Agency, 1982), pp. 139–142, 162–163.

4. See, for example, Sidney D. Drell, "ABM Revisited," *Bulletin of the Atomic Scientists* 40, No. 6 (June/July 1984), pp. 7–8; William E. Burrows, "Ballistic Missile Defense: The Illusion of Security," *Foreign Affairs* 62, No. 4 (Spring 1984), pp. 843–856; Richard L. Garwin, Kurt Gottfried, "Pie in the Sky of Space Defense," *The New York Times*, February 12, 1985; Edward M. Kennedy, "Star Wars vs. the ABM Treaty," *Arms Control Today* 14, No. 6 (July-August 1984), pp. 1, 18–19, 24.

In the early 1960s it was discovered that a ground-launched device could hit an incoming missile and destroy it by nearby detonation or direct collision. This discovery formed the basis for all the efforts at creating systems related to terminal or mid-course defense. The latest developments show that although the available advanced technologies are superior to their predecessors and can employ non-nuclear killing devices[5] in order to avoid nuclear detonations at low altitudes (in which target areas and the surrounding countryside and cities would suffer substantial blast and radiation damage), even in a highly sophisticated arrangement these technologies cannot serve as the sole basis of a nationwide defense. Their use in a narrower mission (i.e., in point defense for covering hardened military targets like MX missile silos) is also questionable because of significant component vulnerability.[6] In the acrimonious debate over the MX missile, even MX proponents showed little confidence in the efficacy of terminal ground defenses. Although reentry ballistic missile defense systems technically have the lowest risk because they can cope more easily with the problem of decoy discrimination than exoatmospheric mid-course systems, their potential payoff is much lower. The possibility of constructing a non-nuclear interceptor with improved accuracy for endoatmospheric defense (and thus circumventing the nuclear release problem) may be increasingly feasible by the end of this decade, but the capabilities created would not go beyond the limits of hard-point defense or small-scale preferential area defense. The assumed military benefits, only slightly above the level achievable in the early 1970s, of complicating the planning of the other side do not seem to balance the negative effects of such an effort. It will initiate a large-scale offense-defense race, destroy the ABM Treaty and enormously complicate international and European security.

The technological developments of the past decade have produced long-wave infrared sensors (for improved tracking) and computers (for on-board data processing and for tracking several dozen incoming objects simultaneously), both of which are seen as new components in a mid-course defense system. Extending the reach of anti-ballistic

---

5. The United States successfully tested a non-nuclear interceptor in June 1984 in mid-course of a ballistic missile flight. The HOE device can be used in terminal defense, too. The test, after three abortive attempts, grew out of six years of research costing about $300 million. The United States has other instruments such as Sprint missiles, LOADS, etc., that can be considered terminal defense systems.

6. Alwyn Young, "Ballistic Missile Defense: Capabilities and Constraints," *The Fletcher Forum* 8, No. 1 (Winter 1984), p. 159.

missile defense into the mid-course also introduces the possibility of a two-layer defense. However, a mid-course defense built upon the traditional concept (i.e., fixed ground-based radars and ground-launched interceptors) is not likely to catch up with the evolving offensive ballistic missile systems and is not able to circumvent such thorny problems as discrimination of decoys, nuclear blackouts and component vulnerability. In mid-course defense interception, operational problems of the system are severe and formidable. New technologies have so far done little to modify previous negative conclusions with respect to a mid-course defense based on traditional concepts. As Sidney D. Drell and Wolfgang Panofsky have pointed out: "Currently, there is no viable concept for a highly effective mid-course defense against a massive threat of thousands of warheads, post-boost vehicles and perhaps many thousands of decoys."[7]

American Considerations and Plans

If, as I briefly summarized, there have been no decisive break-throughs in traditional anti-ballistic missile defense technologies, then what are the factors which led to the renewal of debate about strategic defense programs in the United States? There are two new motives:

- oscillations in American policy, supported and hastened by changes in the decision-making bodies; and

- prospects of a space-based system focusing on boost-phase interception within the framework of a layered defense.

The first factor is connected with a key question: what is the defense for? The political demand for defense varies according to the accepted comprehensive concept of nuclear policy. Without a clear idea of the purpose of a strategic defense within the framework of nuclear policy, it is nearly impossible to evaluate the conditions and criteria of the deployment of a defense system.

President Reagan launched his Strategic Defense Initiative with the declared aim to render nuclear weapons obsolete by providing a comprehensive population defense. In his speech, he proposed to defend the population and thereby to replace deterrence by reliance on offensive nuclear weapons as the bedrock of U.S. national security policy

---

7. Sidney D. Drell, Wolfgang K. H. Panofsky, "The Case Against Strategic Defense: Technical and Strategic Realities," *Issues in Science and Technology* (Fall 1984), p. 60.

and the basis of the Soviet-American military relationship. He did not provide even the vaguest outline of a political scenario that might propel countries toward a "defense-dominated world." Political considerations, which are crucially important in Soviet-American relations and between East and West, were also ignored by Paul Nitze when he later outlined a three-phase transition scenario from the present to a period in which large-scale space defense systems would be deployed.*

Since President Reagan's March 1983 speech, proponents of SDI have enumerated several arguments in order to promote the idea and support its implementation. Various administration spokesmen are promoting their own versions of strategic defense, leaving President Reagan as probably the sole remaining believer in the original vision. Although referring occasionally to the original objective, most administration spokesmen and supporters implicitly reject the idea of population defense or push this goal into the very distant future, strongly emphasizing the argument that strategic defense would enhance deterrence.

The strong support extended by the present administration for strategic defense can best be explained by the shift in military and political thinking among members of the government bodies and within the ruling national security establishment. Part of this shift is connected with the growing and seemingly exaggerated concern about the vulnerability of the U.S. ICBM force. An important contribution to the change has been the raucous voice of those who paint a gloomy picture of the strategic balance between the United States and the Soviet Union, with the implication that it increasingly favors the latter. Some articles have dealt with Soviet anti-ballistic missile defense activities and concluded by saying that "Moscow is accelerating its efforts."[8] Although another group of studies on this issue maintains that a massive Soviet breakout is unlikely in the near future and that neither current Soviet defensive facilities nor those reportedly under research can seriously hinder U.S. retaliation capabilities,[9] high-ranking officials of the Reagan administration like Kenneth W. Dam, then Deputy Secretary of State, have sought to justify SDI as a response

---

* See Appendix.

8. Clarence A. Robinson, Jr., "Soviets Accelerate Missile Defense Efforts," *Aviation Week and Space Technology*, January 16, 1984, pp. 13–16.

9. Sayre Stevens, "The Soviet BMD Program," in Ashton B. Carter and David N. Schwartz, eds., *Ballistic Missile Defense* (Washington, DC: The Brookings Institution, 1984), pp. 182–220; and David N. Schwartz, "Assessing Future Prospects," *Ballistic Missile Defense*, pp. 350–363.

"to the ongoing and extensive Soviet missile defense effort" and "a prudent hedge against any Soviet decision to expand rapidly its ballistic missile defense capability beyond the bounds of the ABM Treaty."[10]

With respect to the vulnerability of U.S. land-based ICBMs, a taxonomy can be established for means of enhancing their survivability. To address the problem the U.S. government has a number of different options, such as adopting a launch-on-attack policy, super-hardening silos, adopting deceptive basing, requesting substantial reductions in Soviet ICBMs, active ballistic missile defense, etc. Although the arguments emphasized by the Reagan administration in favor of invulnerable ICBM forces have been very weak and were questioned by experts (such as the Scowcroft Commission) on several occasions, the administration maintains that the best solution may be active BMD combined with large-scale reductions in Soviet forces to be achieved in arms control negotiations. It is, however, questionable whether an invulnerable ICBM force is a necessity when the United States has a diverse and redundant strategic force. Even then, it is highly doubtful whether invulnerability could be achieved at all. The costs and risks of deploying a nationwide BMD as a solution to ICBM vulnerability clearly outweigh the benefits that might be provided, and would only impel the other side to build new types of offensive weapons and penetration aids. Particularly indicative in this respect is the fact that the United States has strengthened efforts and increased financial support for the Advanced Strategic Missile Systems project, which is designed to assure that American nuclear missiles with new penetration aids can overwhelm a future Soviet defense of any kind.[11] The emphasis attached to the project obviously shows that new developments in the field of defensive forces create a strong incentive to modernize offensive weaponry and thereby initiate an endless offense-defense arms race. The introduction of strategic defense systems does not, however, eradicate the problem of vulnerability but only changes its nature. Although ICBMs can be defended with a certain probability, the components of the defensive system are also vulnerable. SDI deployments will trigger a further spiral of the arms race in anti-defense weapons. As James Thomson of the Rand Corporation

---

10. Address by Kenneth W. Dam, Deputy Secretary of State, before the Foreign Policy Association, New York, January 14, 1985.

11. Bill Keller, "U.S. Seeks Missiles to Evade Defenses," *The New York Times*, February 11, 1985.

concludes, "In an SDI world, the temptation to go first will increase. . . . The key judgment about SDI will be about vulnerability."[12]

Another justification used by strategic defense proponents is that SDI will help arms control. George Keyworth, the former White House scientific adviser, goes even further: "In fact, *deployment* of strategic defense is the *only way* in which the superpowers will be able to achieve very deep arms reductions."[13] A similar argument was employed by Robert C. McFarlane, former Assistant to the President for National Security Affairs, in an address to the Overseas Writers Association: ". . . it was the Strategic Defense Initiative . . . which brought the Soviet Union back to the negotiating table."[14]

Is this standpoint correct? Yes and no. The Soviet Union was ready to resume negotiations on offensive and defensive nuclear forces because SDI created a new, very dangerous situation in international relations. A *New York Times* editorial expressed this view quite succinctly: "The Russians are indeed alarmed at being forced into a ruinously expensive new arms competition that they know will leave neither side safer and probably make the world riskier than ever before. . . . And they must be desperate to learn whether it can still be stopped at a tolerable price."[15] It is a mistake, however, for the United States to think that the Soviet readiness to negotiate has been dictated by fear or that the mere existence of the Geneva talks shows a Soviet willingness to yield to American demands for unilateral or unbalanced concessions in strategic offensive weapons. The Soviet Union, guided by genuine concern about the consequences of the possible collapse of the arms control process, has agreed to discussion and offered radical reductions in offensive forces, including its land-based missiles.

The successful outcome of the Geneva strategic talks is, however, connected with an agreement on "preventing an arms race in space" and a ban on the testing as well as deployment of strategic defensive

---

12. Quoted by David Ignatius, "Analyzing Risks," *The Wall Street Journal*, October 15, 1985.

13. George A. Keyworth, "The Case for Strategic Defense: An Option for a World Disarmed," *Issues in Science and Technology* (Fall 1984), p. 44 (emphasis added).

14. Address by Robert C. McFarlane before the Overseas Writers Association, Washington, DC, March 7, 1985.

15. "It's Still Star Wars," *The New York Times*, February 24, 1985.

weapons. In this respect, there are two problems which seem to be insurmountable without basic changes in the American approach. The first practical problem is that the SDI program envisages field-testing of ABM or space-based components (artfully termed "subcomponents" by the administration) by the early 1990s. Such tests will violate the ABM Treaty, which so far has served as the basis of talks on defensive weapons, and would lead to a point of no return. Once tests succeed, U.S. deployment must be assumed by Soviet planners and reflected in the attitude adopted by the Soviet Union at the Geneva talks.

The second problem is that to date the United States has been unwilling to negotiate seriously on defensive forces, and only willing to "explain" its concept of SDI and a "transition period." The prospect of flight tests, followed by development and deployment of anti-ballistic missile and space weapons, rules out reductions in strategic offensive forces and assures an offense-defense arms race, increasing the temptation of a first strike on both sides.

With respect to the role of SDI in the arms control process, there appear to be at least three main lines of opinion in Washington. First there are those who strongly oppose any effort to reach a modus vivendi with the Soviet Union and proclaim that all past efforts at arms control have been futile.[16] In this group, one can find neoconservatives, fundamentalists, well-known cold warriors, etc. Richard Pipes, an advocate of the hard-line right wing, expressed his view that "such negotiations have been a failure" and "benefited the Soviet Union."[17] For these people, strategic defense would make a dialogue with the Soviet Union and arms reduction negotiations unnecessary. For them, building a strategic defense system is something that the United States can do alone without anyone's agreement and without compromising American interests with another global power. They use uncertainties in the SDI project, difficulties in verification, and the disappointment of arms control in the past few years as a justification for not letting strategic defense become a bargaining chip in the arms control negotiations.

A second, more pragmatic line opposing arms control constraints on strategic defense maintains that the process of negotiating a comprehensive treaty with the Soviet Union may be "very painful" domestically. This group considers the strategic defense issue only the for-

---

16. Ray S. Cline, "Talks are Just Theater for Soviets to Exploit," USA Today, February 7, 1985, p. 3.

17. Interview with Richard Pipes, "Beyond Containment? The Future of U.S.-Soviet Relations," Policy Review 31 (Winter 1985), pp. 15-41.

ward edge of the "official" American attitude toward the Soviet Union. These opponents of constraints on SDI focus on possible asymmetries and Soviet advantages from a comprehensive arms agremeent as well as on the potential domestic benefits of a large-scale high-tech effort. In addition to the concern about the verifiability of compliance with arms control agreements (which is, to a certain degree, legitimate in the case of BMD and ASAT weapons), they demand the investigation and testing of advanced missile defense and ASAT technologies. Tests of some of these technologies, however, will violate the ABM limits. In this respect, a grievous problem is that strategic defense issues are seen and evaluated merely in their military context, neglecting their significance for arms reductions and international relations. In the debate about the relationship between strategic defense and arms reduction, those who favor this view assume that it would be a mistake for the American side to modify or abandon U.S. military programs to meet arms control objectives. International politics, however, has several times compelled decision-makers to recognize that a program which seems to make sense militarily also has political implications that should be taken into consideration and which should, in the final analysis, be paramount.

The third group of U.S. experts tends to look at strategic defense as a bargaining chip. For them, the United States can use SDI to exert pressure on the Soviet Union to reduce the number of its "heavy" (MIRVed, large-payload) ICBMs. Realistically, there is no way to conclude a Soviet-American treaty on the radical reduction of strategic offensive forces without the profound commitment of both parties to limit (preferably to discontinue) the development of strategic defensive forces. One cannot, however, ignore two important aspects of this interrelationship: 1) there is a time frame within which the parties should achieve an agreement before the process of research and development exceeds the limits imposed by the ABM Treaty, which is already threatened with erosion; and 2) even the near-term prospect of a limited defense against strategic offensive missiles would have a damaging impact on prospects for radical reductions in strategic weaponry and would seriously damage the Soviet-American relationship. In my view, the application of the "bargaining chip" concept would first require the reaffirmation of the ABM Treaty and a firm commitment to eliminate its loopholes by negotiating amendments to the treaty. The point is that decisions on weapons systems and items on the agenda of negotiations are primarily political and not military-technical. Moreover, if SDI is presented by the United States as a special "bargaining chip," the Soviet Union is likely to present special bargaining chips of its own.

The appealing strategic vision of a technologically dynamic United States which would acquire "space superiority" and obtain political-military advantages from it has captured the minds of many experts and politicians in the United States.[18] They believe that the United States can achieve durable space and defense superiority based on technological advantage and use this as a means of coercion against the Soviet Union in arms control negotiations and in international political disputes.

There are at least two main lines of argument here. One of them starts with the basic assumption that the United States is better equipped with all the necessary resources and conditions to pursue a successful scientific and technological competition with the Soviet Union in this area. This line is in full harmony with the view expressed several times by military officials and experts like Thomas Moore, John Foster, and Daniel Graham in the 1970s that American "superiority" means, first of all, "technological superiority." In this view, space is just another arena for competition where the United States should act with determination. The establishment of the Air Force Space Command on September 1, 1982, with full presidential support, was interpreted in this view as official recognition of the growing military importance of space. Such a recognition and the basic view of U.S. technological leadership in space are reflected as well in the National Space Policy Directive issued by President Reagan in July 1982.[19] The same line has been repeated by Robert Pfaltzgraff in his summary of the policy and security implications of space defense: "The United States should make a renewed commitment to world leadership in space technology. The United States should build upon the present technological advantage demonstrated in the successful missions already conducted by the Space Shuttle. . . . Deterrence by means of strategic defense in the high frontier of space represents a challenge worthy of American creative energies in strategy, politics and technology."[20]

---

18. "Military Space Doctrine: The Great Frontier," U.S. Air Force Book of Readings, U.S. Air Force Symposium (April 1981); and address by Senator John W. Warner, U.S. Senate, March 24, 1983, *Congressional Digest* (March 1984), p. 47.

19. "White House Fact Sheet on National Space Policy," July 4, 1982, Washington, DC, reprinted in *Weekly Compilation of Presidential Documents*, July 12, 1982, pp. 872–876.

20. Robert L. Pfaltzgraff, "Space and Security: Policy Implications," in Uri Ra'anan and Robert L. Pfaltzgraff, eds., *International Security Dimensions of Space* (Hamden, Conn.: Archon Books, 1984), pp. 264, 268.

A characteristic interpretation of this line was given by then Assistant Secretary of Defense Richard Perle before the Senate Foreign Relations Committee in a hearing on SDI. Having summarized Soviet activities in strategic offensive forces, he went on to say:

> It does not make much sense for the United States to compete with the Soviet Union in an area where the Soviets are strong and we are weak. It does make sense for us to compete with the Soviet Union, in the interest of maintaining a stable strategic balance, by exploiting the areas where we are strong. . . . We do have some advantages, or potential advantages, with respect to high technology. And one of the areas in which it may be possible to bring our technological base to bear is the development of strategic defenses. . . . So rather than match the Soviets in offensive weapons, it seems to me to make sense to see whether we can develop defensive weapons, exploiting one of our areas of strength. . . .[21]

Some experts go even further, stating that the "achievement of U.S. space superiority would help greatly to restore traditional forms of military superiority to their old levels. . . . Military use of space is much more than simply a 'force multiplier'; it is a potential restorer of traditional forms of U.S. military superiority."[22]

This approach shows two serious deficiencies. One is related to the controversy about whether the Soviet Union is at an advantage in the strategic defense race. Some articles have argued that "Moscow is far ahead."[23] In such a situation, then, the maintenance of American technological advantage in space cannot be taken for granted. The other problem is that American R&D programs may be ineffective; technology may fail to live up to present expectations. Even traditional, well-tested systems, where the technologies are understood, can produce unwanted side effects, unexpected delays, or can break down. For a comprehensive, multi-layer defense system, the problems and uncertainties are much greater and more numerous; the technologies as yet are hardly conceptualized. Moreover, a large-scale U.S. R&D

21. Assistant Secretary of Defense for International Security Policy Richard Perle, "Nuclear Strategy, Ballistic Missile Defense and Arms Control," remarks before the Senate Foreign Relations Committee, 99th Cong., 1st sess., November 12, 1985.

22. Barry J. Smernoff, "A Bold Two-Track Strategy for Space: Entering the Second Quarter-Century," in Ra'anan and Pfaltzgraff, eds., *International Security Dimensions of Space*, pp. 28–29.

23. "In Strategic Defense Moscow is Far Ahead," *Backgrounder* (Washington, DC: The Heritage Foundation), February 21, 1985.

program in strategic defense may stimulate more sustainable Soviet programs in strategic defense as well as strategic offensive forces. The basic assumption that the United States has a long-term technological advantage, and will retain that advantage over time, may prove to be false.

Other arguments in favor of SDI are less directly connected with military policy and focus more on the general characteristics of American technological developments. They emphasize the place SDI might take in the historical trend of American industrial development since World War II. In this view, the SDI program can sustain the third wave of pumping a substantial amount of money into industrial R&D programs under government-determined national security guidelines. After the Manhattan Project and the NASA Apollo program, investments in and around the SDI program should give a new impulse to the most energetic high-tech sectors of U.S. industry. As the scale of the SDI program and the investments needed to implement it go far beyond the levels of the two previous projects, the potential results in industrial development are assumed to be more significant.

As the competitiveness of the American economy, especially that of certain manufactured and agricultural products vis-à-vis West European and Japanese goods, declined in the past fifteen years, a growing consensus emerged in the late 1970s that the United States needed a strong program of "reindustrialization" based on a significant improvement in the high-tech sectors of American industry. These sectors are the bedrock of the military industry, too. Those who support the SDI program on such a basis see a possibly fortunate coincidence of three trends or factors in the SDI program: 1) increased public R&D efforts concentrated on the technologies vital to American competitiveness, supported by the White House and—under the popular slogan of defense—by a large section of the American public; 2) a drive for achieving and maintaining technological (and military) superiority over the Soviet Union and creating additional difficulties for Soviet economic development; and 3) the United States regaining and retaining leadership in international science and technology, economics and trade. In this view, the United States could strengthen its leading role in the Western alliance by bringing American industrial technology at least one generation forward, by raising the economy to a new level, by curtailing the flow of new technology to foreign countries, and by involving West European and Japanese researchers in the SDI program (and therefore in the development of U.S. industry).

In order to enlarge nuclear options, and enhance deterrence, a great deal more flexibility has been implemented in American planning since the mid-1970s. Flexibility and selectivity were the key goals sought by U.S. administrations in the past decade. The new, more selective options which have been added to already existing options are designed to minimize collateral damage on the American side and increase the hard-target kill capability of American strategic forces. Changes in the employment policy of American strategic nuclear forces led to a Presidential Directive (PD-59) which, according to former Defense Secretary Harold Brown, formalized the long-developing shift in nuclear strategy toward more flexible attack options.[24] As former Undersecretary of Defense for Research and Engineering William Perry has stated, the United States requires forces "that, first of all, can survive[;] . . . be able to react with whatever flexibility is required[; and] . . . be capable of penetrating whatever defenses the Soviet Union may have."[25] Such a refinement of counterforce doctrine requires a range of nuclear options, significant improvement in command, control, communications and intelligence (C^3I), and survivable strategic forces.

One can conclude that the main U.S. goal in nuclear strategy over the past fifteen years was flexibility—to enhance deterrence, increase American maneuverability on all levels of conflict and thus provide the United States with escalation control. But flexibility has inherent complexities. No one can define the ultimate limits of flexibility; thus, it is easy to argue for more and more of it. But plans to introduce "unlimited" flexibility into strategic planning could create a situation in which the other side perceives these efforts as war-fighting plans or attempts to deny it retaliatory capability. In such a situation, "flexibility" would not enhance deterrence but erode it.

A group of political and military decision-makers and experts argues for strategic defense as a much-needed, organic part of U.S. military policy. The role of strategic defense (both its active and passive elements) would, obviously, differ depending on the type of strategy adopted. It can expand from a role of "supporting force multiplier" to a "substantial role in the ICBM defense," through "the equal element in a combination of offensive and defensive forces" to a "domin-

24. *Report of Secretary of Defense Harold Brown to the Congress on the FY 1981 Budget and FY 1981-1985 Defense Program* (Washington, DC: Department of Defense), February 29, 1980.

25. U.S. Congress, Senate, Committee on Armed Services, *Hearings on Military Posture and H.R. 1872: DOD Authorization for Appropriations for Fiscal Year 1980*, 96th Cong., 1st sess., March-April 1979, p. 186.

ant role." As views of strategy are likely to remain debated in the present decade, the role of strategic defense will continue to be an important element, even the focus, of the strategic discussion.

As early as 1981-1982, the Reagan administration concluded several decisions and signed several documents such as the Strategic Modernization Program (1981), space policy for both civilian and military programs (July 1982), the establishment of a space command (September 1982), and a top secret directive known as the "Defense Guidance," which outlined the administration's official nuclear strategy. The Defense Guidance called for the United States to have strategic nuclear forces that could "prevail and be able to force the Soviet Union to seek earliest termination of hostilities on terms favorable to the U.S. . . . even under the condition of a prolonged war."[26] Such a policy clearly would rely on the application of "coercion" and require the maintenance of a secure strategic reserve force. The authors of and assistants on these documents were precisely those persons (Fred Iklé, Andrew Marshall, Richard Perle, Paul Nitze, Richard DeLauer, Thomas Reed, T. K. Jones) who today are the most vocal advocates of strategic defense. In their view, counterforce targeting strategy under present conditions would alone be unlikely to substantially limit damage and would not facilitate the coerced restraint of Soviet actions. Hence they conclude that unless the United States is committed to a comprehensive defense deployment which can absorb a likely Soviet response, there is no way to establish a favorable escalation control and terminate Soviet activities under terms favorable to the United States.[27] "Denying the Soviet Union information concerning the whereabouts of U.S. forces would also be an important consideration—hence the potential importance of an ASAT (anti-satellite) capability."[28]

At present the Pentagon is devising a nuclear war plan and a new command structure which would integrate strategic offensive forces with the anti-missile defense system being built under the Reagan

---

26. Fred M. Kaplan, *The Wizards of Armageddon* (New York: Simon and Schuster, 1983), p. 387.

27. These are the main findings of the studies on a multilayered defense carried out by the commission appointed by President Reagan: The Defensive Technology Study Team (also known as the Fletcher Commission), "Defense Against Ballistic Missiles, An Assessment of Technologies and Policy Implications" (Washington, DC: October 1983).

28. Keith B. Payne, "What if We 'Ride Out' a Soviet First Strike?" *The Washington Quarterly* 7, No. 4 (Fall 1984), p. 91.

initiative. In accordance with the conclusions of the most extensive nuclear strategy review carried out by the Defense Department in over a decade, a substantial effort is under way to coordinate strategic offensive and defensive forces in a cohesive war plan under the control of a new nuclear war-fighting command.[29] The new plan, which is being worked out under the direction of the Undersecretary of Defense for Policy Fred Iklé, illustrates that the United States is going to create a mix of offensive and defensive strategic forces as soon as it becomes technically feasible to do so.

This new strategic concept envisages combining offensive counterforce capabilities and active and passive defense in order to minimize the vulnerability of U.S. strategic offensive forces and limit damage to the American homeland from absorbing a Soviet retaliatory strike. According to SDI advocates such as Zbigniew Brzezinski and Max Kampelman, an additional advantage of implementing SDI would be the introduction of new uncertainties in Soviet nuclear planning.[30] Some highlight other technological and military effects of the SDI program. In R. A. Poole's view, "SDI-derived technological improvements to U.S. and allied offensive forces, particularly those related to surveillance, acquisition, tracking and kill assessment functions of BMD, are likely to provide important leverage."[31]

It is beyond doubt that with a "limited" SDI the United States could provide some protection to its ICBM forces, which are currently perceived as more vulnerable than they were a decade ago, and could complicate the war planning of the other side. If the measure of deterrence is simply the number of warheads that could penetrate and destroy targets on the enemy's side in retaliation (the lower the number, the stronger deterrence), then any kind of strategic defense would contribute to deterrence. Although there are significant differences between concepts of deterrence—whether it should function through "punishment" or through "denial"—one aspect of deterrence cannot be neglected: stability. The military capabilities of the parties are meant to create stable deterrence. One side should provide assur-

---

29. Richard Halloran, "U.S. Studies Plan to Integrate Nuclear Arms with a Missile Shield," *The New York Times*, May 29, 1985, p. A8.

30. Zbigniew Brzezinski, Robert Jastrow, Max Kampelman, "Defense in Space is not Star Wars," *The New York Times Magazine*, January 27, 1985, p. 51.

31. R. A. Poole, "BMD and Strategic Deterrence," *National Defense* (November 1985), p. 49.

ance to the other not only that its own basic security interests are being protected, but also—at least in an indirect way—that it does not threaten the stability of deterrence, that it recognizes the basic security interests of the other side.

The expansion of strategic defense capabilities can, however, diminish the stability of deterrence. It is not accidental that many experts and politicians such as Congressman Les Aspin, chairman of the House Armed Services Committee, raise the question: "Has the administration really thought through what it is doing to the concept of deterrence?"[32] As the Reagan administration has been calling into question the prevailing concept of deterrence and enumerating the dangers of relying upon it, Aspin asks what the administration's alternative has been, demanding one "that does not really weaken our national security."

Another fashionable rationale provided by SDI supporters has been that even an imperfect ABM system could protect the United States from accidental launches and nuclear terrorists. However, it is obvious that present American efforts are intended to establish a nationwide and space-based, multi-layered system, the capability of which goes far beyond the level required for protection from accidental launch. A terrorist attack using intercontinental ballistic missiles against the United States is highly improbable; to deny such an opportunity certainly does not require a space-based defense.

One cannot but conclude that Reagan's March 1983 speech was motivated neither by moral concerns nor by new technological discoveries. It was an expression and a summary of ongoing changes in U.S. defense policy, intended to set in motion an entire mechanism for strategic defense under a policy which will be supported (as assumed by Reagan at the time) by the American public, Congress and U.S. allies. For the time being, however, there is no clear consensus even within the administration on the role strategic defense ought to play in U.S. strategic policy. Military, foreign policy and arms control implications of the deployment of various defense systems have not yet been comprehensively studied and evaluated in the United States. Differences over SDI are related to uncertainty about how far the United States should and can go along the road of the new nuclear strategy.

In the four years since Reagan's 1983 speech, the SDI program has gained a modest momentum in decision-making bodies and, to a

---

32. Speech by Les Aspin at a "Face to Face" luncheon, U.S. House of Representatives, Washington, DC, January 16, 1985.

lesser degree, in the American public. At the same time, decision-makers and the public have become divided about SDI's goals, feasibility, economic costs and the very rationale announced by the administration to explain the program. The momentum achieved by supporters of strategic defense seems to forecast that attempts to implement the SDI program will not go away easily or in the near future, that the question of strategic defense will remain very much a part of American political life. Divergences in domestic opinion, however, create a climate of indecisiveness which has been making it very difficult for other countries, including the Soviet Union and the NATO allies, to bind the Reagan administration to a comprehensive and detailed arms control proposal on this topic. This seems to hinder the process of reaching an agreement in principle on radical reductions of strategic offensive forces and banning defensive forces.

The Soviet Attitude

The Soviet Union appears unwilling to play along with the American tit-for-tat game of strategic defense. This does not mean that Soviet nuclear planners consider defense meaningless or superfluous. On the U.S. side, many changes have occurred in the field of defense since the early 1960s: many projects were announced and rejected before the present administration claimed that strategic defense is central to its nuclear policy. The Soviet Union has exhibited more calm and consistency in this area. It has always perceived its limited defense as an additional asset to its military capabilities generally and never attached special significance to it. True, the Soviet Union has kept its defense facilities in an operational mode and even upgraded them, but the pace of upgrading has been very slow and the quality of the deployed technologies is far below the level of the American systems already developed. An upgraded version of the original Galosh interceptor (the ATBM-X-3) will probably be operational in the late 1980s and is believed to be equivalent to the Sentinel/Safeguard system deployed in the United States in the mid-1970s.[33] There is virtual agreement among military experts that the ABM system around Moscow, even if it were integrated with the available nationwide air defense, does not offer effective protection against U.S. strikes.

---

33. Thomas K. Longstreth, John E. Pike and John B. Rhinelander, *A Report on the Impact of U.S. and Soviet BMD Programs on the ABM Treaty* (Washington, DC: National Campaign to Save the ABM Treaty, June 1984), p. 12.

Moreover, the maintenance and modernization of the Moscow ABM system fully conforms with the ABM Treaty.

Recently the U.S. administration has been concentrating more and more on evaluating trends in the development of Soviet strategic defense forces. One of the latest U.S. descriptions of Soviet defense programs, issued by the Departments of State and Defense, divided Soviet activities into three categories: 1) R&D on advanced defenses; 2) BMD based on current technologies; and 3) air defense.[34] On the first, the main conclusion is that the Soviet research program "covers many of the same technologies" on which the United States has been focusing "but represents a far greater investment of plant space, capital, and manpower." With respect to existing BMD capabilities, the report emphasizes that the Soviet Union "maintains the world's only operational ABM system around Moscow and . . . began to upgrade and expand that system to the limit allowed by the 1972 ABM Treaty." The American analysis refers to the radar near Krasnoyarsk as "a direct violation of the ABM Treaty," and to surface-to-air missile component tests as well as alleged development of components of a certain new ABM system as "probable violations." Regarding Soviet air defense, the study expresses concern about the possibility that Soviet air-defense missiles might provide the basis for a nationwide ABM system. The study concludes that the SDI program is needed as a response to the Soviet interest in anti-ballistic missile defense and a hedge against any future Soviet "breakout."

Without going into the details of the U.S. debate on Soviet BMD efforts, some points about official U.S. assessments can be made here. The American evaluations do not present reliable data on the Soviet R&D efforts in strategic defense. While the Pentagon report states that the Soviet Union is vigorously developing advanced technologies in strategic defense and implies that the USSR has an edge over the United States, it does not evaluate the quality and possible significance of such technologies.[35] However, the U.S. Undersecretary of Defense for Research has judged the United States "equivalent" to the Soviet Union in directed energy research and announced that the Soviet Union does not surpass the United States "in any of the basic technologies that have the greatest potential for significantly improv-

---

34. U.S. Department of Defense and U.S. Department of State, *Soviet Strategic Defense Programs* (Joint Publication) (Washington, DC: October 4, 1985 [Third Printing]).

35. U.S. Department of Defense, *Soviet Military Power* (Washington, DC: 1985).

ing military capabilities."[36] There are no signs that Soviet research efforts would require tests in the near future that could threaten to violate the ABM Treaty, as the American tests will.

It is true that the Soviet Union has been maintaining and upgrading an operational ABM system—as permitted by the ABM Treaty. But because of its very limited capability, the significance of such a system should not be exaggerated. The ABM Treaty permits the United States to maintain a similar limited defense capacity. The United States decided in the mid-1970s to dismantle its ABM defense center because it was judged ineffective. However, almost immediately after this decision, the United States began new R&D programs in strategic defense and ASAT technologies.[37]

As Soviet surface-to-air missiles (SAMs) become more advanced, they may become somewhat more effective against tactical or intermediate-range ballistic missiles. But this is not a particular Soviet phenomenon. The United States has been spending hundreds of millions of dollars per year on an anti-tactical ballistic missile (ATBM) project. The Defense Department's so-called Hoffman Panel Report emphasizes that the deployment of an ATBM system is an option that will be available to the United States during the implementation of the SDI program. SDI funds are allocated to explore the feasibility of various ATBM systems. The application of Soviet (or American) SAMs in a strategic ATBM role is unlikely even in the long term. The unconstrained development of various ATBM systems, however, do threaten to violate the ABM Treaty. Despite the interpretation of the treaty prevailing in the Reagan administration, the development, testing (in an ATBM mode) and deployment of such systems violate a number of the treaty provisions.

The Krasnoyarsk radar issue has become a disturbing element even for experts who criticize or directly oppose the SDI program. The military significance of one radar in the whole system, however, is marginal and upon its completion it would not give any significant advantage to the Soviet Union. Should the Soviet Union want to fill the gaps in its nationwide strategic defense with point-defense systems, new radars would be needed, requiring the installation of concrete positioning foundations in various parts of the Soviet Union.

---

36. Statements by the Undersecretary of Defense for Research, *The Fiscal Year 1986 DOD Program for R&D and Acquisition*, Hearings, 99th Cong., 1st sess., 1985, pp. 2–4.

37. Some results of this program are now in their testing phase, like the ASAT-weapon MHV (miniature homing vehicle) based on F-15 aircraft.

Well-informed American sources admit that there is no evidence of such foundations, that even if the Soviet Union were to decide to deploy a country-wide system, it would take several years before the system could acquire military significance.[38] CIA officials have testified before Senate committees that they do not consider it likely for the Soviet Union to proceed with such a deployment in the near term.[39]

Soviet statements have explained that the construction of the Krasnoyarsk radar began only in the early 1980s, that the facility will not be fully operational until the late 1980s and that its function is space tracking. The Soviet Union has advised the United States that once the radar is complete, its function of tracking satellites in space will be clear and could be verified on-site by invited international experts. Nevertheless, the Reagan administration has accused the Soviet Union of violating the ABM Treaty. Meanwhile the United States has not provided an appropriate response to a Soviet aide memoire which expressed Soviet concerns about alleged American violations of the ABM Treaty, such as the use of infrared sensors in exoatmospheric testing, Minuteman testing for ABM capabilities, hardening of ABM launcher silos and radar construction on Shemya island in Alaska.

During the Standing Consultative Commission meetings held in 1979-1980, the Soviet Union put forward questions about the phased-array radar systems under construction in Texas and Georgia. The United States replied that these radars would not violate the ABM Treaty, that they are for space tracking. Since then the Soviet Union has been relying on these explanations. The United States has reportedly made alterations in the orientation of those radars. However, because of their size and capability to cover approximately a 240° field, the coverage of the radars includes significant portions of the U.S. homeland and they can be used in a territorial defense system. Therefore, their construction still may be inconsistent with ABM Treaty requirements.

These remarks about near violations of the ABM Treaty clearly show that there are highly sensitive points even at the present stage of

---

38. See Robinson, "Soviets Accelerate Missile Defense Efforts" (fn. 8). These views are supported by the extraordinary on-site inspection of the Krasnoyarsk facility by U.S. experts conducted in September 1987. See William J. Broad, "Soviet Radar on Display," *The New York Times*, September 9, 1987, p. A1.

39. Lawrence K. Gershwin and Robert M. Gates, "Strategic Force Developments," testimony before a joint session of the Subcommittee on Strategic and Theater Nuclear Forces of the Senate Armed Services Committee and Defense Subcommittee of the Senate Committee on Appropriations, *Hearings*, 99th Cong., 1st sess., June 26, 1985, p. 47.

strategic defense research. It would probably best serve the common interests of the two parties if they were to discuss such issues in the Standing Consultative Commission and avoid unnecessary public accusations which can make the debate acrimonious.

What would SDI mean for the Soviet Union and how has it reacted to U.S. efforts to proceed with SDI? Certainly the Soviet Union is not persuaded that President Reagan initiated the program as a noble, moral rationale to prevent nuclear war. Rather, it perceives the project as designed "to confuse Soviet nuclear planning," "to prevent possible Soviet breakout," "to balance U.S. offensive weaknesses," "to redress U.S. inability to protect the retaliatory deterrent," or "to pursue the technological options for active defense." SDI has been portrayed by administration officials as only a "vigorous long-term research program." Many facts, however, contradict such statements. The project has been accompanied by substantial organizational changes in the U.S. armed forces and in its very early phase has already been connected with tests and plans for "system testing." Moreover, it will be difficult, if not impossible, to convince officials and analysts in the Soviet Union and Eastern Europe that a program launched in a nationally televised presidential speech from the Oval Office and described by some of its planners as a central or vital element in future U.S. strategic doctrine and funded at a suddenly increased (by 50 to 200 percent) level is "a mere research program."

The Soviets consider current American efforts at creating a strategic defense as motivated by a unilateral American concept of security which does not take into consideration the security concerns of others and is clearly not based on the notion of shared responsibility for international stability. The American programs are seen as an attempt to force the Soviet Union to restructure its strategic forces and reallocate its available economic resources in order to match the American buildup. According to the advocates of U.S. strategic defense, the United States "must invest in agile counterforce capabilities" (parallel with SDI), "thereby compelling the Soviet Union to make large, expensive, structural alterations in its ICBM-dominated posture, and/or to reconsider the merit of agreeing to negotiate deep reductions in their forces."[40] Strategic defense is seen as part of the transition toward a U.S. nuclear policy in which defense—after a first-strike attempt—would absorb the Soviet retaliatory strike. George Keyworth, the president's former science adviser, said in 1984 that "In a very real sense, the President's SDI completes a cycle that began two years ago with

---

40. Colin S. Gray, "Deterrence, Arms Control, and the Defense Transition," *Orbis* 28, No. 2 (Summer 1984), p. 229.

strategic modernization. I believe this sends a clear message to the Soviets that the era of undisputed superiority of the ICBM is coming to a close."[41] The links between the SDI program and other facets of U.S. military policy have been highlighted by Secretary of Defense Weinberger as well:

> Too frequently criticism fails to look at strategic defense research as a part of America's overarching strategic design. . . . In fact, our research into the possibility of a defense against nuclear attack results from the Reagan administration's broad reassessment of our foreign and domestic policies. . . . Our reassessment led us to believe that a research program into all forms of strategic defense is an absolute necessity.[42]

Several Soviet articles have extensively analyzed the SDI program. In these studies one finds the following arguments:

- the main goals of the SDI program are strategic superiority plus damage limitation;

- the vigorous research and development program for strategic defense is accompanied by similar, well-financed programs for the development of new offensive forces; the United States is planning to combine strategic offensive and defensive forces;

- the SDI program and the development of new defensive weapons are not compelled by technological changes but by political decisions;

- strategic defense is ultimately seen by American military planners as an instrument for enhancing deterrence and upsetting the strategic balance; and

- in addition to long-term goals, the Reagan administration is also considering the deployment of BMD for point defense (i.e., the defense of its ICBMs) as a near-term option.[43]

---

41. George A. Keyworth, "A Sense of Obligation—the SDI," *Aerospace America*, April 1984, p. 59.

42. Caspar Weinberger, Secretary of Defense, "Vision of Strategic Defense," speech before the Philadelphia World Affairs Council, October 3, 1985.

43. See A. Vasyliev, "Program of Aggression in Space," *Mirovaia Ekonomika i Mezhdunarodnye Otnosheniia* 11 (1985), pp. 14–23; Evgenii Velikhov and Andrei Kokoshin, "Nuclear Weapons and Problems of International Security," *MEMO* 4 (1985), pp. 33–43; R. S. Ovinnikov, "The 'Star Wars' Programme—A New Phase in Washington's Militaristic Policy," *International Affairs* 8 (1985), pp. 13-22; R. S. Ovinnikov, "What is Behind the Star Wars Strategy?" *SShA* 11 (1985), pp. 15–25.

The entire SDI program is characterized as destabilizing.[44] Three main features of the SDI program contribute to its destabilizing effect:

- the development of strategic defensive forces will accelerate the development of new offensive weapons and thereupon initiate a new offense-defense arms race;

- space-based defensive weapons can serve as uncontrollable attack weapons against targets on land or in the air; and

- space-based defensive weapons or special ASAT weapons could paralyze the main elements of C^3I.

Soviet analyses predict a decrease in strategic stability in the case of mutual deployment of strategic defense—even if strategic parity is maintained.[45] Soviet analyses conclude that SDI could not provide a comprehensive population defense, but would initiate a new wave of the arms race and upset the superpower strategic balance. Thus, by embarking on the SDI program the Reagan administration has taken an enormous risk with respect to international security.

Moreover, two leading American arms control officials have declared that the ABM Treaty should be changed in light of the SDI project. Paul Nitze has said that the United States offered to discuss with the Soviet negotiating team at Geneva "the implications of new defense technologies for strategic stability and arms control . . . the opportunity to hold the first exchange on the offense-defense relationship since 1972." Kenneth Adelman has expressed the view that "eventually some modifications [to the treaty] may be warranted to permit more definitive demonstrations of the new space-based technologies."[46]

As Article XIV of the ABM Treaty contains the provision that "each party may propose amendments to the treaty," the real question is not whether the treaty may be amended. The key question is for what purpose. The phrasing of the Nitze and Adelman statements clearly

---

44. "Strategic and International-Political Consequences of the Creation of a Space-Based Anti-Missile System Using Directed-Energy Weapons: A Study of the Committee of Soviet Scientists for the Defense of Peace, Against the Nuclear Threat," *SShA* 11 (1985), pp. 112–127.

45. Ibid., p. 126.

46. See "Amending of 1972 ABM Pact is Urged," *The New York Times*, May 31, 1985.

indicates that the United States has been seeking to legitimize the introduction of defensive weapon technologies into the strategic equation in order to create an offense-defense mix. The Soviet Union has rejected the American appeal. "Having embarked on the road that leads toward the scrapping of the ABM Treaty," states Marshal Sergei F. Akhromeev, Chief of the Soviet General Staff, "the Americans are trying to 'exploit' the treaty provisions for possible amendments. . . . The Soviet Union will, of course, not agree to turn the treaty . . . into a cover-up for the U.S. policy aimed at an arms race in space-based anti-ballistic missile systems."[47] However, the Soviet Union would not oppose the amendment of the ABM Treaty in order to eliminate ambiguities, broaden its coverage and tighten its formulation.

As the parties are now engaged in serious talks about strategic forces, one of the first things they could do is reaffirm the ABM Treaty and not press to modify or bypass it. One side's military policies should not undercut existing agreements as long as the other side reciprocates; both sides should not move into unknown terrain before they have in hand at least an agreement in principle.

It is obvious, however, that the SDI project, as presently conceived by the Reagan administration, cannot proceed without at some point violating the ABM Treaty. In order to continue with SDI, the Reagan administration has initiated two additional elements: a three-phase, ostensibly bilateral transition to a "defense-dominated world," and a promise to share U.S. strategic defense technologies with the Soviet Union.

In a major speech before the Philadelphia World Affairs Council, Paul Nitze, special advisor to the president and the secretary of state on arms control matters, advocated the objective of deploying strategic defense systems. "During the next ten years, the U.S. objective is a radical reduction in the power of existing and planned offensive nuclear arms, as well as the stabilization of the relationship between offensive and defensive nuclear arms, whether on earth or in space."[48] He also pointed out the American goal in the talks: substantial reductions in offensive nuclear arsenals, as in the large MIRVed Soviet ICBM forces. With respect to the large-scale deployment of anti-bal-

---

47. Statement of Chief of the General Staff Sergei F. Akhromeev, *Pravda*, June 4, 1985.

48. Paul Nitze, "On the Road to a More Stable Peace," Address to the Philadelphia World Affairs Council (February 20, 1985), reprinted as U.S. Department of State, *Current Policy*, No. 607. (See Appendix.)

listic missile and space systems, the American expert set up two criteria: survivability and cost-effectiveness at the margin. Although Nitze recommended that if the new technologies could not meet these demanding standards, the United States should not deploy them, the criteria have a serious default. They are unilateral standards. They can be interpreted according to the tastes or wishes of any incumbent American administration.

Cost-effectiveness at the margin means that additional defensive systems could be deployed more cheaply than the offensive forces meant to counter them. However, this criterion cannot be evaluated in static economic terms. A technological achievement might lead to a defensive system declared to be cost-effective against a particular kind of offensive system. But it may not be cost-effective against a whole range of offensive forces. Although Nitze implies that cost-effectiveness at the margin would ensure that the best option for the Soviet Union would be to invest heavily in strategic defense, the situation is not so simple. A deeper look into the matter suggests that an offense-defense arms race is the more probable outcome.

Survivability seems to be an even more demanding criterion. The range of threats against strategic defense systems is wide indeed. Even if we assume that defense systems are directed against incoming ballistic missiles (in which case an ASAT ban agreement is needed), one cannot neglect the fact that defensive systems (especially space-based defense systems) threaten each other. If the defensive systems are mutually vulnerable, the strategic defense relationship would be more destabilizing than the current deterrence situation. In my view, it is probably impossible to design and build space-based defensive systems which would effectively work against ballistic missiles but which would be physically unable to cause substantial harm to each other.

Regarding the criteria presented by Nitze and endorsed by the Reagan administration,[49] three additional points need to be made:

- Survivability and effectiveness could be measured against the goals one or another U.S. administration sets for strategic defense systems. The warnings about the difficulties in accomplishing the SDI program may be frank, the criteria may be challenging, but they impose no obligations on future American presidents.

---

49. See Robert C. McFarlane's speech before the Overseas Writers Association (fn. 14), p. 3.

- If the criteria were modified and linked to given force levels, the deployment of strategic defense systems would profoundly destabilize the international system. If they are maintained and met (which seems to me unlikely if they are strictly interpreted), the deployment of strategic defense systems will initiate and sustain an offense-defense arms race with no end in sight.

- A declaration or a mere demonstration that these criteria have been met would not imply that a transition to more defense or to "defense domination" would be stable. Indeed, the most positive element in Nitze's concept is that he looks at the so-called "transition period" as a "cooperative endeavor" with the Soviet Union. The problem here, however, is that cooperation on such a crucial issue requires an atmosphere of mutual confidence which cannot be achieved without across-the-board improvement in Soviet-American relations—not to speak of an arms agreement. In strictly military terms, the Soviet Union would respond to the deployment of American strategic defense systems with specific countermeasures: 1) to restore the balance in defense; 2) to reduce the effectiveness of the emerging U.S. strategic defense; and 3) to preserve its retaliatory capability.

The notion of sharing strategic defense technologies was advanced by President Reagan during a news conference in 1984. Some months later this whim was apparently abandoned by the Reagan administration. During the preparatory phase of the November 1985 summit meeting, the idea again came into public sight in modified form: the United States would share defense technologies with the Soviet Union "at a cost" in the final phase of the transition. American experts tend to claim such an action is unlikely. If the Reagan administration is seriously thinking about sharing defense technologies, the best way of doing it would be to use regular bilateral scientific channels from the very start of the new strategic defense programs and establish "joint ventures" in relevant applied science areas. An increased exchange of scientific knowledge would promote better understanding. However, recent American decisions to tighten restrictions on technology transfer, pressure Western European countries and Japan to enlarge the COCOM list, and establish specific rules for curtailing the export of American licenses, know-how, etc., seem to show very different guidelines for technology-sharing. Moreover, the established policy of the Reagan administration, which calls for the United States to be preeminent in all space activities, including civilian areas, does not facilitate cooperation and sharing.

SDI's Impact on European Security

In the debate among American experts about active defense in the late 1970s, there was no extensive discussion of the impact of an American strategic defense on European security or the security of the NATO allies. Moreover, there was not the slightest mention of creating an active defense covering the West European part of the alliance or building a special comprehensive anti-tactical ballistic missile (ATBM) defense in Western Europe. Some proponents of anti-ballistic missile defense argued that American strategic defense would help the United States strengthen its security guarantees to its allies in Western Europe, but the majority maintained that "while this argument is structurally persuasive, there are few if any concrete cases in which actually prevailing political perceptions and relationships would suggest significant results of this kind."[50] In a seventy-five-page special report written by three prominent proponents of active defense, published in December 1979, there was no mention of its possible effects on European security, even though their task was—as reflected in the title of the report—to deal with the implications of a ballistic missile defense.[51]

In President Reagan's 1983 speech, there was a tangential reference to U.S. allies when he expressed the wish: "We could intercept and destroy strategic ballistic missiles before they reached our own soil or *that of our allies*."[52] The immediate West European reaction was a rejection, expressing growing alarm over the American "Star Wars" plan. This might have been an unexpected development for President Reagan, whose advisors assured him that a plan for strategic defense "would lead to a revival of faith in the effectiveness and reliability of the U.S. deterrent and hence would be viewed as a godsend to their [West European] security interests."[53] However, experts who had

---

50. Donald G. Brennan, "BMD Policy Issues for the 1980s," in *U.S. Strategic Nuclear Policy and BMD: The 1980s and Beyond* (Cambridge: Institute for Foreign Policy Analysis, 1980), p. 32.

51. Leon Goure, William G. Hyland and Colin S. Gray, *The Emerging Strategic Environment: Implications for Ballistic Missile Defense* (Cambridge: Institute for Foreign Policy Analysis, 1979).

52. "Peace and National Security," President Reagan's address to the nation (March 23, 1983), reprinted as U.S. Department of State, *Current Policy*, No. 472. (See Appendix.)

53. Daniel O. Graham, *High Frontier: A New National Strategy* (Washington, DC: The Heritage Foundation, 1982), p. 87.

sufficient knowledge about West European security interests recognized that the U.S. initiative would rekindle old fears and create new ones among the NATO allies. These European concerns* can be summarized as follows:

1. How can the geographical unity of NATO be maintained and a division of the allies into two (protected and unprotected) categories be avoided?

2. Once the Soviet Union inevitably develops a matching defense and the United States acquires a false sense of security, Europe will be left as a possible battlefield. This is especially true if American concepts of a "limited war" emphasized in the early 1980s constitute an organic part of U.S. nuclear planning and because of the greater range of the conventional and nuclear weapons deployed in Europe.

3. As it is highly doubtful whether a reliable area defense can be deployed for the European NATO territory, concerns over whether an American deployment downgraded to a point defense against Soviet short- and medium-range missiles would be technically feasible at acceptable cost or worthwhile at all should prevail.

4. American plans to deploy a leakproof strategic defense on American soil will give greater impetus to the renewed West European debate on "decoupling" and undermine the consensus on NATO strategy.

5. A strategic space-based defense will violate the ABM Treaty and will lead to an intensified arms race.

6. American efforts will undermine the military and political value of the French and British nuclear forces and would weaken any hopes of a relatively independent West European attitude in East-West security (and political) matters.

7. The continuation of strategic defense programs in the United States leading to testing and deployment will jeopardize arms limitation and disarmament talks and may arrest progress toward radical reduction of strategic and intermediate-range weaponry.

---

* See Appendix for documents expressing West German and British views.

In 1984, the Reagan administration became aware that the strategic defense idea could not be sold on a moralistic basis to its NATO allies and that its advertised military value was questioned by many experts and government officials in these countries. It therefore changed its tactic. Since then, three new arguments supporting SDI have been used.

The most important military argument has been that protection for the West European NATO allies against a Soviet missile attack should be seen as a natural complement to U.S. strategic defense and that it could be accomplished by upgrading the Patriot and Hawk missiles. According to American military estimates, a "system of perhaps 1,000 Patriots with sophisticated sensors and two airborne radars could cover a significant fraction of key NATO installations."[54] The so-called Hoffman Report argued for an anti-tactical ballistic missile system as an intermediate option for mid-course and terminal defense: "inclusion of such an option . . . should reduce allied anxieties that our increased emphasis on defenses might indicate a weakening of our commitment to the defense of Europe."[55] In the NATO Nuclear Planning Group meeting at Cesme, Turkey, in April 1984, U.S. Secretary of Defense Caspar Weinberger reportedly advised his partners that the Patriot missile would be available as a basic weapon in an ATBM system for NATO Europe. In an article published only a week after the Cesme meeting, Clarence Robinson described the American project for an ATBM system as a "phased approach" in which "NATO countries are expected to participate." According to Pentagon officials, the anti-tactical missile program is considered a priority effort by both the United States and its allies.[56]

From a strictly military point of view, a defense system using upgraded Patriot and Hawk missiles will provide only point defense or at most a very selected area-defense capacity. Therefore, its development and deployment would not solve the defense problems of the

---

54. Quotation from an American estimate used in an unpublished paper by Hans-Guenther Brauch presented at the 26th International Studies Association convention in Washington, March 5–9, 1985.

55. Fred S. Hoffman, *Summary Report: Ballistic Missile Defense and U.S. National Security* (Washington, DC: Department of Defense, October 1983).

56. Clarence A. Robinson, "U.S. Develops Anti-tactical Weapon for European Role," *Aviation Week and Space Technology*, April 9, 1984.

European NATO allies. It would, however, be seen by Eastern Europe as an addition to the NATO capability supporting recent doctrinal shifts toward a stronger emphasis on "deep strike" and as such it would likely be counterbalanced by WTO efforts.

From an arms control viewpoint a NATO ATBM system raises two serious concerns. In accordance with Article IX of the ABM Treaty, "each party undertakes not to transfer to other states and not to deploy outside its national territory, ABM systems or their components limited by this Treaty."[57] Thus, the deployment of upgraded U.S. Patriot missiles produced in the United States or in cooperation with U.S. NATO allies against tactical ballistic missiles in Western Europe will violate the ABM Treaty. Moreover, in accordance with a 1972 U.S. unilateral statement on the understanding of the phrase "tested in an ABM mode," the testing of an ABM Patriot must be considered as a test in an ABM mode because it would be flight-tested "to an altitude inconsistent with interception of targets against which air defenses are deployed."[58] Based on these understandings, the participation of any West European NATO ally in the research and testing of an ABM system with some inherent SLBM and IRBM capabilities in cooperation with the United States will lead to the abrogation of the ABM Treaty—irrespective of interpretations issued by the Pentagon.[59]

The second kind of justification provided by U.S. government officials maintains that the West must show unity in supporting American strategic defense programs in order to deny the Soviet Union leverage in the Geneva talks. The American request for an early public commitment of West European governments to support SDI was motivated by U.S. concern over intensified domestic debate on SDI as well as fear of effective Soviet proposals at Geneva aimed at gaining support from Western Europe in order to change American stubbornness in strategic-defense-related issues. The interrelationship of the three issues under negotiation in Geneva was, however, well understood by the West European countries; they did not want to incur the risk of an early stalemate by making a public commitment to SDI before they

57. See fn. 3.

58. Unilateral statement by the U.S. delegation on the phrase, "Tested in ABM Mode," delivered on April 7, 1972, in ibid., pp. 146–147.

59. Bill Keller, "Pentagon Asserts Star Wars Tests Won't Break Pact," *The New York Times*, April 20, 1985, p. A1.

had had an opportunity to make a detailed evaluation of its long-term political and strategic implications.[60]

So far the most appealing U.S. proposal for ensuring West European support for SDI has been an invitation extended to several West European governments and Japan to participate in U.S. strategic defense research and development programs. A common statement on this invitation has not been issued, either by the ministerial meeting of the Western European Union (WEU), which took place in Bonn, April 22–23, 1985, or by any other multilateral forum of European NATO members. The WEU countries were reluctant to admit that they were put under duress by the ultimatum-like invitation delivered by U.S. Defense Secretary Weinberger, requiring them to declare within two months whether they were interested in taking part in SDI research. Fears of an increasing technology gap between the United States and Western Europe as a result of American strategic defense research promote European cooperation. The West European reactions can be divided into three main categories:

1) participation of different private companies conditioned, guaranteed and supervised by the government under a framework agreement between that government and the U.S. administration (Great Britain has chosen this way and other countries like West Germany, Italy, Japan and Israel are tending to follow);

2) participation of private companies without governmental endorsement (France seems to exemplify such an experiment); and

3) outright rejection of the U.S. invitation for participation (Greece, the Netherlands, Austria and several other countries have already expressed their refusal).

---

60. This uncertainty was expressed by West German Chancellor Helmut Kohl in his policy statement to the Bundestag on April 18, 1985. "Nobody can yet judge with certainty whether President Reagan's SDI will prove to be a method of greatly reducing and ultimately outlawing nuclear weapons." He referred to the Geneva talks, saying that "It is in our interest that the superpowers should negotiate in Geneva on strategic defense systems in connection with the offensive nuclear weapons without blocking or impeding progress towards promising solutions by establishing one-sided and inappropriate links. . . . The arms control function of the Strategic Defense Initiative is of central importance to us. We shall steadfastly promote this view in our dealings with our American allies." (See Appendix.)

The three main West European governments have had major reservations about SDI and have provided only conditional support for the U.S. program. The anticipated but dubious gains from participation in strategic defense research might provide an incentive for embracing the American invitation, but they fail to mollify the serious strategic and political anxieties and risks associated with SDI. There are differences not only in the attitudes toward SDI between the West European countries, but most of their societies are domestically divided as well. Reasons for this division are both economic-technological and political-military.

From an economic-technological point of view, many experts do not see prospects for the West Europeans or Japan to become equal partners with the United States. Past experience in joint weapons procurement is not a promising basis for such two-way cooperation. The most probable form of participation will be research commissions to West European and Japanese companies in areas where their previous accomplishments are equal to or better than those of American firms. In such cases, it is very difficult to predict whether participation would bring benefits to a country or divert important research capacities from national programs. As Konrad Seitz has concluded, "What is clear . . . is that this kind of participation would not lead to a technological step-up."[61]

From a political-military standpoint, West Europeans are concerned that as participants they would share political responsibility for the concept of strategic defense without having a greater say in the outcome of the American program. Since SDI testing will be inconsistent with the ABM Treaty, West European participants would contribute, although inadvertently, to the erosion of the treaty. As yet it cannot be seen how a proper anti-missile defense for the European NATO countries could be established; the American program, therefore, does not promise improvements for the protection of Western Europe. Many NATO countries have expressed concerns that just the present debate about the deployment of strategic defense—and the debate alone—weakens present NATO strategy and diverts attention and resources from building a stronger conventional defense.

At two points, the economic-technological and political-military aspects coincide: 1) the SDI program strongly militarizes basic and

---

61. Konrad Seitz, "SDI: The Technological Challenge for Europe," *The World Today* (August/September 1985), p. 157.

applied research while the direct benefits of civilian research may be more significant than the spinoffs from military R&D; and 2) a combined political and technological solution should be found for West Europe to meet the challenge of SDI, i.e., a common (Western) European program for technological development should be established. With the Eureka program, the West European countries have taken a step toward this objective.

Thus far, circumstances have not compelled the East European members of the Warsaw Treaty Organization to make a comprehensive analysis or full official consideration of strategic and space defense in their governmental announcements. These countries, unlike some West European members of NATO—the U.K., France, the FRG—do not have the capability to build a ground- or space-based defense. Their concerns, as expressed in articles by experts and in various remarks by state officials, stem from anticipation that the American strategic defense plan would:

- decrease stability in Soviet-American relations;

- introduce new destabilizing elements into European security and disarmament;

- lead to an intensified arms race;

- enhance the probability of war on European soil; and

- by furthering the division of Europe, undermine the main achievements of the Helsinki process.

With respect to strategic defense, their special interests lie in their concerns about its menace to political, economic and human contacts between the nations of Europe. Because of their geographic location, limited military capabilities and their membership in the WTO, the only realistic *military* approach for these countries is and will be a policy coordinated with the Soviet Union. This was also expressed by former Soviet Foreign Minister Andrei A. Gromyko in a television interview in January 1985. To a question about the security interests of the allies of the Soviet Union, he replied: "We will fully take them into account. The Soviet Union speaks to Western countries and to the U.S. in her own name and in the name of her allies. . . . This is a concerted policy. We are speaking for ourselves and for them, we consider that their security interests must also be fully protected in the same manner as those of the Soviet Union will be protected."[62]

---

62. Gromyko's conversation with political observers, *Pravda*, January 14, 1985, pp. 4, 5.

For the East European countries, strategic and tactical defense will clearly be dangerous. They will be less effectively defended than the United States or the Soviet Union because of the geographical proximity of American short- or medium-range missiles deployed in the Western part of Europe. Even a space-based WTO defense cannot significantly change this assessment.

For the time being the military aspects of strategic defense are of secondary importance to the East European countries; their attention has turned toward its economic-technological and political features. Since the East European countries have no military or technological drive to build their own strategic defense, budget outlays for such purposes would clearly be seen as throwing money away. The resources that might be allocated for such programs are needed elsewhere in their civilian economies. Thus, the American initiative has been criticized by the public in these countries as a deliberate attempt to dry up economic resources which could be used for achieving higher domestic standards of living. Increased international tension in the early 1980s, the general problems in the world economy, and defects in their national economic performances already have slowed down economic growth in several East European countries. The prospect of additional burdens stemming from the strategic defense race is not attractive. They would certainly respond to the technological part of the strategic defense challenge by upgrading and enlarging their individual and joint efforts in the relevant areas of science and technology. While some of these areas are significant for the technological level of their economies, the drive for national technological revival and keeping pace with the rest of the world in scientific-technological development covers much broader areas, as has been shown by the recently approved long-term CMEA cooperation project in science and technology.

Cooperation in science and technology is widely sought by all of these countries, although in different degrees and ways. The ongoing process of technology transfer between East and West has become an almost built-in element in national economic planning. The subjugation of this channel to strategic defense programs would substantially curtail the exchange of scientific information and technology. Even the existence of the Eureka program with its possible military applications has raised concerns among East European economists and political experts. Some predict that because of Eureka and the association of several West European companies with SDI, East-West technology transfer may decrease in the coming years. Although this might be one undesirable consequence of SDI, the Eureka program itself should not lead to such results, as it is basically a civilian research and development program. It may, rather, serve as a new vehicle in all-European cooperation, along with the CMEA joint program.

Politically, the most important issue for the East European countries is that the implementation of the SDI program together with its West European aspects would further strengthen the division of Europe. Therefore, mutual concerns about this problem among East and West European countries may strengthen the common wish of these countries that the Soviet Union and the United States achieve agreement in Geneva on meaningful limitations and reductions of strategic arms.

The Future of Space and Strategic Defense Arms Control

The future developments in strategic and space arms control are basically determined by two processes: 1) what general course Soviet-American relations will take and 2) how strongly the United States will push for strategic defense and what kind of defense it will prefer or find feasible. The two processes are, of course, interconnected, but for the sake of this analysis can be separated.

What has become apparent from the 27th Communist Party Congress and the Geneva and Reykjavik summit meetings is that the Soviet Union has a clear preference for improved relations with the United States. The most important factors leading the Soviet Union to reduce tension in Soviet-American relations are the growing responsibility of both countries for international security and stability; the fact that the parties must strive for maintaining political dialogue even under tense circumstances; and the fact that a calm international system is the most favorable condition for implementing a large-scale social transformation and radical economic reform program in the Soviet Union. General Secretary Gorbachev expressed this conclusion in his speech at the 27th Party Congress:

> To ensure security is increasingly seen as a political problem and it can only be resolved by political means. In order to progress along the road of disarmament what is needed is, above all, the will. Security cannot be built endlessly on fear of retaliation, in other words, on the doctrines of "containment" or "deterrence." Apart from the absurdity and amorality of a situation in which the whole world becomes a nuclear hostage, these doctrines encourage an arms race that may sooner or later go out of control. In the context of the relations between the USSR and the USA, security can only be mutual, and if we take international relations as a whole it can only be universal. The highest wisdom is not in caring exclusively for oneself, especially to the detriment of the other side. It

is vital that all should feel equally secure. . . . Our countries [the USSR and the United States] have quite a few points of coincidence and there is the objective need to live in peace with each other, to cooperate on a basis of equality and mutual benefit and there is no other basis.[63]

Both the United States and the Soviet Union have been undergoing significant changes. In many ways, they are not the same countries they were during the era of detente. Therefore it is unclear what kind of relationship is possible between them. From the Soviet point of view, the preference for an improvement is not unconditional. Soviet readiness to achieve such an objective derives not from weakness or from fear and does not involve renouncing the Soviet Union's global role. Rather, this Soviet policy is motivated by its sense of responsibility for international security and by the sheer interest of getting the clearest assessment of the international options available to it as it enters a phase of profound change in its society. On the American side, the Reagan administration has to consider an alternative to its current Soviet policy. There is a moment of opportunity to find an alternative course which may lead to balanced agreements and a significant improvement in the relationship. The United States is again in a situation in which serious thinking is needed about what kind of Soviet Union is in U.S. interests. Both countries have a very modest capacity to influence the course of policy the other side takes and carries out. Using this capacity prudently and responsibly requires a long-term perspective and taking some distance from the current domestic political situation.

Yet the time factor cannot be neglected here. With swift changes in the world, if hopes dim for progress there will be a growing inclination to conclude that the United States is not prepared to negotiate seriously on the central issue of our day—how to eliminate nuclear weapons, how to avoid a nuclear war. It is not a question of putting the onus on the United States or blaming the Soviet Union for wrongdoing, but a question of will—to find the best way, acceptable to all countries involved.

A phased process of reducing nuclear weapons pursued by the two parties could lead to several consecutive, synergistic actions and agreements. In the first phase, the most urgent steps are the reaffirmation of the ABM Treaty and the preservation of the other arms control

---

63. Mikhail Gorbachev, "Political Report of the General Secretary to the 27th CPSU Congress," *Pravda*, February 26, 1986.

agreements observed so far. The Soviet Union came forward with comprehensive new proposals in January 1986. In order to achieve the elimination of all nuclear weapons the Soviet leadership is ready to negotiate and concentrate on three main areas: banning nuclear testing; prevention of an arms race in outer space; a radical, phased reduction of the existing nuclear weaponry of intercontinental, medium and short range, supported by significant reduction in conventional forces. The elimination of medium-range nuclear weapons from Europe will have been secured by the signing of the U.S.-Soviet INF treaty in December 1987. From a political point of view, which part of the complex arms balance is touched upon by the negotiating parties next is almost insignificant. There are two points which really matter. A first step should be made, a compromise agreement should be reached. And no one action or decision is permissible which might threaten the arms control process before the next successful step is taken. Therefore, all those plans, disputes and possible decisions connected with a "broader" interpretation of the ABM Treaty, an early deployment of a point-defense system, or outer-space testing of anti-ballistic missile weapons would be counterproductive and would threaten the opportunities of achieving further significant reductions in nuclear weapons. Based on self-restraint and efforts by the parties to increase mutual understanding and confidence, work can be accelerated in the second phase—in accordance with the 1985 Geneva summit commitment—in all those areas of arms control where agreements seems to be feasible in a three-to-five year period. The most promising possibilities are a comprehensive nuclear test ban following the ratification of less comprehensive agreements already signed in this area, reductions of conventional forces in Europe, and a cut in short-range nuclear weapons deployed in Europe. By the time the research work in strategic and space defense would enter the testing phase, the parties should establish a clear division line between research and development and reach an agreement which may allow basic research work in laboratories and clearly separate such work from field-testing. In the meantime, talks should be maintained to promote progress on such debated issues as compliance with the ABM Treaty, verification methods, etc. The most important achievement of this second stage may be an agreement on maintaining the ABM Treaty for another decade at least.

Before the third phase of the process may commence, the United States should decide whether the risks of developing and deploying strategic and space defense weapons are worth taking and really necessary for U.S. security. In evaluating the needs of U.S. security, it should be taken into consideration that the Soviet Union is clearly in favor of a "sufficient" level of weaponry, i.e., the lowest possible level for maintaining its own security. This would be the phase when the Soviet Union should decide whether there is any kind of large-scale strategic defense deployment that will not jeopardize its security and will not put international stability under unbearable pressure and risks. It is the phase when the parties may reach an agreement on the radical reduction of strategic offensive weapons and embark on the road leading to a lower level or the possible elimination of nuclear weapons without upsetting international stability.

3

Ballistic Missile Defense, U.S.-Soviet Relations and European Security

VLADIMIR BILANDZIC

I. Anti-Ballistic Missile Defense in the U.S.-Soviet Strategic Equation: Past and Present

Since the late 1950s, the ultimate guarantee that the superpower competition will not escalate into military conflict has been the threat of mutual nuclear annihilation. Mutual vulnerability and insecurity have become the basis of superpower security. This paradoxical yet probably unavoidable state of affairs has become known as mutual assured destruction (MAD).[1] In the individual strategic policies of each superpower, the objective situation of MAD has found its expression in the strategy of *deterrence*, whereby each side has kept such a quantity and variety of nuclear weapons so as to ensure that it could absorb a first strike and still be capable of delivering a punishing retaliatory blow. Therefore, the preservation of an assured retaliatory capacity is a central element of a credible deterrence policy. Any attempts to protect oneself from retaliation by defensive measures and/or to knock out the opponent's offensive capacity in a single (first) strike would undermine deterrence and create strategic instability, fueling the reciprocal fear of surprise attack.

---

1. "MAD has often been misleadingly characterized as a deliberate governmental policy of maximizing population damage in the event of war—so as to maximize deterrence—and of voluntarily leaving populations vulnerable. . . . But mutual assured destruction is more accurately understood as an inherent consequence of the awesome destructive potential of each side's nuclear stockpile." Peter A. Clausen, "SDI in Search of a Mission," *World Policy Journal* 2, No. 2 (Spring 1985), pp. 251-252.

Still, as the history of the nuclear arms race shows, neither side has been able to resist the temptation to "improve" its own deterrent and search for alternatives in case deterrence fails. One of the options repeatedly considered by both sides has been the possibility of defense against nuclear ballistic missiles.

It is hardly surprising that the superpowers found it very difficult to accept mutual assured destruction as a permanent state of affairs. It was not only the risk of a failure of deterrence entailing the likely destruction of their societies that bothered them, but also the fact that MAD had put significant constraints on their foreign policies, especially their policies towards each other. Former U.S. Secretary of Defense Harold Brown has stated that, judging from his own experience, "the fact of American vulnerability . . . affects all of our national security policies and limits our military and diplomatic behavior."[2] There is no reason to doubt that similar constraints are felt on the Soviet side.

Thus, nuclear weapons, which became the basis of the superpowers' status, providing them with a special position in the international arena, have also become a burden for them. To possess the absolute weapon and be unable to use it, except as a threat against its use by an adversary, is not readily accepted.

As a country which once enjoyed a (brief) monopoly over atomic weapons, the United States found it very difficult to accept the fact that it not only had lost its nuclear monopoly, but that it had become vulnerable to a possible nuclear attack by ICBMs, which the Soviet Union acquired before the United States. One of the American responses (besides building up its offensive nuclear weapons to bridge the perceived "missile gap") was to try to develop an anti-ballistic missile defense system. The first U.S. ABM program was presented to Congress in 1955, and in 1958, a year after the Soviet Union had launched its first ICBM, the Nike-Zeus system was in full-scale development. However, in 1963, after five years of research, this system was abandoned because it was thought that "it could not cope with the Soviet threat envisioned for the late sixties."[3] At the same time, the so-called "missile gap" was replaced by U.S. strategic superiority,

---

2. Harold Brown, *The Strategic Defense Initiative: Defensive Systems and the Strategic Debate*, unpublished paper, p. 3.

3. James F. Bryden, "The Emerging BMD Debate: Dèja Vu or Not?" *Air University Review* (November-December 1984), p. 43.

which probably decreased the sense of urgency for developing an ABM defense.

Nevertheless, U.S. ABM programs continued, first with the Nike-X system, which represented an attempt to develop a population defense. The Nike-X effort was followed in 1968 by the Sentinel program, which in turn was replaced in 1969 by the more modest Safeguard project. In Safeguard, a long-range Spartan rocket was designed to destroy incoming reentry vehicles beyond the atmosphere, while the short-range Sprint rocket was to be used for lower-level interception. Although considered vulnerable and of marginal effectiveness, the Safeguard system became partly operational in 1975 (one site to protect ICBM silos in North Dakota), only to be dismantled after a few months.

Although Soviet work on a BMD program reportedly started as early as the late 1940s or early 1950s,[4] the first Soviet ABM missile, the Griffin, was displayed to the public in 1963. Although intended for deployment around Leningrad, it never became operational. The second Soviet ABM missile, Galosh, was exhibited in a military parade in Red Square in November 1964, its size indicating that it was an exoatmospheric interceptor with a range of several hundred miles. The construction of the ABM system using the Galosh missile for Moscow proceeded in the late 1960s. The system became operational in 1970 or 1971, but apparently on a scale smaller than originally planned. Construction was initiated on eight launch sites that would have included 128 missiles, but only four complexes involving sixty-four missiles were actually completed.

The experience with developing both Soviet and American ABM defenses in the 1960s shows that both sides came to the conclusion that such systems had, at best, very limited strategic value, and that they might even be counterproductive, since they might provoke offensive countermeasures by the other side. This conclusion was reached, however, only gradually, after both sides had acquired large offensive and defensive forces, and after they had debated the question of the relationship between the two forces before and during the SALT I talks (1969-1972). In this respect, it is interesting to note that the arguments against ABM defense developed simultaneously with, and probably as a result of, the buildup of formidable offensive strategic forces on both sides.

---

4. Sayre Stevens, "The Soviet BMD Program," in Ashton B. Carter and David N. Schwartz, eds., *Ballistic Missile Defense* (Washington, DC: The Brookings Institution, 1984), p. 191.

The United States, the first to build huge offensive strategic forces, was also officially the first to endorse the principle of mutual assured destruction as the ultimate basis of its strategy of deterrence. This type of deterrence—deterrence by punishment—was articulated in the 1960s by then U.S. Secretary of Defense Robert McNamara. In a speech in San Francisco in September 1967, for example, he claimed that "assured destruction" was "the very essence of the . . . deterrence concept" and implied that strategic nuclear capabilities had grown to the point that the United States and the Soviet Union could deter each other (mutual assured destruction).[5]

The Soviet Union, which at the time seriously lagged behind the United States in the construction of offensive strategic forces (at the beginning of 1967, the USSR had 750 strategic launchers, compared to 2,280 launchers for the United States), did not publicly endorse the concept of MAD and apparently was not fully convinced of the futility of efforts to build an ABM defense. For instance, during his trip to London in February 1967, Soviet Prime Minister Alexei Kosygin stated that defensive systems were not "a cause of the arms race" and that their purpose was to save "human lives." At his meeting with U.S. President Lyndon Johnson later that year in Glassboro, Kosygin maintained his position in favor of ABM defense; however, it seems that the Soviet prime minister only expressed the view that in future negotiations anti-missile systems should not be singled out for limitation, but considered together with limitations on offensive forces.[6]

As a rule, Soviet statements in favor of ABM defense, which were even more unequivocal in the early 1960s,[7] when ABM technology was rudimentary and the United States was taking the lead in the buildup of offensive forces, should not be interpreted as the Soviet repudiation of deterrence as such, but as an element of the doctrine of "deterrence by denial." This type of deterrence fit more conveniently with traditional Soviet military doctrine and probably seemed more credible than deterrence by punishment, for which the necessary precondition—formidable offensive strategic forces—had not yet been developed by the Soviet Union. In such a situation, Soviet military

---

5. Quoted in Bryden, "The Emerging BMD Debate."

6. Raymond L. Garthoff, "BMD and East-West Relations," in Carter and Schwartz, eds., *Ballistic Missile Defense*, p. 297.

7. For example, then Soviet Minister of Defense Marshal Malinovsky noted in 1961 that "the problem of destroying enemy missiles in flight has been successfully resolved." (Quoted in Stevens, "The Soviet BMD Program," p. 194.)

planners probably considered the development of ABM systems as compensation for Soviet inferiority in offensive strategic weapons.

However, as the Soviet Union was approaching nuclear parity with the United States and by the time the SALT I talks were under way, the concept of MAD started to be acknowledged indirectly in the Soviet Union, primarily in the statements of political leaders, but also in some military writings. For example, in a May 1969 article in the Soviet journal *Military Thought*, it was claimed that the "existing level of development of nuclear missile weapons" makes it "impossible to prevent an annihilating retaliatory strike."[8] This was an obvious departure from some earlier statements by Soviet military theorists, such as one in 1964 claiming that "the creation of an effective anti-missile system enables the state to make its defenses dependent chiefly on its own possibilities, and not only on mutual deterrence, that is, on the goodwill of the other side."[9]

Of course, neither the Soviet Union nor the United States enthusiastically accepted the reality of MAD. The debate over whether this state of affairs should be recognized as permanent and unavoidable continued in both countries throughout the 1970s—in different ways and with varying degrees of openness. Furthermore, the military postures and strategic doctrines of the superpowers (especially their nuclear targeting policies) were not based exclusively, or even primarily, on the notion of mutual assured destruction, but rather on limited nuclear options and counterforce strategies.

The successful conclusion of the SALT I talks and above all the acceptance of a treaty limiting the anti-missile defense systems of both superpowers were generally interpreted as proof that both the United States and the USSR implicitly, but nevertheless officially, accepted that mutual vulnerability and the threat of retaliation formed the basis of their security. By agreeing that they would not endeavor to look for protection from ballistic missile attack, the two powers, in effect, made deterrence based on the principle (and reality) of mutual assured destruction their common concept of security.

This important doctrinal implication of the ABM Treaty has been widely recognized by officials and experts in both East and West. Polish observers at the time noted that by concluding the ABM Treaty, the United States and USSR fully secured the effectiveness of the

---

8. Cited in Garthoff, "BMD and East-West Relations," p. 309.

9. Cited in David Holloway, "Soviet Policy and the Arms Race," in Gwyn Prins, ed., *The Nuclear Crisis Reader* (New York: Vintage Books, 1984), pp. 111–112.

retaliatory strike, which discourages both sides from undertaking an attack and thus constitutes a proof of mutual confidence.[10] Former U.S. Secretary of State Henry Kissinger even attributed to the ABM Treaty "revolutionary significance" because it meant that for the first time in history two great powers intentionally based their security on mutual vulnerability.[11]

Apart from its strategic-doctrinal importance, the additional significance of the ABM Treaty, especially for the Soviet Union, has been political. The SALT I agreement, with the ABM Treaty as its central element, was considered the main basis for the development of detente between the two superpowers. Soviet and East European observers argued that there was a close interrelationship between the SALT I agreement and the breakthrough to detente, and that it was not "by accident" that the SALT I agreements and Declaration on the Basic Principles of U.S.-Soviet Relations, which accepted "peaceful coexistence" as the foundation for the development of these relations, were concluded at the same time. Judging from official Soviet statements and writings, the lapse of time and the deterioration of Soviet-American relations did not in any way diminish the importance and crucial role of the ABM Treaty in Soviet eyes. Almost without exception, Soviet officials and experts emphasize the fact that the ABM Treaty is a solemn undertaking of indefinite duration, viewing it as a formal recognition and guarantee of strategic parity with the United States. They still consider the ABM Treaty as a unique agreement in the field of strategic arms limitation and call it a symbol of the achievements in the mutual understanding between the United States and USSR in the delicate and complex field of national security. Soviet commentators repeatedly emphasized that there is a close link between this treaty and the possibility of detente and mutual cooperation between East and West.[12]

Although the ABM Treaty at best only partially slowed the strategic arms race, its continued importance is underscored by most arms control specialists in Western Europe. Lawrence Freedman, one of the leading British experts in the field, has characterized the ABM

---

10. A. Gradziuk and A. Towpik, "SALT: Present Results, Significance and Perspectives," *Sprawy Miedzynarodowe* (December 1974), pp. 20–74.

11. Henry Kissinger, *Years of Upheaval* (New York: Little, Brown and Company, 1982), p. 256.

12. A. G. Arbatov, "Ogranichenie protivoraketnikh sistem—problem, uroki, perspektivi," *SShA* 12 (1984), pp. 16–28.

Treaty as "arms control's most impressive achievement thus far," underlining its link with "what used to be called detente and is now referred to as East-West dialogue."[13] However, the interest of Western Europeans in preserving the ABM Treaty stems not only from its political importance in the context of East-West relations but also, at least as far as Great Britain and France are concerned, from its contribution to maintaining the credibility of their own strategic forces.

The majority of arms control specialists in the United States also considers the ABM Treaty to be the cornerstone of stability in the superpower strategic balance and believes that the agreement, which has been called "a milestone in the political approach to preventing nuclear war," should be preserved.[14] However, despite official assurances that it does not intend to depart from the treaty, the Reagan administration has shown growing skepticism about the ability of the ABM accord to enhance U.S. security. President Reagan himself considers all arms control agreements concluded so far within the framework of SALT, including the ABM Treaty, detrimental to U.S. security, while U.S. Secretary of Defense Caspar Weinberger has publicly stated that he had "never been a proponent of the ABM Treaty."[15] His insistence on the so-called "broad" interpretation of the treaty, which would allow development and testing of SDI components using previously unknown, "exotic" technologies, gradually prevailed in the administration, although it still faces opposition in the Senate and Congress.[16] Whatever the result of this debate, it is obvious that by launching SDI the Reagan administration has not simply called into

---

13. Lawrence Freedman, "NATO and the Strategic Defense Initiative," *NATO's Sixteen Nations* 29, No. 6 (November 1984), p. 19.

14. Sidney D. Drell, Philip J. Farley, and David Holloway, "Preserving the ABM Treaty: A Critique of the Reagan Strategic Defense Initiative," *International Security* 9, No. 2 (Fall 1984), p. 55. (See also John B. Rhinelander, "How to Save the ABM Treaty," *Arms Control Today* 15, No. 4 [May 1985], pp. 1–12.) Of course, this view is not unanimous and the criticism of the ABM Treaty in the United States has become, if not wider, then at least more vocal in recent years, coming mainly from the conservative side of the political spectrum. For example, one of the main supporters of Reagan's SDI, physicist Robert Jastrow, has claimed that "it takes a person with an idealized view of the world to think up something like the ABM Treaty." (*High Frontier Newsletter* 3, No. 1 [January 1985], p. 4.)

15. Quoted in Wayne Biddle, "How High Will Star Wars Fly," *The New York Times*, December 30, 1984.

16. "U.S. Moves Towards Arms Treaty Rethink," *The Times* (London), February 10, 1987, p. 3.

question the permanence of the ABM Treaty as a legal instrument, but challenged the basic philosophy of deterrence underlying the treaty, which was considered the main guarantee of peace in the nuclear era.

What are the main reasons for this renewed interest in ballistic missile defense and what are the main arguments for the Reagan administration to pursue with such determination its search for replacing deterrence by strategic defense?

Before answering this question, it should be pointed out that both superpowers have continued their research in the field of BMD, even after the ABM Treaty was signed, and that this research was explicitly allowed by the treaty. Evidently, the logic of the arms competition, which was not substantially limited by the SALT I and II agreements, has demanded that both superpowers keep up their efforts in the field of ABM defense, ostensibly in order to prevent a possible breakthrough by the other side. It is difficult to assess whether either side is on the verge of a breakthrough, but as far as existing ABM technologies are concerned, it seems that neither of the two powers has a meaningful advantage that would affect the present strategic balance. Although the Soviet Union, unlike the United States, has kept one ABM system (as allowed by the ABM Treaty), the capacity of the Soviet system is rather limited, and certainly not of such a scale that it would make a major difference as far as the overall U.S.-Soviet strategic relationship is concerned. On the whole, even a cursory comparison of Soviet and American R&D programs with possible ABM applications makes clear that there is no gap between the two powers that would necessitate such a massive effort on the American side as that which is envisaged by SDI.[17] If this rationale for SDI is not convincing, what about the other arguments in favor of SDI which its initiators and proponents advance?

The most frequently and forcefully used argument in favor of a shift towards defense, i.e., in favor of SDI, deals with the "erosion" of the deterrence concept based on MAD. The notion of the "erosion of deterrence," when used by the Reagan administration and its supporters, means that the credibility of the U.S. strategic deterrent has diminished and that the Soviet Union has acquired, or is about to acquire, a first-strike capability against American land-based ICBMs. Furthermore, it is argued, Soviet military doctrine, which has not

---

17. Sidney Drell et al., "Preserving the ABM Treaty," p. 64; Congress of the United States, Office of Technology Assessment, *Ballistic Missile Defense Technologies*, September 1985, pp. 17-18.

accepted the idea of mutual assured destruction, emphasizes nuclear warfighting. Even Henry Kissinger, who has interpreted the ABM Treaty as the formal recognition by both the United States and the USSR of mutual vulnerability, now argues that the Soviet Union does not believe in MAD and that "it is absurd to base the strategy of the West on the credibility of mutual suicide."[18]

Although some articles and statements by Soviet military experts could be interpreted as an acceptance of the possibility of prevailing in a nuclear war, these date mainly from earlier years. The notion of victory in a nuclear war has been categorically rejected in the last decade not only by Soviet political leaders, but also by its high-ranking military officials. Some of these statements, such as the following one by former Chief of the General Staff Marshal Nikolai Ogarkov, actually amount to an implicit acceptance of the concept of MAD, although the actual term is not explicitly used. As Ogarkov wrote in September 1983:

> With the modern development and dispersion of nuclear arms in the world, the defending side will always retain such a quantity of nuclear means as will be capable of inflicting "unacceptable damage," as the former Defense Secretary of the U.S.A. Robert McNamara characterized it in his time, on the aggressor in a retaliatory strike. . . . In contemporary conditions only a man bent on suicide can wager on a first nuclear strike.[19]

Of course, it can be argued that in this respect there is still a certain lack of consistency in Soviet military thinking. For example, Marshal Ogarkov himself had written earlier, in the 1982 brochure *Always Ready to Defend the Motherland*, that "the experience of past wars convincingly demonstrates that the appearance of new means of attack has invariably led to the creation of corresponding means of defense. . . . this applies fully even to the nuclear-missile weapons."[20] Nevertheless, on the highest level, Soviet statements have remained quite clear and unambiguous. According to the January 5, 1983, declaration of the Political Consultative Committee of Warsaw Treaty

---

18. Kissinger's speech at a conference on "NATO—The Next Thirty Years," held in Brussels on September 1, 1979.

19. Cited in Holloway, "Soviet Policy and the Arms Race," p. 112.

20. Quoted in David B. Rivkin, Jr., "What Does Moscow Think?" *Foreign Policy* 59 (Summer 1985), p. 100.

member states, "there can be no winners in a nuclear war once started."

More recently, one of the chief Soviet specialists on strategic forces, Lt. General Victor Starodubov, made the same point in a statement published in a French military journal. According to him, "we [the Soviets] consider that a nuclear war is inadmissible and that it must never be started. We think that it is neither possible to have an all-out war, war of long duration, nor a preventive strike. . . . in such a war there would be no winner."[21]

American military strategic doctrine has also often been at variance with deterrence based exclusively on massive retaliation. As a matter of fact, U.S. targeting policy, even in McNamara's day, reflected more "counterforce" than "countervalue" strategies, while more recent strategic concepts such as "protracted nuclear war" are more closely associated with "nuclear warfighting" than with deterring a nuclear war.[22] However, such strategies, whether they are openly declared or implied by one or the other superpower, do not necessarily mean that either side thinks it could win a nuclear war, but rather that it believes that preparedness to fight a nuclear war can most effectively deter such a war.

Another argument used to explain the "erosion of deterrence"—a first-strike ICBM capability by the Soviet Union—is also seriously disputed by many American experts. The Soviet Union has always relied on much heavier warheads to compensate for their lesser accuracy, and in the last decade has substantially increased both the accuracy and penetrability of their ICBMs by applying MIRV techniques. Still, it is by no means certain that this has given the USSR such a marked advantage as to warrant speculations that it has achieved an actual first-strike capability. Moreover, this advantage in land-based ICBMs is probably going to be offset when the American MX missile

---

21. Quoted in Thierry Garcin, "L'Etat-Major Soviétique Entre la Parité Nucléaire et L'ids," *Défense Nationale* (March 1986), p. 37.

22. ". . . [T]hrough successive refinements by the Nixon, Carter, and Reagan administrations, deterrence became increasingly equated with these nuclear warfighting capabilities. The Carter administration embraced a strategy of 'countervailing' deterrence, based on selective nuclear options that would allow the United States to respond to Soviet attack at any level of conflict. The Reagan administration has carried this approach one step further, advocating a U.S. force structure that can 'prevail' in a protracted, controlled nuclear conflict." Peter A. Clausen, "SDI in Search of a Mission" (see fn. 1), p. 255.

is fully deployed. However, according to the findings of the Scowcroft Commission, even now the Soviet Union does not have a first-strike capability. Furthermore, the vulnerability of Minuteman missiles in their silos has been exaggerated.[23] Even if ICBM vulnerability were to become a serious problem, this could be counteracted by other means—such as mobile basing—which would enhance the survivability of the ICBM leg of the U.S. triad. This alleged vulnerability could also be compensated for by increasing the survivability of the other legs of the triad, such as SLBMs. At present, in fact, the United States is doing both by developing Midgetman and Trident II missiles.

Of course, it is quite plausible that the strategic buildup in the last decade, characterized by the increased counterforce capability of nuclear weapons and a new emphasis on warfighting strategies, has made the maintenance of a credible nuclear deterrent more complicated and more uncertain over the long term. However, given the present level of nuclear arms on both sides, mutual assured destruction is not a function of choosing a particular doctrine or policy, but a condition which cannot be escaped in the foreseeable future.[24]

All this does not mean that deterrence by nuclear retaliation should be advocated as a permanent guarantee of peace in the nuclear age. Indeed, while it has preserved the peace, deterrence has done so by the constant increase of nuclear weapons. The arms race is closely linked to deterrence because in order to be credible and to deter, nuclear arms must be perceived as usable, even if only as a last resort. And since deterrence is a matter of perception, neither side can allow itself to feel inferior or refrain from efforts to gain advantage. Unless and until the political rivalry between the two superpowers is reduced, and until a degree of mutual trust is established, it will be very difficult for them to escape the vicious circle of the arms race. As a British diplomat observed some years ago, the two nuclear powers "are doomed to watch one another like hawks, to negotiate constantly by

---

23. See S. Smith, "The Mathematics of Counterforce," *Coexistence* 19, No. 4 (October 1982); also Mathew Bunn and Kosta Tsipis, "The Uncertainties of a Preemptive Nuclear Attack," *Scientific American* (November 1983), pp. 38–47; William Kincade, "Missile Vulnerability Reconsidered," *Arms Control Today* 2, No. 5 (May 1981), pp. 1–2, 5–8.

24. "There is no military need for parity: at the present level of nuclear armaments, margins of numerical superiority are militarily meaningless. The demand for parity is a political demand; both sides fear that if they are seen to be inferior, their position in the world would be in some ways weakened." *World Armaments and Disarmament. SIPRI Yearbook 1985* (London: Taylor and Francis, 1985), pp. 25–26.

day for strategic parity and to plot ceaselessly by night for strategic advantage. Since neither can nor will feel fully confident unless its parity is more equal than the other side's parity, dynamic instability is inherent in the very static stability they seek."[25] Therefore, the question of "morality" or "immorality" of nuclear deterrence is not the central issue, although it is important. Indeed, deterrence by threat of annihilation cannot be morally acceptable, not only because it holds hostage the population of two superpowers, but even more because it threatens the survival of other nations that are not part of the superpowers' rivalry and the nuclear arms race.[26] Unwillingness to accept deterrence by MAD also stems from the fact that this kind of nuclear peace cannot withstand a single major failure, whether as a result of intentional risk-taking, accident or error. An escape from this situation can be achieved only by gradually negotiating lower levels of deterrence, and not through a search for even "more absolute" counterweapons.

However, given the present state of U.S.-Soviet relations and the high priority given SDI by the Reagan administration (thereby making it almost impossible for future administrations to cancel a program which has gained such strong momentum), one can realistically assume that in the years to come the search for new, more effective types of BMD will have a significant impact on the strategic and political relationship between the United States and the USSR.

II. The Strategic Defense Initiative and U.S.-Soviet Relations

Assessing the long-term implications for superpower relations of the possible development and deployment of a new type of strategic defense is necessarily a highly speculative exercise. There are many

---

25. Former U.K. Ambassador to Washington Peter Jay, quoted in *International Herald Tribune*, January 7, 1985, p. 4.

26. This point of view is reflected in the Political Declaration of the Eighth Summit Conference of Nonaligned Countries: "For approximately forty years, the survival of mankind has been held hostage to the perceived security interests of a few nuclear-weapon states, in particular the superpowers and their allies. . . . The idea that world peace can be maintained through nuclear deterrence, a doctrine that lies at the root of the continuing escalation in the quantity and quality of nuclear weapons and which has, in fact, led to greater insecurity and instability in international relations than ever before, is the most dangerous myth in existence." Para. 32 of the Declaration, *Review of International Affairs* (Belgrade), No. 875 (September 1986), p. 40.

unknown variables which are of crucial importance in any serious attempt to foresee the likely impact of BMD development on U.S.-Soviet relations. These variables include, *inter alia*, the following: What will be the scope and effectiveness of a new BMD system(s)? Will they be developed and deployed simultaneously by both superpowers and with comparable performance characteristics or will there be a significant difference in that respect? How will the superpowers develop their other categories of strategic forces? What will change in the general state of U.S.-Soviet relations? The picture gets even more complicated when we take into account the fact that these variables are not independent of each other—that they are influenced by each other in such a way that the distinction between cause and effect cannot always be easily determined.

Therefore, in order to simplify our analysis we shall not give equal attention to all the possible scenarios as far as the development of a strategic "shield" is concerned, but instead focus on the situation that will most likely emerge from SDI in the next decade or two.

An extensive reading of the ever increasing technical literature on the subject leads to the conclusion that a perfect defense against nuclear weapons is an unattainable goal, not only in the near term, but also in the more distant future.[27] This assessment is made not only by the critics of SDI, but also by officials directly involved in the program, like General James Abrahamson, the Director of the Strategic Defense Initiative Office (SDIO). While strongly advocating a system of defense for strategic weapons, Abrahamson clearly stated that "a perfect astrodome defense is not a realistic thing."[28]

If we eliminate from our analysis as a plausible hypothesis the possibility that SDI would result in a comprehensive and totally reliable population defense, it would also be unrealistic to think that the present situation will remain unchanged indefinitely and that nothing will come out of the SDI program (or from the efforts that the Soviet Union has been investing in this field). The high priority that the Reagan administration has assigned to SDI, the large funds being allocated for this purpose and the growing support within the U.S.

---

27. For a technical appraisal of SDI see, for example, Ashton B. Carter, *Directed Energy Missile Defense in Space*, Background Paper, Congress of the United States, Office of Technology Assessment (April 1984); John Tirman, ed., *The Fallacy of Star Wars* (New York: Vintage Books, 1984); Sidney Dell, Philip J. Farley, and David Holloway, *The Reagan Strategic Defense Initiative: A Technical, Political and Arms Control Assessment* (Center for International Security and Arms Control, Stanford University: 1984).

28. *Science*, August 10, 1984.

arms control community for some limited BMD system make it highly unlikely that this program will be completely abandoned by future administrations.

Thus, the SDI program, though at the moment characterized only as a research effort, but with accelerated movement towards testing and eventual deployment,[29] will inevitably influence Soviet-American relations in the years to come, even if it leads to a limited deployment of a partial, land-based anti-missile defense. This influence will probably be negative or at least destabilizing, as indicated already by the initial Soviet reaction to SDI.

The Soviet Reaction to SDI

The Soviet Union reacted to President Reagan's speech of March 23, 1983, with sharp criticism voiced by its leader, Yuri Andropov, only four days after Reagan had launched his strategic defense initiative. In an interview in *Pravda* on March 27, 1983, the Soviet general secretary denounced Reagan's plan, pointing out that it would most likely lead to an unrestrained arms race and undermine the entire process of limiting strategic arms. Emphasizing the importance of the 1972 ABM Treaty for strategic stability between the two nuclear powers, Andropov stressed that by this treaty both sides have "recognized the fact that it is only mutual restraint in the field of ABM defenses that will allow progress in limiting and reducing strategic systems," and warned that the United States intended to sever this relationship between limiting defensive and offensive weapons. This criticism of the SDI project was later repeated on several occasions by Andropov himself, and then by his successors Konstantin Chernenko and Mikhail Gorbachev, as well as other prominent Soviet military and civilian officials. The basic argument that SDI would open the gate for an unrestrained arms race was supplemented by additional arguments supporting the view that SDI is an extremely dangerous move jeopardizing world peace and stability. For example, in an article in *Pravda* published on November 19, 1983, then Soviet Minister of De-

---

29. According to U.S. Defense Secretary Caspar Weinberger, a missile-defense test that is scheduled for 1988, if successful, could lead to partial SDI deployments as early as 1993 or 1994. John H. Cushman, Jr., "1988 Test Cited as Key to Deployment of SDI," *International Herald Tribune*, February 26, 1987.

fense Dimitri Ustinov charged that SDI is intended to secure for the United States the ability "to deliver a first nuclear strike against the Soviet Union with impunity." This view of the motivations and aims of SDI was repeated even more clearly by Chernenko in one of his last statements, published on January 31, 1985. Chernenko said that the U.S. space defense program is actually "an aggressive concept" designed to "disarm the other side and deprive it of the capability to retaliate in the event of nuclear aggression against it."[30]

The main Soviet arguments against SDI were further elaborated and substantiated in numerous articles in Soviet newspapers and periodicals.[31] In addition, a group of prominent Soviet scientists and foreign policy experts in April 1984 completed a study examining the feasibility of an American space-based ballistic missile defense system and its strategic, political and legal implications.[32] The thrust of the technical analysis, based mainly upon published American sources, was that the construction of a space-based anti-missile defense system might be technically feasible, but that it would be very costly, unreliable and vulnerable. The political and strategic impact of such a system was assessed, not surprisingly, as highly negative. In particular, the Soviet scientists argued that it would increase the danger of a first (preemptive) strike and set off a chain reaction in the making of modern weapons systems. Only in one sentence of the study was it indirectly recognized that a large-scale anti-missile system might have some conditional stabilizing role, in the event that "the Reagan administration, simultaneously with taking a decision on its development, were to renounce the buildup and improvement of nuclear offensive forces."[33] However, this statement was contradicted later in the text where it was stated (although in a different context) that even if the American side were prepared to "conclude mutually acceptable and equitable agreements on the limitation and reduction of strategic weapons, the existence of the tested and deployed components of

30. *The New York Times*, February 1, 1985.

31. See, for example, A. G. Arbatov, "Ogranichenie protivoraketnikh sistem—problemy, uroki, perskpektivy, *SShA* 12 (1984), pp. 16-28; S. Stashevskii, "Predotvratit' militarizatsiiu kosmosa," *Mirovaia ekonomika i mezhdunarodnye otnosheniia* 1 (1984), pp. 28-38; A. Platonov, "Militarizatsiia kosmosa—ugroza chelovechestvu," *Mezhdunarodnaia zhizn'* 1 (1985); "Ugroza zvezdnykh voin," *Novoe vremia*, February 15, 1985.

32. Roald Z. Sagdeev and Andrei A. Kokoshin, *A Space-Based Anti-Missile System with Directed Energy Weapons: Strategic, Legal and Political Implications* (Moscow: Committee of Soviet Scientists for Peace, against the Nuclear Threat, April 1984).

33. Ibid., p. 23.

SBAMs [space-based anti-missile systems] even on a limited scale may . . . reduce chances for a timely Soviet-American understanding."[34] In any case, neither in this report nor in Soviet public statements was a possible stabilizing role for space-based missile defense ever mentioned again, either directly or indirectly.[35]

The Soviet strategy in countering Reagan's SDI has been threefold: (1) to deliver warnings about Soviet countermeasures; (2) to try to stop SDI through arms control talks with the United States, which was most evident in the bold arms reductions proposals submitted by Gorbachev at the Reykjavik summit; and (3) to appeal to Western Europeans to oppose the American project.

With respect to countermeasures, the Soviet Union has not indicated that it would build its own strategic shield. Rather, it has suggested that it would take steps that would make any future U.S. missile defense ineffective and create an even more precarious situation as far as U.S. security from a nuclear attack is concerned. Among the steps indicated by the USSR as a possible response is the buildup of Soviet strategic forces, which is the same kind of response that former U.S. Secretary of Defense McNamara had recommended in the 1960s as the most appropriate American answer to a possible Soviet massive BMD. Similarly, Soviet spokesmen today are warning the American side that the Soviet Union is "not going to sit on [its] hands and wait until [the United States] decides whether or not it would be worthwhile to deploy such a system" but that it will "start perfecting [its] strategic offensive arms."[36]

In an article released by the Soviet news agency Novosti on May 5, 1986, one Soviet analyst emphasized, as possible responses to space defense, submarine-launched ballistic missiles flying on flat trajectories, as well as cruise missiles in different basing modes. He claimed that "not one of the space weapons now being developed in the United States can reliably detect and intercept low-flying small cruise missiles." He also added that the Soviet Union could seek to exhaust

34. Ibid., p. 27.

35. Soviet commentator Aleksandr Bovin has acknowledged, but only as a theoretical possibility, such a role for ABM systems, if both "the Soviet Union and the United States were to obtain reliable anti-missile systems 'suddenly' and at the same time, which is improbable." Aleksandr Bovin, Let's Speak Frankly (Moscow: Novosti Press Agency, 1985), p. 18.

36. Statement by Col. Gen. Nikolai Chervov, a senior member of the Soviet General Staff, quoted in The Washington Post, March 6, 1985.

a space-based missile defense system by launching ICBMs that would force it into early action. As a result, "the energy resources of space-based ABM elements will be considerably exhausted" and "this will also lead to the discharge of X-ray lasers and electromagnetic railguns and to other premature losses in the firepower of an ABM system."[37]

In addition to referring to the possibility of neutralizing strategic defense by overwhelming it with an increased number and variety of strategic offensive arms (SLBMs, cruise missiles, bombers), Soviet articles have indicated a number of other possibilities to protect Soviet retaliatory capabilities if an American strategic defense is deployed. Besides measures also discussed in American studies on this issue— e.g., shortening the boost phase of the missile flight, rotating the missiles as they ascend, employing decoys, etc.—other, less familiar measures were mentioned, such as basing missiles at lake bottoms or even deploying rockets on the lunar surface.[38]

As far as the arms control approach to SDI is concerned, it is widely believed that Soviet interest in stopping SDI played a major role in the Soviet decision to resume comprehensive arms control talks with the Reagan administration. Nevertheless, the Soviet Union has made it clear that the final results of the Geneva talks will depend on U.S. willingness to compromise on SDI. Although the Soviet Union no longer insists as strongly as it did previously on the close linkage between the three sets of issues (strategic offensive arms, inter-mediate-range nuclear forces and space weapons), the proposals it has made with respect to the reduction of offensive strategic arms are linked to restrictions on SDI. And although the Soviet Union has backed away from its initial position by no longer insisting on banning all research on space defense systems, the Soviet proposal of June 16, 1986, clearly aims at preventing the testing and deployment of space weapons. It specifies that research should be limited to laboratories and that both sides should pledge to abide by the ABM Treaty for at least another fifteen years.

This Soviet position was maintained in the proposals and offers that Gorbachev made at the Reykjavik summit in October 1986. The Soviet leader proposed the elimination of all offensive strategic arms

---

37. Tony Berber, "Soviet Analyst Lists Possible Responses to Space Weapons," *Reuters*, May 5, 1986.

38. V. Falin, "Kosmos—moment istini," *Izvestiia*, December 14, 1984.

in a ten-year period and, at one point, even the elimination of all nuclear weapons of any type, including short-range weapons and gravity bombs, provided SDI research and testing remain restricted to the laboratory and both sides remain bound by the ABM Treaty. The U.S. side instead proposed the elimination of ballistic missiles in a ten-year period, but without limits on SDI research and with the provision that each side would be free after that period to withdraw from the ABM Treaty and deploy anti-missile defense. This basic divergence over SDI prevented an agreement. In a comment, Gorbachev observed that "it would have taken a madman to accept" SDI research and testing outside the laboratory while offensive arms were being reduced.[39]

There are a number of reasons which help explain the adamant Soviet opposition to American plans to develop and deploy strategic defenses. The Soviet concern is not so much that the United States will create a perfect defensive shield that would make all nuclear weapons obsolete (although it seems that they fear American technology more than do many U.S. critics of SDI). Rather, the USSR is alarmed that it would result in a partial but relatively effective point defense that would negate the effectiveness of Soviet land-based ICBMs. Many Soviet officials privately (and even publicly) concede that the USSR has an advantage over the United States in this particular category of weapons, but they consider this advantage necessary in order to maintain overall strategic parity, because of American technological and/or numerical advantage in other categories of strategic weapons—SLBMs, bombers and long-range cruise missiles. The Soviet concern that the implementation of the SDI program, combined with the current and future U.S. buildup of its offensive strategic forces (MX, Trident II, the B-1 and Stealth bombers), would result in U.S. strategic superiority is undoubtedly reinforced by the fact that domestic support for SDI in the United States is most vocal in those conservative circles which see the program as a device that would "cancel out years of Soviet investment in ICBMs," thereby "pushing the USSR back to the rank of a second-rate power."[40]

---

39. Don Oberdorfer, "How U.S., in Iceland, Improvised the Most Important Arms Proposal in History," *International Herald Tribune*, February 18, 1987. (See also Gorbachev's press conference in Reykjavik, excerpted in the appendix to this volume.)

40. See for example, Gregory A. Fossedal, "The Reagan Doctrine," *The American Spectator* 18, No. 3 (March 1985), pp. 12–15.

One of the clearest Soviet statements to the effect that SDI would undermine strategic parity was enunciated in a lengthy unsigned article in *Izvestiia* on January 25, 1985. After warning that peace can be maintained only by strategic parity and recalling that parity was achieved only at the beginning of the 1970s when the United States was "finally deprived of the possibility to blackmail the Soviet Union," the article claims that both sides then came to the conviction that "in conditions of parity in strategic offensive arms, any additional strengthening of defensive capabilities of one side would amount to gaining advantage in inflicting the first strike."[41]

Of course, the Soviet Union is unlikely to opt out of this new stage of the strategic arms race, but efforts to match new U.S. strategic programs would impose a heavy burden on its economic, scientific and technological resources, especially if the Soviet Union feels compelled to develop its own strategic defense (although it claims that it does not have such plans). In view of the territory to be protected and keeping in mind that the USSR is within reach not only of U.S. ICBMs, but also of U.S. forward-based nuclear forces stationed in and around Western Europe, the costs of deploying such a system for the USSR would be even greater than for the United States. Therefore, it is likely that Soviet concern about SDI is also motivated by the wish to avoid additional, possibly unbearable, pressures on its economy.

Finally, Soviet opposition to SDI stems also from its wish to preserve the ABM Treaty, which the USSR views not only as the formal acknowledgment of strategic parity, but also as an implicit confirmation of its status as an equal political partner with the United States.

SDI and Strategic Stability

That a shift from offensive nuclear arms to a mix of offensive and defensive systems, and especially a shift to a perfect defense, would tremendously increase strategic stability is one of the most frequently cited arguments in favor of SDI. Even if we could imagine, for analytical purposes, the possibility of complete reliance on defense systems, and that this would enhance strategic stability and the prevention of war, the road from the present reliance on MAD to a state of "mutual assured survival" would be extremely complicated and risky; so risky,

41. "On the So-Called 'Strategic Defense Initiative' of the U.S.," *Izvestiia*, January 25, 1985, p. 5.

in fact, that it would not warrant a search for new weapons technology (even if defensive) whose implications cannot yet be fully grasped.

The risk inherent in the attempt to replace nuclear deterrence by building defensive systems stems, first of all, from the fact that it is highly unlikely that both sides would develop and deploy defensive technologies in a simultaneous and coordinated way. Instead, as past experience has shown, one side would obtain a temporary advantage, which would prompt the other to try to devise countermeasures or devise its own system, or both. Consequently, instead of an orderly replacement of nuclear arms by non-nuclear defensive systems, the transition period would be another even more unstable and tense stage of an offense-defense arms race. The side that, rightly or wrongly, considered its retaliatory capacity to be eroding might— especially in a crisis situation—be under extreme pressure to preempt before the shift in the strategic balance became irreversible.

The only scenario in which the dangers of the uneven transition period are substantially decreased would be one in which the side that has first embarked upon and taken the lead in the deployment of defensive technologies would reduce its offensive forces in much larger proportion, unilaterally or by agreement, in order to reassure the other side that it was not attempting to achieve first-strike capability. However, such a scenario is difficult to imagine, since the side that initiated SDI is not only improving and upgrading its offensive capabilities, but asking the other side to significantly reduce its offensive forces.

The proposition that the uncertainties during the transition phase would be reduced by assurances that the side possessing the defense technology would give that technology to the other side lacks credibility. Why in an adversarial relationship would the side that gains an advantage immediately give it away? How could the other side have enough trust in this offer to refrain from devising its own countermeasures, especially when this offer is made upon the precondition that the side which has not yet developed its own defense system first give up its offensive systems?[42] In other words, 'before I provide you with a shield, you should lay down your sword.' A much safer way, but admittedly also a difficult and long one, would be to create

---

42. In recent interviews, Caspar Weinberger and Fred Iklé have made it clear that the idea of "sharing defense technology with the Soviet Union" would make sense only when the United States had entirely perfected and deployed its defense system, and while the Soviet Union had, as a preconditon, drastically reduced its offensive nuclear arms.

the conditions in which there would be need for neither sword nor shield.

However, even if we could imagine that both sides had deployed defensive systems, it is not necessarily true that a future non-nuclear world (which would differ from the present one only by the fact that nuclear arms were made "obsolete") would be safer than the present "MAD world."[43] First of all, one should not forget that defensive strategic systems are *weapons* systems, and that there are no exclusively defensive weapons which could not also be used for offensive, destructive purposes, especially if they are based on using large amounts of directed energy, as future space-based weapons most probably will be. According to some views, directed-energy weapons from space could be used not only against ballistic missiles, but also against other military targets and command and control facilities, against such "soft" ground targets as power plants, industrial centers and even grain fields, creating such destruction that it would "take an industrialized country back to an 18th-century level in 30 minutes."[44] Knowing that such harmful consequences as radiation and the "nuclear winter" effect would be absent, inhibitions about their use could be far smaller than is presently the case with nuclear weapons; consequently, the risk of war would increase. In this case the eternal objective of nuclear powers to devise an absolute but usable weapon would, at least in their minds, be achieved in the form of directed-energy weapons.

However, even if defensive systems were to make nuclear weapons obsolete without creating new dangers of war in (or from) space, the danger of conventional war would not automatically decrease if old animosities and suspicions persisted. On the contrary, it is more realistic to assume that the two rivals would be much more prone to risk-taking if their mutual fears of nuclear retaliation were done away with. If, on the other hand, rivalry were replaced by understanding, this could raise fears among smaller powers about the danger of super-power collusion and condominium.

Risks inherent in the attempts to reach perfect defenses are also present in the case of trying to develop a more limited, partial BMD system, especially as far as the uncertainties of the transition period are concerned. The danger that one side would perceive the efforts

43. See, for example, Charles L. Glaser, "Star Wars Bad Even If It Works," *Bulletin of the Atomic Scientists* 41, No. 3 (March 1985), pp. 13–16.

44. Philip M. Boffey, "Dark Side of 'Star Wars': Systems Could Also Attack," *The New York Times*, March 7, 1985.

of the other side as an attempt to gain a first-strike advantage would be very real. This would increase the risks of "preemptive" strikes by one side in order to prevent the other side from protecting its offensive forces.

On the other hand, the side which first acquired a limited, but relatively effective BMD might be tempted to use this newly acquired but relatively small and potentially short-term advantage. It is hard to disagree with the argument that "an effective but imperfect ABM on one side would exacerbate the risk because the side that did have an ABM might calculate that it would be better off if it struck first and used the ABM defense to deal with the weakened response," and that the "same calculation would affect both sides, if both possessed ABM."[45] General Brent Scowcroft, former Assistant to the President for National Security Affairs under President Ford, has pointed out that "any potential defense was likely to be more effective against an attacking missile force already crippled by a highly destructive surprise attack." Hence, he concluded "such a defense system could become an 'inducement' to surprise attack."[46]

In the face of this compelling logic, the argument that even partial BMD would reinforce deterrence by creating additional uncertainty for the potential attacker[47] seems flawed. It is not so much uncertainty that is the essence of deterrence, but certainty, in the minds both of potential attacker and potential victim, that a first strike would be answered by a massive retaliatory strike.

The deployment of a partial BMD with some space-based elements might have other adverse effects for crisis stability and war prevention. There is a consensus among technical experts that BMD systems based on new technologies would be even more effective against satellites than against missiles. This would pose a significant threat to the satellites, which serve not only as the backbone of each superpower's sophisticated command, control and communications network, but also as the best available means for mutual surveillance, inspection and monitoring of compliance with arms control agreements. The increased vulnerability of satellites would mean an increased danger of misunderstanding, miscalculation and surprise moves by either superpower.

---

45. Sidney Drell et al., "Preserving the ABM Treaty" (see fn. 14), p. 81.

46. *The New York Times*, February 28, 1985.

47. Kenneth Adelman, "Toward A Defense Strategy," *The New York Times*, March 10, 1985.

The high probability that a space-based anti-missile system would have to react automatically, even in a pre-programmed way, to a missile attack, could mean that the decision to launch a nuclear war would be made by computers, and not by human judgment. The danger of an accidental nuclear war also might be increased, rather than decreased, if there were a failure in such a highly complex system which could be activated by itself or against a mistakenly perceived missile launch or missile test by the other side.

It is probably true that even a partial BMD could reduce the danger of a nuclear threat by small nuclear powers, and thus serve as a disincentive against nuclear proliferation, but it is much less certain that a partial BMD or point defense would substantially reduce damage in case of a "nuclear exchange" between the two superpowers. Even if we disregard the "nuclear winter" theory, the consequences for the populations of the two superpowers, even if only a few nuclear warheads got through, would be devastating. And even if all the incoming nuclear warheads were destroyed before reaching their targets (missile silos), possible and probable nuclear detonations in midair or at high altitudes also would create catastrophic effects such as an electromagnetic pulse, the destruction of the ozone layer and radioactive fallout.

A change in nuclear strategy, or nuclear targeting policy, which would probably occur if a highly effective point defense were deployed by one or both superpowers, could also result in increased risks to their populations. As Ashton Carter points out, if a superpower possessed defense capable of intercepting all but a few of the opponent's nuclear warheads, the other side might retarget its forces to inflict the most destruction possible with its few penetrating warheads in order to maximize the loss of population and destroy the fabric of the other side's society.[48]

The uncertainties of shifting from a system of deterrence based on offensive weapons to a mixture of offensive and defensive forces, or even to the domination of the latter, indicate that the emphasis should not be placed on efforts to reduce the consequences of a nuclear war (thus making it psychologically more acceptable), but rather on efforts to *prevent the outbreak* of war, by dealing with its possible causes. In other words, arms control and the general improvement of overall relations between the superpowers should take priority over attempts to find in technology a substitute for real security.

---

48. Ashton Carter, *Directed Energy Missile Defense* (see fn. 27), p. 56.

SDI and Arms Control

The superpowers' present ballistic missile defense programs are stretching the limits of the ABM Treaty.[49] It is not only the phased-array radars controversy (American complaints about the Krasnoyarsk radar and Soviet complaints about the U.S. Pave Paws radars) that indicates possible "breakouts" from the treaty, but also advances in other weapons technologies, ostensibly developed for other purposes, such as anti-satellite weapons and anti-tactical ballistic missiles (ATBMs). The testing and development of these systems could easily breach Article VI(a) of the ABM Treaty, which prohibits upgrading air defense and other non-ABM systems and components to give them an ABM capability. Of course, once the SDI program moves from research into the testing stage, which may occur before the end of this decade, it will clearly run up against ABM Treaty provisions and will call into question the treaty's entire philosophy, even if this is not the intention of SDI's initiators. In view of the weapons technologies contemplated for space-based anti-ballistic missile defense (lasers, particle-beam weapons), the testing and certainly the deployment of such a system would not only abrogate the 1972 ABM Treaty, but probably also breach the 1967 Outer Space Treaty and possibly even the 1963 Partial Test Ban Treaty.[50] Also, because of the similarities to ASAT weapons, the development of ABM technologies would preclude any possibilities for achieving a meaningful treaty prohibiting attacks against satellites.

Even if one were to take a highly negative view of the achievements of arms control so far and consider present arms control and disarmament agreements not worth preserving at any price, it is by no means probable that the present impasse in arms control would become easier to overcome by resorting to missile defense, as claimed by some respected arms control specialists such as Henry Kissinger.[51] On the

---

49. See Thomas K. Longstreth and John E. Pike, "U.S., Soviet Programs Threaten ABM Treaty," *Bulletin of the Atomic Scientists* 41, No. 4 (April 1985), pp. 11–15.

50. Article IV(1) of the Outer Space Treaty prohibits: a) to place in orbit around the Earth any objects carrying nuclear weapons or any other kind of weapons of mass destruction; b) to install such weapons on celestial bodies; and c) to station such weapons in outer space in any other manner.

51. Saying that arms control theory is at a dead end and that the stalemate in negotiations reflects an impasse in thought, Kissinger considers that perhaps the most compelling argument in favor of some missile defense is its possible beneficial effect on arms control. Henry A. Kissinger, "Limited 'Star Wars' Defense May Help Deter an Attack, Encourage Arms Control," *International Herald Tribune*, September 24, 1984.

contrary, it is more probable that the search for a comprehensive strategic defense, even if it materializes in a modest form, would provoke a new spiral in the arms race on both sides. As has been pointed out, an overwhelming majority of arms control experts and former U.S. government officials considers that the U.S. move to deploy a strategic defense would provoke a Soviet response in the form of a buildup of their offensive strategic weapons. For example, former U.S. Secretary of State Cyrus Vance, testifying before the Senate Foreign Relations Committee, has said that the Soviet reaction to the development and deployment of a space-based defense system "will almost certainly be a large increase in the number of their offensive weapons, which we will then be compelled to match, and the arms race will be ratcheted upwards."[52] Soviet spokesmen themselves have made the same warning. In an interview in the leading Hungarian daily, *Nepszabadsag*, Georgi Arbatov, Director of the Institute for the Study of the U.S.A. and Canada and one of the Soviet Union's top Americanologists, has said that "it is already clear that [the Soviet Union] will not agree to decrease strike weapons if [the United States] doesn't give up the anti-missile system."[53]

However, even if the Soviet Union would not resort to countermeasures, the absurd, and yet, it seems, inescapable logic of the arms race is such that the side which initiates a particular program of weapons innovation tries to match in advance the other side's anticipated countermeasure. For example, while the United States is embarking upon a program aimed at making Soviet ballistic missiles "impotent and obsolete," it is at the same time developing a missile technology that would assure that American nuclear missiles never meet the same fate.[54] In addition, scientists at the U.S. government's Lawrence Livermore National Laboratory claim that the United States might embark upon building heavier and more powerful nuclear warheads in order to overcome possible Soviet defenses.[55]

As a result of the same logic, the announcement of SDI, followed by assertions that it might be vulnerable to "air-breathing" nuclear

52. *The New York Times*, February 5, 1985.

53. *International Herald Tribune*, February 18, 1985.

54. "U.S. Seeks Missiles to Evade Defense," *The New York Times*, February 11, 1985.

55. Fred Hiatt and Rick Atkinson, "SDI May Mean Bigger Bombs," *International Herald Tribune*, June 6, 1986, p. 2.

systems, has prompted the Pentagon to claim that there is a need to restore U.S. air-defense systems (the cost of which, in terms of rebuilding and sustaining, would amount, according to an estimate by former Secretary of Defense James Schlesinger, to at least $50 billion per year).[56] If such a drive towards an arms buildup accompanies the first steps of SDI, what can be expected if and when this program enters its more advanced stages? Judging by the history of the arms race and present developments, there is every reason to agree with those like Stanley Hoffmann, who warn that SDI is "a recipe not for arms control but for the endless escalation of the arms race."[57]

III. SDI and Europe

The announcement of U.S. strategic defense plans has been received in Europe, especially in Western Europe, with apprehension and dissatisfaction. The fact that SDI has provoked the most intense debate in the Western part of Europe is hardly surprising. Western countries, having based their security on their alliance relationship with the United States, have felt most affected by the possibility of radical changes in NATO strategy, the central pillar of which is deterrence by the possible use of nuclear weapons. Although President Reagan's initial statement and numerous subsequent statements by U.S. officials were designed to reassure American allies that the U.S. research effort will provide them with some protection against nuclear missiles (it was even suggested that the ABM defense for Western Europe might be achieved earlier than for the United States), these assurances seemed to have had only a limited effect. Western European skepticism about the project has not disappeared, either in the official positions of the majority of Western European governments, or among large sections of public opinion.

The criticism voiced against SDI by different European countries has not evolved into a definitive, common Western European stand on the subject. Nevertheless, in the intra-NATO debate over SDI there are two different lines of thinking—American and Western Euro-

---

56. "Weinberger Says a Space Defense Also Needs a Counter to Bombers," *The New York Times*, January 17, 1985.

57. Stanley Hoffmann, "'Star Wars' Means Only Trouble," *The New York Times*, February 25, 1985.

pean—which are quite divergent. According to some Western European observers, the differences in approach to SDI on the two sides of the Atlantic are such that "the transatlantic relationship between the United States and its European allies is about to be subjected to the most severe strain it has endured since the alliance was established."[58] Whether that will really be so will depend on a number of factors—the magnitude and direction of the U.S. program (total defense or point defense); the pressures and incentives that could be applied by the U.S. government in order to generate alliance solidarity on the issue; the directions and results of Soviet BMD efforts; developments at the Geneva negotiations, etc. Still, whatever the interplay of these factors, it is unlikely that the issue of SDI, as a potential bone of contention, will disappear from public debate in the alliance.

SDI will remain a potentially divisive issue not only between Washington and its allies, but also between the Western Europeans themselves. Among Western European members of NATO, the response to the U.S. offer to participate in SDI research on a governmental level has been far from uniform. So far, four countries—Norway, Denmark, Greece and France—have rejected the offer. Two others—Great Britain and the FRG—after fairly lengthy deliberations and internal debate have signed memoranda on cooperation with the United States, while the others have yet to give their answers. It is important, however, to note that participation or non-participation in SDI research should not be equated with the acceptance or rejection of a new concept of strategic defense. On this issue, the reservations of Western European governments, although somewhat less pronounced than initially, still clearly show that the present security arrangement is preferred to the uncertainties of a transition to a defense-dominated world.

So far the most outspoken European members of the Western alliance have been France, Great Britain and the Federal Republic of Germany. Their views on the subject initially had many common elements, but they have been modified by specific individual features stemming from the different positions and roles of these countries within the alliance (e.g., the fact that France and Britain are nuclear powers, while the FRG relies heavily on the U.S. nuclear deterrent for its security).

58. Geoffrey Smith in *The Times* (London), March 23, 1986.

France

Among these three major Western European countries, France has been the most outspoken and most consistent critic of SDI, although it seems that even its criticism has been somewhat toned down by the passage of time (and by the 1986 change of government). Instead of simply rejecting Reagan's initiative, France has also pointed to an alternative—an increased, independent Western European role in developing new SDI-type technologies and conducting space research.

France has based its repudiation of the concept of a space-based missile defense, such as SDI, on two main considerations. First, it has been seen as a threat to strategic stability, which is based on nuclear deterrence, and a factor provoking a new cycle of the arms race in offensive weapons. These concerns were officially enunciated in a statement by the French representative to the Geneva Conference on Disarmament in the spring of 1984. The representative also made specific proposals for limiting BMD and ASAT activities, such as strict limitations on ASAT systems, especially those that can reach high orbits, and the prohibition, for a renewable period of five years, of tests and deployments of guided-energy weapons systems capable of destroying ballistic missiles or satellites at very long range.[59] At the highest level, France has also voiced similar concerns over the implications of SDI. In his first public statement on the issue, President Mitterrand described the SDI program as "overarmament" and stressed the importance of leaving space safe for the unimpeded function of satellites as a means of observation.[60] Particular French concern with this aspect was reflected in a proposal, advanced in early 1985, that combined an ASAT ban with a suggestion to create an International Satellite Monitoring Agency, an idea designed partly to attract the interest of European neutrals (there is already French-Swedish cooperation on the commercial SPOT satellite).

Secondly, French officials have warned about the possible implications of SDI for security and the regional balance in Europe. For example, former French Defense Minister Charles Hernu, speaking at the *Wehrkunde* conference in Munich in February 1985, stated that the development of a successful missile defense could lead the superpowers into a "complicity" that "would rid them of any rivalry" in

---

59. For the text of the French statement see *Survival* 26, No. 5 (September/October 1984), pp. 235–237.

60. *Le Monde*, December 13, 1984.

the strategic arena, leaving Europe with a less stable situation than the present one based on nuclear deterrence.[61] These French concerns were also clearly spelled out in an analysis by French military specialist Jacques Vernant:

> . . . the militarization of outer space and the deployment of an anti-ballistic system would have as a result the accentuation of the military-technical distance between the United States and the European members of the Atlantic alliance: command, control and communications will be more than ever the appanage of the United States. This situation will consolidate the bipolar structure of the international system and subordinate specific European interests to American interests.[62]

The initial French criticism of the SDI project remains valid today, although it has become in the meantime more moderate, even before the change of government. It seems that the moderation of the initial French criticism of SDI was influenced by two factors: 1) the assurances that the United States had given to the French that it would not agree to any inclusion of independent French nuclear forces in the Geneva negotiations, and 2) the realization that the shock created in Europe by the SDI announcement provided a real opportunity for Western Europe to pool its efforts and potential, under French leadership, and develop its own space program for peaceful and possibly military purposes.

Nevertheless, in substance the reserved French attitude toward SDI has not actually changed, in spite of more positive remarks about it by French Prime Minister Jacques Chirac. His statements, it seems, are mainly politically motivated and do not reflect a change in the French government's strategic thinking. In any case, President Mitterrand remains as opposed to SDI as ever. In essence, French opposition to plans like SDI is deeply embedded in Gaullist military and political-strategic thinking and will almost certainly persist and even increase if the U.S. (and possibly Soviet) drive towards space-based BMD gains irreversible momentum. Indeed, it is doubtful that any government in Paris would endorse a plan which could possibly render French deterrent forces obsolete.

---

61. "French Minister Warns Against 'Star Wars' Plans," *The Washington Post*, February 10, 1985.

62. Jacques Vernant, "La 'Guerre des Etoiles' . . . et Nous," *Revue de défense nationale*, December 1984, p. 141.

Great Britain

In comparison with the French attitude, the British stand on SDI has been less critical, but not fully supportive, although Prime Minister Margaret Thatcher has firmly backed U.S. research into new defense technologies.

However, while backing U.S. research into new ABM technologies, the U.K. government has set out four basic conditions for the development and possible deployment of a new defensive system, which Prime Minister Thatcher spelled out during her meeting with President Reagan in December 1984. These four points (which, according to the British prime minister, were agreed to by Reagan) were 1) that the U.S. and Western aim was not to achieve superiority but to maintain balance, taking account of Soviet developments; 2) that the SDI-related deployments would, in view of treaty obligations, be subject to negotiation; 3) that the overall aim is to enhance, not undermine, deterrence; and 4) that East-West negotiations should aim to achieve security with reduced levels of offensive systems on both sides.[63]

In one important respect—possible European participation in the U.S. research program on SDI—the attitude of the U.K. clearly differed from the French stand. Unlike France, which has been advocating that Europe should develop its own technologies in this field, the United Kingdom has suggested, as its defense minister stated in Paris on April 2, 1985, that there was potential Western European interest in joining the U.S. research effort in view of possible technological gains. Therefore, it was not surprising that the United Kingdom became the first Western European country to sign (December 6, 1985) an agreement (or confidential memorandum of understanding) with the United States on the participation of British companies and research institutions in the SDI program. In order to counter criticism that this act signified the acceptance of a new strategic doctrine, the then British Minister of Defense Michael Heseltine emphasized in the House of Commons that U.K. government policy toward SDI remained firmly based on the four points agreed to by Thatcher and Reagan at Camp David in December 1984.[64] However, by officially becoming a partner in SDI research, Britain is likely to find it more difficult to express its own views on the security implications of the program.

---

63. *International Herald Tribune*, December 24-25, 1984.

64. *The Times* (London), December 10, 1985, p. 4. (See Appendix.)

The Federal Republic of Germany

The third major Western European country in which SDI has pro-voked an intensive debate is the Federal Republic of Germany, where opinions on the issue, compared to France and the U.K., seem to be more divided, both within the governing coalition and among the public at large. Because of its geostrategic position and because it does not possess nuclear weapons, the FRG relies much more heavily on the U.S. nuclear deterrent. Not surprisingly, therefore, it initially reacted to SDI with great skepticism. The clearest indication of such an approach was the statement made by FRG Minister of Defense Manfred Woerner at the meeting of the NATO Nuclear Planning Goup in April 1984 in Cesme, Turkey. Woerner voiced his doubts that SDI could provide greater protection or stability, saying that he was only hoping that it would provide an incentive for arms control.[65]

However, at the *Wehrkunde* Conference in Munich in February 1985, Chancellor Helmut Kohl made a statement generally interpreted as cautious approval for SDI. He also argued very strongly for Western European participation in the research program, pointing out that SDI, irrespective of its final results, would give the United States a big technological advantage.[66]

Still, Chancellor Kohl's qualified support for SDI apparently did not reflect a unanimous government view on the subject. A written statement by the West German Foreign Ministry signed by Foreign Minister Hans-Dietrich Genscher contained an indirect yet clear critique of the SDI concept,[67] while FRG President Richard von Weiz-saecker expressed his skepticism about SDI at an Anglo-German con-ference in Konigswinter as much "as constitutional niceties permitted" him to do.[68] In a way, his view was close to the stand of the opposition parties, the SPD and the Greens, which also declined to support SDI

65. *The New York Times*, April 14, 1984.

66. "Kohl Gives the U.S. Guarded Support on Space Defense," *The New York Times*, February 10, 1985.

67. "Genscher Voices Reservations over Space Weapons Strategy," *Financial Times*, March 19, 1985.

68. *The Times* (London), March 25, 1985.

research and opposed West German involvement in the U.S. research program.[69]

On the other hand, some influential West German politicians from the governing coalition, like the head of the Christian Social Union (CSU), Franz-Josef Strauss, have supported SDI without any reservations. Nevertheless, the statements of Chancellor Kohl, such as the one made in the Bundestag on April 18, 1985, confirmed that the official West German position remained one of cautious support, delaying a firm commitment. The reluctance of the West German government to take an earlier, more definite stand stemmed, it appears, from four main considerations—its close ties with France and the wish not to damage its relations with the USSR on the one hand, and its solidarity with the United States and the attractiveness of participation in SDI research on the other. As one commentator remarked, "the issue has pushed the Germans into what is for them the most uncomfortable of positions—having to choose between America, their protector, and France, an old enemy but now the other half of a partnership that anchors Europe's political and economic stability."[70]

After much deliberation, Bonn has made its choice by, in effect, opting for both. It gave support to the French-initiated project Eureka, but also became the second European government to sign an agreement joining SDI research. After months of negotiations, the agreement of March 27, 1986, was signed by U.S. Defense Secretary Caspar Weinberger and FRG Economics Minister Martin Bangemann. The fact that the West German defense minister did not sign the agreement was yet another indication of Bonn's efforts to portray its participation as motivated primarily by economic considerations, not military-strategic ones. In any case, the FRG seems to be convinced that the technological spinoffs from research on BMD technologies will pave

---

69. In its 1985 statement "SDI and Europe's Interests" (see Appendix), the Parliamentary Group of the SPD had expressed its opposition to SDI in ten points which include, *inter alia*, the following considerations: the building of a strategic defense system in space will fundamentally alter NATO's defense strategy and call into question the ABM Treaty; participation in SDI research involves political responsibility for the system's development and deployment; SDI would probably not improve the protection of Europe; SDI will make the U.S.-Soviet arms control talks more difficult; SDI will militarize basic research; and Western Europe must take up the American technological challenge and find a response of its own. See also "Les Allemands et la 'guerre des étoiles'," *Le Monde*, April 6, 1985.

70. John Newhouse, "The Diplomatic Round: Europe and Star Wars," *The New Yorker*, July 22, 1985, p. 37.

the way for a new technological revolution and that European countries should not risk being left behind. The West Germans also seem to be confident that Western Europe, and especially the Federal Republic, have the resources and know-how needed for active participation in SDI research and that such participation would bring immediate financial benefits and lead to a more equitable and more balanced flow of technology between the United States and Western Europe.

Keeping in mind the uncertainties and dilemmas with regard to the advantages and disadvantages, military-strategic and technological, for Western Europe, it is not surprising that all these countries have not been and probably will not be able to formulate a joint stand on the issue, either in full support or complete rejection. Whether the possible technological and financial benefits might, if not buy, then at least "rent" the European governments' support for SDI remains to be seen.[71] The reluctance or rejection of some smaller Western European countries, such as Denmark or Norway, to accept the American offer to take part in research could indicate that political and security uncertainties over the implications of SDI have been deemed more important than the potential technological benefits or financial gains.[72] Although this example was not followed by all major Western European countries, their doubts about the security implications of SDI cannot be dispelled simply by joining in the research.[73] These doubts, if they remain, will probably not lead to a joint negative stand against SDI, mainly because of the risks such a stand would entail for transatlantic solidarity. Western Europeans still prefer to leave the job of limiting or cancelling SDI to the U.S. Congress, arms negotiations in Geneva, and the inherent technological uncertainties.

---

71. George W. Ball, "The War for Star Wars," *The New York Review of Books*, April 11, 1985, p. 41.

72. According to an unnamed Pentagon official, Western European defense companies and research institutes could receive contracts worth $2.6 billion from the SDI program or roughly 10 percent of its total budget for the first stage, which is $26 billion. This calculation is based upon the assumption that the European countries would play a leading role in constructing a ground-based defense against short-range missiles (*Reuters*, June 17, 1986). By comparison, the value of the first ten projects which were agreed to at the second ministerial "Eureka" conference in Hanover in November 1985 is estimated to be roughly $500 million.

73. A European participant at the annual conference of the London-based International Institute for Strategic Studies in Avignon (September 13–16, 1984) pointed out, with reference to SDI, that Western Europe objects to any change in a security system that seems to be working well enough as it is. Therefore, the burden of proof is on those who propose the change.

Neutral / Nonaligned

The European countries that do not belong to the military-political alliances and which base their security on their own defense efforts and not on nuclear deterrence did not feel obliged to take an official stand on SDI. However, the tone of their media commentary and official positions on the question of the arms race and the militarization of space leaves no doubt that they were very concerned with SDI's repercussions on security and stability, not only in the relations between the superpowers and the two alliances, but in the world as a whole. Therefore, in arguing for the demilitarization of space, the non-bloc countries emphasized the fact that space is the common heritage of mankind and that the question of preventing an arms race in space cannot be left entirely to the superpowers. In that respect, "the group of 21" in the Geneva Conference on Disarmament (CD), which included neutral Sweden and nonaligned Yugoslavia, pressed in the CD since 1982 for the establishment of a working group dealing with the question of preventing an arms race in outer space. Their efforts were instrumental in the creation of such a group in April 1985, although it was unable, due to the U.S. position, to take up effective work.

During the work of the CD in 1983 and 1984, Sweden frequently appealed for negotiations to dismantle existing ASAT systems and prohibit the establishment of new ones. Sweden has particularly pointed to the dangers inherent in efforts to develop a space-based anti-ballistic missile system, saying that such a research and development program would not only be a waste of resources, but could also increase international tensions, lead to countermeasures and hence give rise to a new cycle of the arms race.[74] While emphasizing that Sweden questions nuclear deterrence policies and philosophies as such, the Swedish delegate at the CD nevertheless pointed out the destabilizing effects of the search for new ABM systems which could undermine mutual deterrence and international security. As possible measures to stop such developments and prevent the arms race in space, Sweden had suggested, *inter alia*, that as one of its main tasks the Conference on Disarmament should negotiate an international treaty banning all space weapons, including weapons directed against targets in space. Sweden also suggested that the ban upon development, testing and deployment of space-based ABM systems, as agreed

---

74. *The United Nations Disarmament Yearbook*, Vol. 8 (1983), p. 324.

upon in the 1972 ABM Treaty, should be reiterated in a multilateral treaty.[75]

The statements of Yugoslav representatives in the CD voiced the same concern. Yugoslavia associated itself with the analysis given by the Swedish delegate with regard to the implications of military space systems,[76] and proposed steps to prevent the militarization of outer space from assuming irreversible proportions. Yugoslavia's position has been that the arms race cannot be solved by technical means and that, therefore, the introduction of new weapons technology would provoke the development of counterweapons, thereby accelerating the arms race and disrupting the balance between the superpowers. According to this view, every new establishment of balance, which is inevitable, would hardly bring more security for the rivals. Furthermore, it would only accentuate the military-technological gap between the two superpowers and their alliances on the one hand, and the rest of the world on the other.

The views of Yugoslavia on this issue are also reflected in the relevant documents of the movement of nonaligned countries, to which this country belongs. Most recently, in the political declaration from the nonaligned summit in 1986, the nonaligned countries "called upon all states, in particular those with major space capabilities, to adhere strictly to the existing legal restrictions and limitations on space weapons, including those contained in the Outer Space Treaty and the 1972 U.S.-Soviet Treaty on Anti-Ballistic Missiles, and to refrain from taking any measures aimed at developing, testing or deploying weapons and weapons systems in outer space."[77]

As a country which bases its security on the concept of total national defense, Yugoslavia cannot be indifferent to the prospect that massive research in new space weapons technologies would almost certainly have spinoffs in the field of conventional arms, thereby making the defense of smaller and medium-sized non-bloc countries much more difficult. Huge networks of satellites, even without new types of armaments and used "only" for BMD command and communications purposes, nevertheless could be used for monitoring the military activities

---

75. Conference on Disarmament/Provisional Verbata, hereafter cited as CD/PV.252, March 22, 1984, p. 16.

76. CD/PV.254, March 29, 1984, p. 36.

77. *Review of International Affairs* (Belgrade) 875 (September 20, 1986), p. 41.

and installations of other states and using this information in conventional operations against them.

Besides these military-strategic implications, the militarization of space has an additional political and international legal dimension, which makes it unacceptable for reasons of principle for nonaligned countries like Yugoslavia. Placing new weapons systems in orbit around the Earth would be another example of the superpowers' military presence outside their own national territories, from which they could directly threaten the security of third countries (for example, by interrupting their lines of communications).

Two other European neutral states, Austria and Finland, which are not members of the UN Conference on Disarmament, have expressed their views at the CD on the question of preventing the arms race in space. They have also emphasized the priority of this task, noting that the Conference on Disarmament is the proper body to deal with it. They also show concern that space weapons technology could create strategic instability and provoke a new, dangerous dimension of the arms race. To prevent such a development, the Finnish representative has emphasized the need for "a comprehensive approach which would as far as possible fill the gaps in the treaty system and prohibit the extension of the arms race to outer space,"[78] while the Austrian representative has also pointed to the usefulness of earlier-mentioned French proposals at the CD.[79] One neutral country which has largely refrained from taking up official or semi-official views on SDI-related issues has been Switzerland.

Nevertheless, on the whole, the views of the European neutral and nonaligned countries on the subject of preventing the arms race in space, including programs such as SDI, have much in common, resembling, in a way, the similarity of their positions within the Conference on Confidence- and Security-Building Measures and Disarmament in Europe (CDE). Although this subject, unlike confidence- and security-building measures, is not of a direct security concern to them, their attitude reflects the sense of urgency they attach to the subject and their view that it is too important to be left entirely to a narrow circle of powers for solution.

---

78. CD/PV.242, February 16, 1984, p. 14.

79. CD/PV.276, July 26, 1984, p. 22.

IV. Further Implications

Europe has found or at least is trying to find an answer to SDI's technological challenge by launching its own project—Eureka. However, a corresponding answer to the possible security implications of SDI has yet to be found. It is unrealistic to assume that such an answer could be found now, while the SDI program is in its initial stage and while views about its effects are necessarily speculative and divergent. In spite of this diversity of views, it is clear that concerns about the potential negative implications of SDI outweigh the views that anti-ballistic missile defense would have a positive effect on the security of Europe.

An overview of the attitudes of different European countries to SDI shows that many of their objections and reservations on this project mirror domestic U.S. criticism and, indeed, Soviet reactions. We have in mind here such implications of SDI as the negative impact on strategic stability; the dangers of the transitional period; the possible new impetus given to the arms race, with a corresponding adverse impact on superpower arms control negotiations and agreements; and further increases in tension in East-West relations.

The Decoupling Issue

Although President Reagan's initial SDI speech contained a clause which mentioned the protection of U.S. allies and was followed by numerous administration assurances that the envisaged protective shield would cover Western Europe, the chronic Western European fear of "decoupling" was not reduced. Rather, it began to grow as U.S. research plans for new BMD technologies materialized.

Theoretically speaking, in the unlikely event that the United States succeeds in building a highly effective ballistic missile defense, the return to an era of American nuclear invulnerability could restore the credibility of the U.S. threat to resort to nuclear weapons in case of an attack on Western Europe. The logic of such an argument, often used by SDI proponents in the U.S. administration, has been recognized by certain Western Europeans. For example, former British Defense and Foreign Secretary Francis Pym has noted: "Until now the argument has been that the Americans would be reluctant to use nuclear weapons in the defense of Europe because of their own vulnerability to a retaliatory nuclear attack by the Soviet Union. If they become invulnerable as a result of SDI, the cause of their reluctance would have disappeared or been much reduced."[80] However, he has stated, reflecting a typical Western European concern, that this would also leave the West Europeans more exposed to the larger conventional forces of the East and place new limits on the options available to the West under the doctrine of flexible response.

However, if the development of new defense technologies would lead to a relative invulnerability of one superpower, or both of them on the strategic level, this would not exclude and might even increase the possibility of nuclear threats or "limited nuclear exchange" on a regional level, when their forces are confronted. In that case, the danger of decoupling would be replaced by an increased risk of limited nuclear war, an even more frightening prospect for the Europeans.

Still, the prevailing view among Western Europeans is that the drive towards SDI would stimulate isolationist tendencies in the United States, creating a "Fortress America" mentality that would lead to the subordination of Western European security interests to U.S. foreign policy priorities. Former French Foreign Minister Claude Cheysson has asked in this respect: "Could the Europeans still have faith in American protection from a United States believing itself to be protected by an anti-missile network?"

In view of the devastation that Europe suffered in two world wars, the ultimate aim of SDI—a return to a "non-nuclear world"—does not suggest for most Europeans an idyllic peace, but rather evokes memories of destruction and suffering. In the words of a former French ambassador to Washington, "Europeans do not believe in conventional deterrence. Twenty centuries of history have taught us that conventional deterrence does not work."[81] Laurence Freedman also points out that without the risk of nuclear war hanging in the background, deterrence is diminished, making Europe much "safer" for conventional warfare.[82] If the basic rivalry between the superpowers remains unchanged while the threat of nuclear confrontation is drastically reduced (or the consequences of such a confrontation made "bearable"), it is quite conceivable that rivalry could produce a conventional conflict, either in Europe, where the forces of the two blocs are directly opposed, or in some other crisis spot in the world.

---

80. Francis Pym, *The Strategic Defense Initiative—A European View.* The Ira D. Wallach Lecture Series (New York: Institute for East-West Security Studies, 1985), p. 16.

81. "'Star Wars' Plan Worries Envoy," *The Washington Post*, October 30, 1984.

82. Lawrence Freedman, "NATO and the Strategic Defense Initiative" (see fn. 13), p. 19.

British and French Forces

If the "decoupling" or "coupling" effects of SDI still lie largely in the realm of the hypothetical, the implications of new BMD technologies, even if only partially deployed, seem to be somewhat clearer for the effectiveness of French and British nuclear forces. Even if the USSR would not react to U.S. SDI deployments with a highly effective missile defense, a partial defense would be quite sufficient to drastically reduce the value of the French and British deterrents.[83] This concern is also voiced by certain British and French officials and specialists. Following its discussion with British Defense Minister Michael Heseltine about SDI's possible effects on Britain's plans to modernize its nuclear forces, the House of Commons Defense Committee concluded that "in the event that both superpowers were to proceed down this road of defensive space-based systems, this would not only be destabilizing between the superpowers but, if effective, it would negate what we have in mind to do."[84] Similarly, French author Jacques Vernant expressed the concern that space-based BMD systems could be effective against the nuclear forces of middle powers not in a position to saturate these defenses. This would have two negative political consequences for France and Europe. First, it could show that France does not have any other choice but to reintegrate itself in the NATO military organization which De Gaulle left in 1966; second, it would lead to the military-technological supremacy of the superpowers and the subordination of European to American interests.[85]

However, the view that future BMD developments will make the French nuclear deterrent obsolete is rejected by other French defense specialists, such as General Pierre Gallois. His confidence in the continued credibility of the French nuclear deterrent is based on two assumptions: one, that there are no technical possibilities for the superpowers to develop perfect defenses; and two, that the current French modernization program will multiply its nuclear capabilities.[86] French

83. See, for example, Charles Glaser, "Star Wars Bad Even If It Works" (see fn. 43), p. 16.

84. Quoted in Paul E. Gallis, Mark M. Lowenthal, and Marcia S. Smith, *The Strategic Defense Initiative and United States Alliance Strategy*, Congressional Research Service, The Library of Congress, February 1, 1985, p. 23.

85. Jacques Vernant, "La 'Guerre des Etoiles,'" pp. 140–141.

86. For similar views see Pascal Boniface and Jean-Michel Gaillard, "Le bouclier ou la passoire," *Le Nouvel Observateur*, February 15–21, 1985, p. 15.

defense experts also point out that French nuclear strategy will remain "countervalue"-oriented and that its retaliatory credibility would not be diminished by a partial BMD, useful only for point defense.[87] On the British side, it is suggested that the modernization of British strategic forces would increase their penetration capabilities and enable them to overcome the improved capability of the Moscow ABM system. Consequently, the credibility of the British (and French) deterrents is not seen as an issue in the foreseeable future.[88] However, this view is based on the assumption that the Soviet Union would not, at least in the near future, develop and deploy a full-scale missile-defense system.

Whatever the final effect of possible SDI-related developments on the credibility of nuclear forces of third parties, it could very well lead to an intensification of the nuclear arms race on the regional European level. If the USSR would respond to SDI with efforts to expand its own BMD systems, Britain and France would probably step up the modernization and expansion of their nuclear forces to assure their retaliatory capacity. In response, the Soviet Union could retarget some of its strategic forces on Western Europe, thereby undermining the rationale for an INF disarmament agreement. Refusal to take the potent French and British forces into account could also further complicate efforts to work out bilateral agreements on strategic forces.

ATBM

The argument that SDI would lead to a reduced risk of nuclear war in Europe is based upon two propositions—that strategic defense would reinforce deterrence, including extended deterrence, and that technologies will be developed and deployed that could effectively deal with missiles aimed at Europe. However, both of these propositions are highly doubtful. In an earlier section we listed the reasons which call into question the argument that SDI would strengthen deterrence. As far as the second proposition is concerned, there are a number of factors which make an effective missile defense for such a relatively small area quite improbable.

---

87. Michel Tatu, "La 'Guerre des Etoiles': le rendez-vous de Genève," *Le Monde* (International Edition) No. 1897, March 7–14, 1985, pp. 1–4.

88. Francis Pym, *The Strategic Defense Initiative—A European View*, p. 17.

A multilayered space-based defense would provide defense for Europe only from the layer which is supposed to deal with incoming missiles in their boost or post-boost phase (two other layers, the mid-course and reentry phase, would not cover Europe, but the area between Europe and the United States). Since this layer would employ technologies based on directed-energy weapons, it is highly doubtful whether and when it could be deployed and how effective it could actually be.

Turning to the possibilities of developing defense against short- or intermediate-range weapons, which concerns both Western and Eastern Europe, we should like to point out that, although it seems feasible to develop an ATBM system based on existing technologies, such a defense would be faced with extreme limitations. The greatest obstacle would be the extremely short warning time. While a strategic ballistic missile defense would have approximately thirty minutes to perform its function, ATBM systems in Europe would have as little as three to ten minutes to detect, identify, track, target and attack incoming missiles. In such a situation, the decision to intercept would have to be practically automatic, even preprogrammed, which would leave no possibility for retreat in case of error and actually could increase the risk of inadvertent or accidental war. An interceptor launched by accident could be mistaken for a nuclear missile by the other side, thereby provoking a nuclear response. Politically, of course, it would mean that the decision of war and peace in Europe would be even more removed from the Europeans and put into the hands of the superpowers.

Furthermore, it is doubtful that the ATBM defense in Europe could deal effectively with the problem of tactical nuclear weapons (e.g., artillery shells) and so-called "suitcase bombs." Therefore, a consequence of ATBM development could be the proliferation of battlefield nuclear weapons, especially along the central front, air-launched and sea-launched cruise missiles (this would also affect the security of countries on the flanks, including non-bloc members) and other sorts of weapons which could evade this defense system. According to many European arms control specialists, such as Lawrence Freedman, battlefield nuclear weapons are more threatening, in terms of triggering a nuclear war, than intermediate-range ones. Of course, all this does not mean that the risk of a limited nuclear war in Europe will be dramaticlly increased (actually, the probability of any war in Europe is rather low). However, if, in the long run, this nuclear buildup in Europe were coupled with the deployment of a comprehensive or even limited BMD by the superpowers, the risk of a limited nuclear war in Europe (or some other part of the world) could become a real possibility.[89] And if only one superpower were to develop and deploy a BMD defense, the other superpower could try to compensate for this strategic imbalance by trying to gain decisive superiority on a regional, i.e., European, level.

"Limited" Deployments and European Security

Of course, impenetrable defenses, as stated earlier, are not a likely immediate or even ultimate result of SDI. Does this then mean that partial defenses would have no adverse effects as far as the risk of conventional war is concerned? Not necessarily. The development and deployment of a partial BMD could create real or perceived imbalances on the strategic level which, even if temporary, would increase the importance of the conventional balance (or imbalance) for security. This would likely lead to increased pressure by both superpowers on their allies to assume an even greater share of the burden of upgrading conventional forces, not only in terms of arms modernization, but probably also in terms of increasing manpower. If not raising the risk of conventional war, this would at least strain the detente process in Europe and prevent the possibilities for any meaningful arms limitation or arms reduction agreements.

Although the strategic arms control negotiations have continued and even brought some fresh proposals (particularly from the Soviet side) in spite of the continued U.S. commitment to SDI research, this does not change the basic proposition that the continuation of such BMD plans, on a global and a European level, would seriously burden the arms control process, endangering the results that have been achieved so far (such as the ABM Treaty and the forthcoming INF treaty) and preventing further agreements. As shown in Reykjavik, the readiness of the Soviet Union to accept the idea of radical reductions of offensive strategic arms is directly connected to the limitation of SDI to laboratory research (and continued adherence of both powers to the ABM Treaty).

Therefore, although a way out from the reliance on nuclear deterrence should be sought, the way to do it is not by exploring possibilities

---

89. " . . . SDI could certainly not eliminate the threat existing as a result of nuclear battlefield weapons or short-range missiles. In other words, the regionalization of a nuclear conflict, the confinement of a nuclear exchange to the battlefield would become a conceivable option." "SDI and Europe's Interest," Statement of the Parliamentary Group of the Social Democratic Party of Germany on President Reagan's "Strategic Defense Initiative" (see fn. 69), p. 5. (See Appendix.)

for neutralizing nuclear arms by new counterweapons, but by nuclear arms reduction, accompanied by reductions in conventional weapons. Any serious attempt to find a defense against nuclear weapons, be it on the strategic (SDI) or regional (ATBM) level, or on both, would trigger an action-reaction process that would manifest itself as a defense-offense arms race in all three major categories of nuclear weapons—strategic, intermediate-range and battlefield. Inevitably, this race would spill over into the conventional field.

This new arms race, apart from torpedoing what is left of the arms control process, would clearly endanger the security of small European states outside the blocs and force them to undertake new efforts in the defense field. Some of the measures which the superpowers and military alliances could employ in order to develop strategic or tactical defense, or to counter the opponent's defense systems, could pose a direct threat to the security of non-bloc countries. For example, if ATBM defenses were developed and deployed for the area of central Europe, the natural military response would be to try to find alternative flight trajectories on the flanks, thus increasing the risk that missile trajectories would cross the territories of third countries. This would impose on non-bloc countries the costly and difficult task of acquiring the technology to intercept and destroy these missiles. Another military response to ATBM systems—an increased number of sea-launched cruise missiles deployed in European waters—would have the same negative effect on the security of the coastal non-bloc countries.

In sum, it is very difficult to see how the process initiated by SDI could lead to greater stability in Europe and better security for Europeans. The introduction of new weapons technologies, even if considered defensive, could very well take us in the opposite direction.

V. Conclusions

Since its official launching in 1983, the Strategic Defense Initiative has evolved from an idea in President Reagan's speech to a research program with its own organization and large funding. Despite the fact that the notion of developing the missile shield has remained controversial, both in the United States and abroad, and that its financing is subject to budgetary restrictions,[90] the research program is

---

90. The U.S. administration's request for SDI research, development, testing and evaluation funds for 1988 was $5.68 billion, but the joint House and Senate authorization conference voted to approve $3.9 billion—a figure subsequently accepted by the president.

slowly gaining momentum and is unlikely to be stopped; on the contrary, it will continue until at least some initial results are reached. Few people, including supporters of the program, believe it will ever lead to the near-perfect population defense envisaged in Reagan's speech. However, the fact that the aims of the program seem to be less ambitious and its scope less comprehensive makes the whole project more realistic and increases the probability that it will materialize in one form or another. Most observers—both critics and supporters—agree that SDI research could lead to a new type of point defense which should, according to those who are sympathetic to the idea, enhance deterrence, which has allegedly been rapidly eroding over the last decade.

What are the possibilities that a negotiated solution, which would be acceptable to both sides and satisfy the concerns of third countries, could be found at the Geneva arms control talks?

Since the reopening of the arms control dialogue between the two superpowers some important moves have been made, especially at the Reykjavik summit in October 1986. In spite of different reports it is clear, and it is claimed by both sides, that the leaders of the USSR and the United States came very close to an agreement on a number of important issues—major (50-percent) reductions of offensive ballistic missiles, nuclear testing and, in particular, intermediate-range nuclear forces (INF). However, differences over SDI remained an obstacle to any agreement. The American president showed no intention of foregoing the SDI option, while the Soviet leader maintained the view that anything beyond laboratory research in this field precludes agreement on offensive arms reduction.

Therefore, while it is true that Reykjavik was not a failure, because it showed that both sides could do away with most of their nuclear weapons without upsetting the balance, it also confirmed that the possibilities of reaching a compromise on SDI remain unclear and very difficult to envisage at this point.

Considering the firm commitment of the Reagan administration to the SDI program and the equally firm Soviet opposition to it, a comprehensive arms reduction agreement such as the one contemplated in Reykjavik does not seem possible in the near future. Progress on strategic issues presupposes that differences on SDI are narrowed, and not widened.

Clearing up misunderstandings regarding compliance with the ABM Treaty and its interpretation seems to be a step which is indispensable for making some headway in addressing the SDI issue. The establishment of a working group in the Geneva talks for this purpose is a welcome sign. Another step forward would be the cancellation of programs which raise doubts over compliance with the treaty. Therefore, the reported removal of controversial radars at the Sary-Shagan missile test center in the Soviet Union, combined with the on-site inspection of the controversial Krasnoyarsk radar site by U.S. experts in September 1987, should certainly contribute towards increased ABM Treaty credibility.[91] On the other hand, the decision of the Reagan administration in favor of a "broad" interpretation of the treaty would lead in the opposite direction.

Keeping the SDI project within the limits of research seems to be necessary for preserving the prospects for agreements that opened up in Reykjavik. Although it is true that verification of a ban on research is difficult if not impossible, the effective limitation on funds available for research could serve the same purpose. Since unilateral restraints are unrealistic to expect, this argues in favor of proposals to freeze and cut military budgets. Of course, this would require more openness on the military level by all powers concerned, and an agreement on generally accepted criteria for comparing military expenditures.

Also, if the United States is not willing to back down on its SDI plan, it should at least not energetically pursue its offensive arms projects, such as MX and Trident II. It is quite unrealistic to expect that one side would reduce its strategic forces if faced with both an offensive and defensive buildup by the opposite side. In any case, it seems that a halt or at least a substantial slowing down of the pace of strategic modernization on the part of the superpowers is urgently needed to give arms control negotiations the chance to catch up with technology. Since a freeze seems to be difficult to agree upon, a partial substitute for it, such as a comprehensive test ban or ban on all missile tests for an agreed period, should be undertaken as a first step.

A suggestion was also made with reference to the Geneva talks that the United States should indicate a willingness to forego a first-strike capacity against Soviet land-based intercontinental missiles, in the hope that the Soviet Union would reciprocate.[92] However, while such a mutual pledge could have the beneficial effect of ameliorating the atmosphere and creating greater confidence, it would also have serious shortcomings. Such a pledge would be of limited value without a change in force postures. Also, any declaration to forego the use of

91. R. Jeffrey Smith, "Soviet Removes Radars Cited as Risk to Treaty," *International Herald Tribune*, February 26, 1987.

92. Stephen J. Solarz, "If the Arms Talks Are to Succeed," *The New York Times*, January 21, 1985.

a particular weapons category might imply that the use of other weapons is not prohibited, and might weaken the general international obligation not to use force. Finally, a bilateral agreement of this kind between the superpowers, even if it included all types of nuclear weapons, might imply that nuclear strikes against third countries are not prohibited.

If the SDI program would be confined in the next few years strictly to research, this would open up the possibility to create such conditions in superpower relations that the testing or deployment of new anti-missile weapons systems, either in space or ground-based, would be perceived as politically undesirable by the side acquiring this capacity. In other words, one should strive for an "across-the-board" improvement of U.S.-Soviet relations, for the establishment of mutual confidence and for concrete arms control results in all fields. In a way, this would be a race against time, a race to create a favorable political environment before technology's momentum brings destabilizing results. Therefore, two conditions must be met: speeding up the arms control process on the one hand, and slowing down military research on the other. While the scaling down of military research and development is largely dependent on domestic factors, both political and economic, it would undoubtedly be helped by positive results from the arms control process.

In the field of intermediate-range nuclear weapons in Europe, the conclusion of a U.S.-Soviet treaty eliminating such systems, scheduled for December 1987, represents a hopeful sign. The withdrawal of Soviet and American missiles from Europe would, among other things, weaken the argument that the development of a missile-defense system for Europe is necessary and in this way indirectly weaken the rationale for a space-based defense for strategic missiles.

Progress in some other areas of arms control—such as a chemical weapons ban or conventional force reductions in Europe—also seems to be within the realm of the possible. Of course, the impact of these agreements on prospects for the solution of strategic offensive and space weapons questions would be only marginal. Still, results in these areas, if achieved relatively soon, would create a climate of confidence which would facilitate the tackling of more difficult questions.

However, these achievements would not help much if the Geneva talks on strategic and space weapons fail to take advantage in the meantime of the meeting of minds that was achieved in some areas in Reykjavik. Therefore, it seems imperative to reach an agreement in this area, even an interim one, until the conditions for a more lasting solution are ripe. One element of such an agreement has to be the meaningful reduction of strategic offensive nuclear armaments; another should be the limitation of exploration of new BMD technologies to the research stage only. This is not, however, a classical tradeoff situation, because radical reductions in offensive arms are now an objective of both sides, while as far as defensive systems are concerned nothing tangible can be traded away at the moment. Nevertheless, it is very difficult to imagine the possibility of an agreement in one area without an agreement in the other. The simplest solution would be to combine an agreement on the reduction of strategic offensive weapons with another to prolong the notice of withdrawal from the ABM Treaty from six months, as it stands now, to at least five to ten years. The explicit restriction of space-based BMD programs such as SDI to research only would not be necessary in this case because the ABM Treaty in its present form does not allow the development and testing of mobile ABM systems. (Of course, this presupposes that the so-called broad interpretation of the treaty is not legally valid.)

If the process of offensive arms reductions were to proceed without dramatic breakthroughs in research on space-based defense, a more lasting and more radical agreement could be negotiated. Such an agreement could combine reductions of strategic arms to the level of minimum deterrence with a ban on the development and deployment of any missile-defense system, space-based or land-based.[93] Additional elements of such a comprehensive agreement should be an agreement on prohibiting the development and testing of ASAT systems (because of their close connection with ABM technologies) and an agreement banning all nuclear tests.

Of course, the prospects for arms limitations and disarmament in the field of offensive and defensive strategic weapons will remain uncertain if the SDI project is pursued with the firm intent to deploy such systems. Therefore, SDI will remain, at least for the time being, a major risk for the future of arms control. On the other hand, the controversy which has surrounded the idea since its inception has contributed to focusing attention in the right direction—on some of the most basic issues of arms control and disarmament, including the problem of replacing nuclear deterrence with a more acceptable and

---

93. This idea was proposed by the former director of the Stockholm International Peace Research Institute (SIPRI), Frank Blackaby, who has rightly observed that "if ABM development and deployment is a bad idea, the sensible thing is to stop it altogether." Frank Blackaby, "Space Weapons and Security," *World Armaments and Disarmament. SIPRI Yearbook 1986* (Oxford: Oxford University Press, 1986), p. 94.

sound basis of security. Whether and when such a basis will be found depends on many factors. Some of the most crucial among them go beyond the area of arms control and beyond the bilateral framework of superpower relations. One thing, however, is certain: although the ultimate solution has to be radical—the abolition of nuclear weapons— the road toward this goal has to be pursued very carefully and with the awareness that the solution has to be political, not technical.

Finally, it should be repeated that the discussion of the issue of the demilitarization of space is not the sole privilege of the superpowers. They have a responsibility in this area to all the other countries, stemming from the fact that outer space is the common heritage of all mankind, not just the *domain preserve* of those who possess space technology. The need to begin appropriate international negotiations with a view to preventing an arms race in space was affirmed in the Final Document of the Tenth Special Session of the UN General Assembly devoted to disarmament. The UN resolution, entitled "Prevention of an Arms Race in Outer Space" (Res. 38/70, para. 4), reiterated that the Conference on Disarmament "has a primary role in the negotiation of an agreement or agreements . . . on the prevention of an arms race in all its aspects in outer space." The importance of this issue is such that its general political and international legal implications cannot and should not be left exclusively to bilateral negotiations between the superpowers, whatever their outcome may be.

Appendix

1

On March 23, 1983, U.S. President Ronald Reagan outlined his vision of the Strategic Defense Initiative for the first time. The following is an excerpt from the text of his address to the nation, "Peace and National Security" (as provided by the U.S. Department of State, Bureau of Public Affairs).

Now, thus far tonight I've shared with you my thoughts on the problems of national security we must face together. My predecessors in the Oval Office have appeared before you on other occasions to describe the threat posed by Soviet power and have proposed steps to address that threat. But since the advent of nuclear weapons, those steps have been increasingly directed toward deterrence of aggression through the promise of retaliation. This approach to stability through offensive threat has worked. We and our allies have succeeded in preventing nuclear war for more than three decades.

In recent months, however, my advisers, including, in particular, the Joint Chiefs of Staff, have underscored the necessity to break out of a future that relies solely on offensive retaliation for our security. Over the course of these discussions, I've become more and more deeply convinced that the human spirit must be capable of rising above dealing with other nations and human beings by threatening their existence. Feeling this way, I believe we must thoroughly examine every opportunity for reducing tensions and for introducing greater stability into the strategic calculus on both sides.

One of the most important contributions we can make is, of course, to lower the level of all arms and particularly nuclear arms. We are engaged right now in several negotiations with the Soviet Union to bring abut a mutual reduction of weapons.

I will report to you a week from tomorrow my thoughts on that score. But let me just say, I am totally committed to this course. If the Soviet Union will join with us in our effort to achieve major arms reduction, we will have succeeded in stabilizing the nuclear balance. Nevertheless, it will still be necessary to rely on the specter of retaliation, on mutual threat. And that's a sad commentary on the human condition. Wouldn't it be better to save lives than to avenge them? Are we not capable of demonstrating our peaceful intentions by applying all our abilities and our ingenuity to achieving a truly lasting stability?

I think we are. Indeed, we must. After careful consultation with my advisers, including the Joint Chiefs of Staff, I believe there is a way. Let me share with you a vision of the future which offers hope. It is that we embark on a program to counter the awesome Soviet missile threat with measures that are defensive. Let us turn to the very strengths in technology that spawned our great industrial base and that have given us the quality of life we enjoy today.

What if free people could live secure in the knowledge that their security did not rest upon the threat of instant U.S. retaliation to deter a Soviet attack, that we could intercept and destroy strategic ballistic missiles before they reached our own soil or that of our allies?

I know this is a formidable, technical task; one that may not be accomplished before the end of this century. Yet, current technology has attained a level of sophistication where it is reasonable for us to begin this effort. It will take years, probably decades of effort on many fronts. There will be failures and setbacks, just as there will be successes and breakthroughs. And as we proceed, we must remain constant in preserving the nuclear deterrent and maintaining a solid capability for flexible response.

But isn't it worth every investment necesary to free the world from the threat of nuclear war? We know it is. In the meantime, we will continue to pursue real reductions in nuclear arms, negotiating from a position of strength that can be ensured only by modernizing our strategic forces.

At the same time, we must take steps to reduce the risk of a conventional military conflict escalating to nuclear war by improving our non-nuclear capabilities. America does possess—now—the technologies to attain very significant improvements in the effectiveness of our conventional, non-nuclear forces. Proceeding boldly with these new technologies, we can significantly reduce any incentive that the Soviet Union may have to threaten attack against the United States or its allies.

As we pursue our goal of defensive technologies, we recognize that our allies rely upon our strategic offensive power to deter attacks against them. Their vital interests and ours are inextricably linked. Their safety and ours are one. And no change in technology can or will alter that reality. We must and shall continue to honor our commitments. I clearly recognize that defensive systems have limitations and raise certain problems and ambiguities. If paired with offensive systems, they can be viewed as fostering an aggressive policy; and no one wants that. But with these considerations firmly in mind, I call upon the scientific community in our country, those who gave us nuclear weapons, to turn their great talents now to the cause of mankind and world peace, to give us the means of rendering these nuclear weapons impotent and obsolete.

Tonight, consistent with our obligations of the ABM [anti-ballistic missile] Treaty and recognizing the need for closer consultation with our allies, I'm taking an important first step. I am directing a comprehensive and intensive effort to define a long-term research and development program to begin to achieve our ultimate goal of eliminating the threat posed by strategic nuclear missiles. This could pave the way for arms control measures to eliminate the weapons themselves. We seek neither military superiority nor political advantage. Our only purpose—one all people share—is to search for ways to reduce the danger of nuclear war.

My fellow Americans, tonight we're launching an effort which holds the promise of changing the course of human history. There will be risks, and results take time. But I believe we can do it. As we cross this threshold, I ask for your prayers and your support.

2

*On February 20, 1985, Paul H. Nitze, Special Adviser to the President
for Arms Reduction Negotiations, defined the criteria to be satisfied
before any deployment of strategic missile defenses could begin. The
following is his speech on the subject to the Philadelphia World Affairs
Council, "On the Road to a More Stable Peace" (as provided by the
U.S. Department of State, Bureau of Public Affairs).*

Since the dawn of the nuclear age 40 years ago, there have been countless
proposals to eliminate nuclear weapons from the face of the earth. That has
been the professed objective of both the Soviet Union and the United States,
but, until recently, it has not been a practical goal.

The President is determined to do more, to look even now toward a world
in which nuclear weapons have, in fact, been eliminated. The present situation—in which the threat of massive nuclear retaliation is the ultimate sanc-
tion, the key element of deterrence, and, thus, the basis for security and
peace—is unsatisfactory. It has kept the peace for 40 years, but the potential
costs of a breakdown are immense and, because of continuing massive Soviet
deployments of both offensive and defensive weaponry, are not becoming
less. If we can, we must find a more reliable basis for security and for peace.

This concern prompted the President's decision to proceed with the
Strategic Defense Initiative (SDI). He has directed the scientific community
to determine if new cost-effective defensive technologies are feasible which
could be introduced into force structures so as to produce a more stable
strategic relationship. We envisage, if that search is successful, a cooperative
effort with the Soviet Union, hopefully leading to an agreed transition toward
effective non-nuclear defenses that might make possible the eventual elimination of nuclear weapons.

The Strategic Concept

In preparing for Secretary Shultz's January meeting with Foreign Minister
Gromyko, we developed a strategic concept encompassing our view of how
we would like to see the U.S.-Soviet strategic relationship evolve in the future.
That concept provides the basis for our approach to next month's talks in
Geneva. It can be summarized in four sentences.

> During the next 10 years, the U.S. objective is a radical reduction in the power
> of existing and planned offensive nuclear arms, as well as the stabilization of
> the relationship between offensive and defensive nuclear arms, whether on earth
> or in space. We are even now looking forward to a period of transition to a more
> stable world, with greatly reduced levels of nuclear arms and an enhanced ability
> to deter war based upon an increasing contribution of non-nuclear defenses
> against offensive nuclear arms. This period of transition could lead to the eventual
> elimination of all nuclear arms, both offensive and defensive. A world free of
> nuclear arms is an ultimate objective to which we, the Soviet Union, and all
> other nations can agree.

It would be worthwhile to dwell on this concept in some detail. To begin
with, it entails three time phases: the near term, a transition phase, and an
ultimate phase.

The Near Term

For the immediate future—at least the next 10 years—we will continue to base deterrence on the ultimate threat of nuclear retaliation. We have little choice; today's technology provides no alternative.

That being said, we will press for radical reductions in the number and power of strategic and intermediate-range nuclear arms. Offensive nuclear arsenals on both sides are entirely too high and potentially destructive, particularly in the more destabilizing categories such as the large MIRVed [multiple independently-targetable reentry vehicles] Soviet ICBM [intercontinetal ballistic missile] and SS-20 forces.

At the same time, we will seek to reverse the erosion that has occurred in the Anti-Ballistic Missile (ABM) Treaty regime—erosion that has resulted from Soviet actions over the last 10 years. These include the construction of a large phased-array radar near Krasnoyarsk in central Siberia in violation of the ABM Treaty's provisions regarding the location and orientation of ballistic missile early warning radars.

For the near term, we will be pursuing the SDI research program—in full compliance with the ABM Treaty, which permits such research. Likewise, we expect the Soviets will continue their investigation of the possibilities of new defensive technologies, as they have for many years.

We have offered to begin discussions in the upcoming Geneva talks with the Soviets as to how we might together make a transition to a more stable and reliable relationship based on an increasing mix of defensive systems.

The Transition Period

Should new defensive technologies prove feasible, we would want at some future date to begin such a transition, during which we would place greater reliance on defensive systems for our protection and that of our allies.

The criteria by which we will judge the feasibility of such technologies will be demanding. The technologies must produce defensive systems that are survivable; if not, the defenses would themselves be tempting targets for a first strike. This would decrease rather than enhance stability.

New defensive systems must also be cost-effective at the margin—that is, they must be cheap enough to add additional defensive capability so that the other side has no incentive to add additional offensive capability to overcome the defense. If this criterion is not met, the defensive systems could encourage a proliferation of countermeasures and additional offensive weapons to overcome deployed defenses instead of a redirection of effort from offense to defense.

As I said, these criteria are demanding. If the new technologies cannot meet these standards, we are not about to deploy them. In the event, we would have to continue to base deterrence on the ultimate threat of nuclear retaliation. However, we hope and have expectations that the scientific community can respond to the challenge.

We would see the transition period as a cooperative endeavor with the Soviets. Arms control would play a critical role. We would, for example, envisage continued reductions in offensive nuclear arms.

Concurrently, we would envisage the sides beginning to test, develop, and deploy survivable and cost-effective defenses at a measured pace, with particular emphasis on non-nuclear defenses. Deterrence would thus begin to rely more on a mix of offensive nuclear and defensive systems instead of on offensive nuclear arms alone.

The transition would continue for some time—perhaps for decades. As the U.S. and Soviet strategic and intermediate-range nuclear arsenals declined significantly, we would need to negotiate reductions in other types of nuclear weapons and involve, in some manner, the other nuclear powers.

The Ultimate Period

Given the right technical and political conditions, we would hope to be able to continue the reduction of nuclear weapons down to zero.

The global elimination of nuclear weapons would be accompanied by widespread deployments of effective non-nuclear defenses. These defenses would provide assurance that, were one country to cheat—for example, by clandestinely building ICBMs or shorter range systems, such as SS-20s—it would not be able to achieve any exploitable military advantage. To overcome the deployed defenses, cheating would have to be on such a large scale that there would be sufficient notice so that countermeasures could be taken.

Were we to reach the ultimate phase, deterrence would be based on the ability of the defense to deny success to a potential aggressor's attack. The strategic relationship could then be characterized as one of mutual assured security.

Comments

Having thus outlined our strategic concept, let me offer some comments and perhaps anticipate some of your questions.

First, the concept is wholly consistent with deterrence. In both the transition and ultimate phases, deterrence would continue to provide the basis for the U.S.-Soviet strategic relationship.

Deterrence requires that a potential opponent be convinced that the risks and costs of aggression far outweigh the gains he might hope to achieve. The popular discussion of deterrence has focused almost entirely on one element—that is, posing to an aggressor high potential costs through the ultimate threat of nuclear retaliation.

But deterrence can also function if one has the ability, through defense and other military means, to deny the attacker the gains he might otherwise have hoped to realize. Our intent is to shift the deterrent balance from one which is based primarily on the ultimate threat of devastating nuclear retaliation to one in which non-nuclear defenses play a greater and greater role. We believe the latter provides a far sounder basis for a stable and reliable strategic relationship.

My second comment is that we recognize that the transition period—if defensive technologies prove feasible and we decide to move in that direction—could be tricky. We would have to avoid a mix of offensive and defensive systems that, in a crisis, would give one side or the other incentives to strike first. That is precisely why we would seek to make the transition a cooperative endeavor with the Soviets and have offered, even now, to begin talking with them about the issues that would have to be dealt with in such a transition.

My third comment is that we realize that a world from which nuclear weapons have been eliminated would still present major risks. The technique of making nuclear weapons is well known; that knowledge cannot be excised. The danger of breakout or cheating would continue. Moreover, there would also be the potential problem of suitcase nuclear bombs and the like.

But even if all risks cannot be eliminated, they can be greatly reduced. Nothing is wholly risk free; one must compare the alternatives. It seems to me that the risks posed by cheating or suitcase bombs in a world from which nuclear arms had been eliminated from military arsenals would be orders of magnitude less than the risks and potential costs posed by a possible breakdown in the present deterrence regime based upon the ultimate threat of massive nuclear retaliation.

The Geneva Talks

U.S. and Soviet delegations will meet in Geneva in roughly 3 weeks' time to begin negotiations on nuclear and space arms. In those talks, we will advance positions consistent with and designed to further the concept I have outlined.

At the end of January, I was asked by the press whether I was confident about the outcome of the upcoming talks. I replied that I was more confident than previously—that is, before the Geneva meeting between Mr. Shultz and Mr. Gromyko—but I still wasn't very confident. We must bear in mind that there are profound differences of approach between the two sides.

In Geneva, Mr. Gromyko stated the Soviet position clearly and unambiguously. It has, since then, been repeated by many Soviet commentators. The Soviets insist on the "nonmilitarization" of space; by that, they mean a ban on all arms in space that are designed to attack objects in space or on earth and all systems on earth that are designed to attack objects in space. They have expressed opposition to research efforts into such systems, in spite of their own sizable efforts in this field, which include the only currently operational ABM and anti-satellite systems.

As to offensive arms reductions, the Soviets have yet to acknowledge the legitimacy of our concern about the threat we see in their large, highly MIRVed ICBM force. They continue to demand compensation for British and French nuclear forces and assert that U.S. Pershing II and ground-launched cruise missiles somehow represent a more odious threat than that posed to NATO Europe by the hundreds of SS-20 missiles now deployed.

In addition, the Soviets maintain that the three subject areas—strategic nuclear, intermediate-range nuclear, and defense and space arms—must not only be discussed in their interrelationship, but that it is not possible to implement an agreement in one area without agreement in the others. We believe otherwise; if the sides come to agreement in one area, we see no sense in a self-denying rule that would prevent the sides from implementing an agreement that would serve the interests of both.

There are obvious differences. We will present our views and listen carefully to Soviet proposals. We do not expect the Soviets to accept immediately our viewpoint or our concept as to how the future strategic relationship should evolve. The negotiators have their work cut out for them; the process will be complex and could well be lengthy. But with persistence, patience, and constructive ideas, we hope the Soviets will come to see the merits of our position—that it will serve their national interests as well as ours.

Conclusion

At the beginning of my remarks, I noted that the elimination of nuclear weapons has often seemed an impractical goal, one which has received little more than lip service. As you can see, the United States is going beyond that; the President has initiated a serious effort to see how it can be accomplished.

We do not underestimate the difficulties in reaching that objective. Quite frankly, it may prove impossible to obtain; and, even if we do eventually reach it, it will not be for many, many years—perhaps well into the next century.

But we cannot be anything but uneasy about the current situation, in which the nuclear arsenals of the world total tens of thousands of nuclear weapons. We owe it to our children, our grandchildren, and—in my case—to my great-grandchild to hold out for and to work toward some brighter vision for the future.

3

On October 12, 1986, following the breakup of the "pre-summit" meeting in Reykjavik, Iceland, between President Reagan and Soviet General Secretary Mikhail S. Gorbachev, the Soviet leader held a press conference in which he gave a detailed exposition of his views on strategic missile defense and nuclear arms control. What follows are the relevant passages from the general secretary's remarks (as translated by the Foreign Broadcast Information Service from the Soviet newspaper Pravda, *October 14, 1986, pp. 1, 2).*

One more problem in view of our setting about the practical abolition of nuclear weapons is such: Each side should have a guarantee that during that time the other side will not be seeking military superiority. I think that it is a perfectly fair and legitimate requirement both politically and militarily.

Politically, if we begin reductions, we should take care that all existing brakes on the development of new types of weapons be not only preserved, but also strengthened.

Militarily: Indeed, care should be taken to preclude the following situation: Both sides have reduced the nuclear potentials and while the reduction process is underway, one of the sides secretly contemplates and captures the initiative and attains military superiority.

This is inadmissible. I apply this to the Soviet Union. We have all rights to lay similar demands on the American side.

In this connection, we raised the question in the following way: When we embark on the stage of a real deep reduction and, after ten years, of the elimination of the nuclear potential of the Soviet Union and the United States, it is necessary that this period should not seek the shaking of the mechanisms restraining the arms race, above all such as the ABM Treaty. These mechanisms should be consolidated.

Our proposal was reduced to the following: The sides consolidate the ABM Treaty of unlimited duration by assuming equal pledges that they shall not use the right to break out of the treaty within the next ten years.

Is this proposition correct and logical? It is logical.

Is it serious? It is serious.

Does it meet the interests of both sides? It does meet the interests of both sides.

Simultaneously, we suggested that all ABM requirements be strictly observed within these ten years, that the development and testing of space weapons be banned and only research and testing in laboratories be allowed.

What did we mean by this?

We are aware of the commitment of the American Administration and the President to SDI. Apparently, our consent to its continuation and to laboratory tests offers the President an opportunity to go through with research and eventually to get clear what SDI is, and what it is about, although it is already clear to many people, ourselves included.

It was at that point that a true battle of two approaches to world politics, including such questions as the termination of the arms race and a ban on nuclear weapons, began.

The American Administration and the President insisted to the end that America should have the right to test and study everything involved in SDI not only in laboratories but elsewhere, including outer space.

But who will agree to this? A madman? But madmen, as a rule, are kept where they should be, where they're given medical care. Anyway, I do not see any in posts of leadership, especially at the helm of states.

We were on the brink of taking major, historic decisions, because up to then the point had always been merely arms reductions. We took decisions on ABM, SALT-I, SALT-II, etc.

Since the U.S. Administration, as we understand now, is confident of U.S. technological superiority and is hoping to achieve through SDI military superiority, it has gone even so far as burying the accords already achieved. We suggested that instructions were given for drawing up treaties with a view to their practical fulfillment. They could be signed during a meeting in Washington. But the American side torpedoed all this.

I told the President that we were missing an historic chance. Our positions had never been so close.

Bidding me goodbye, the President said that he was disappointed and that I had from the outset come unwilling to look for agreements and accords. Why do you display such firmness on SDI and the problem of testing, all that range of problems, because of one word? But I think that the matter is not words but substance. Herein lies the key to the understanding of what the U.S. Administration has on its mind. I think that it has on its mind what, as I now see, is on the mind of the American military-industrial complex. The Administration is captive to the complex and the President is not free to take such a decision. We made breaks and held debates and I see that the President was not given support. That was why our meeting failed when we already were close to producing historic results. . . .

The positions were drawing closer. But when there occurred a rupture on the question of ABM, when all the discussion was broken off and the search was suspended, we stopped our meeting. . . .

Question (Icelandic radio and television): After the negative result of the summit, will the Soviet Union counter the American SDI program with something else and will it not launch its space arms program full blast?

Reply: I think that you have understood the essence of the Soviet position. If now we have approached a stage at which we start a drastic cut in nuclear weapons, both strategic and medium-range missiles (we have already approached understanding with the Americans to do this in the next decade), we have the right to demand that we should be guaranteed in this period that nothing surprising and unforeseen will take place. This also includes such a sphere as space and deployment of a space-based ABM system.

I told the President (maybe I will slightly open the curtain over our exchange of opinions) that the SDI does not bother us militarily. In my opinion, nobody in America believes that such a system can be created. Moreover, if America eventually decides to do this, our reply will not be symmetrical. True, I told him: Mr. President, you know that I have already been turned into your ally in the SDI issue. He was surprised by this. It turns out, I tell him, that since I so sharply criticize the SDI, this offers you a convincing argument that the SDI is needed. You just say: If Gorbachev is against it, this means that it is a good thing. You win applause and financing. True, cynics and sceptics have appeared who say: What if this is Gorbachev's crafty design—to stay out of the SDI and to ruin America. So you figure this out yourself. But we are not scared by the SDI in any case.

I say this with confidence, since it is irresponsible to bluff in such matters. There will be reply to the SDI. An asymmetrical one, but it will be. We shall not sacrifice much at that.

But what is its danger? For one thing, a political danger. A situation is created right away, which brings uncertainty and fans up mistrust for each other and suspicion. Then the reduction of nuclear weapons will be put aside. In short, quite another situation is needed for us to take up thoroughly the question of reducing nuclear weapons. Second, there is a military aspect after all. The SDI can lead to new types of weapons. We also can say this with competence. It can lead to an entirely new stage of the arms race which is unpredictable for its serious consequences.

It turns out that, on the one hand, we agree to start reduction of nuclear weapons—at present the most dangerous and dreadful, and, on the other— we should bless research, and even conduct it in space, on location, so as to create the latest weapons. This does not agree with normal logic. . . .

Question (American TV company ABC): Mr. General Secretary, I don't understand why, when you had an opportunity to achieve with President Reagan agreement on cuts in nuclear weapons, the Soviet side did not agree to SDI research. You yourself said in Geneva that you were ready to pay a high price for nuclear arms cuts. Now, when you had such an opportunity, you missed it.

Answer: Your question contains an element of criticism, so I will answer it in some detail.

First, the U.S. President came to Reykjavik with empty hands and empty pockets. The American delegation, I would say brought us trash from the Geneva talks. It was only thanks to the far-reaching proposals of the Soviet side that we were about to reach most major agreements (they were not formalized, mind you) on cuts in strategic offensive weapons and on medium-range missiles. Naturally, we hoped in that situation—and I think it is perfectly clear to a politician, a military man and any normal person in general— that if we are to sign such agreements on major cuts in nuclear weapons, we should take care to ensure that nothing could thwart that difficult process, towards which we had been moving for decades. Then we raised the question that we stood for strengthening the ABM Treaty. The American side is constantly burrowing under the ABM Treaty.

It has already called in question SALT II and would now like to stage a funeral of the ABM Treaty in Reykjavik, moreover, with the participation of the Soviet Union and Gorbachev. That will not do. The world as a whole would not understand us, it is my conviction.

All of you who are sitting here, all of you are convinced that if we begin to attack the ABM Treaty in addition to everything else, the last mechanism which has contributed so much to constraining, in spite of everything, the process of the arms race, we are worthless politicians. But it is not enough to preserve its terms at a time when deep cuts in nuclear weapons are initiated. We think that the treaty must be strengthened. We proposed a mechanism of strengthening it—not to use the right to pull out of the ABM Treaty during the ten years in which we will totally reduce and destroy the nuclear potentials in our countries.

At the same time, to ensure that neither the Soviet Union seeks to overtake America in space research and achieve military superiority nor America seeks to overtake the Soviet Union, we said that we agreed to laboratory research and testing but opposed to the emergence with that research and testing of components of space-based ABM defenses into outer space. This is our demand. Our demand in that case also was constructive and reckoning with America's stand. If she agreed, she would get an opportunity to resolve her problems within the framework of continued laboratory research but without attempts to develop space ABM defenses. I think there is iron logic here, as the children say, and sometimes we should learn even from children.

4

On October 27, 1987, Marshal Sergei F. Akhromeev, Chief of the Soviet General Staff, gave an interview to **The New York Times,** *during which he made the following comments on the Strategic Defense Initiative. (Source:* **The New York Times,** *October 30, 1987, p. A6).*

Q. Why does President Reagan's space defense program seem to give Soviet leaders and strategists so much political trouble, especially if so many on both sides believe it cannot work for 20 or 30 years?

A. . . . It is not a matter of political obstacles caused to the Soviet leadership. The thing is, we are deeply convinced that creating a space-based ABM defense to cover the territory of the United States would radically step up the military threat toward the Soviet Union. In that case, the United States would have the strategic defense of its territory, which according to the opinion of the U.S. Administration is intended to defend only the United States from an attack on the part of the Soviet Union.

At the same time the United States would have in its hands the strategic forces capable of delivering a strike against Soviet territory. That is, the United States would have a nuclear sword and a space-based nuclear shield, which means an eternal, never-ending arms race. In which case there can be no talk whatsoever about increasing security for both sides.

Q. From the scientific advice you get, do you believe that a shield would ever be anywhere near effective, even in theory?

A. The United States is working concurrently to solve two problems: to create a space-based nuclear shield for itself, and at the same time to cut down the number of strategic forces to a certain level, 6,000 warheads on each side. Given this number of warheads on each side, it is possible, at least in theory, to create a space-based nuclear shield.

Q. Does this mean that, in Soviet view, that if strategic offensive missiles are not reduced, it would be impossible to create an effective shield?

A. I share this view. If one of the sides will keep increasing the number and improving the quality of strategic nuclear forces, then creating a protective shield against these forces is either impossible or will not become practical until the distant future.

But I think the Administration of President Reagan in trying to carry out the Strategic Defense Initiative is pursuing at the same time other objectives, both political and economic, namely an intention to get military superiority over the other side and an attempt to slow down the social-economic progress of Soviet society. That's beyond my field of competence, which is military affairs, but I think the objectives being pursued in the strategic defense program are more than just military ones.

Q. What if both sides reduce their warheads, and both deploy defenses in space?

A. One cannot answer this question with great certainty. But based on my experience in the negotiating process and judging from the public response around the world, I think that if we manage to put a stop to the realization of the Strategic Defense Initiative for a period of 10 years and at the same [time] cut strategic offensive forces by 50 percent, this would make the whole process of nuclear arms reduction irreversible. Thus, the world would proceed to the complete liquidation of nuclear weapons. . . .

5

On April 18, 1985, West German Chancellor Helmut Kohl delivered an official policy statement to the Bundestag on the Strategic Defense Initiative. His complete statement, as translated by the German Information Center, follows.

1. President Reagan's strategic defense initiative (SDI) will be the dominant security issue in the years ahead and greatly influence both East-West relations and the relationship between the United States and Europe.

In his speech on March 23, 1983, President Reagan called for research to establish whether it might be possible with the aid of modern technology to become less reliant on offensive nuclear weapons without jeopardizing one's security. In a very far-sighted manner he has created a model for assured defense with non-nuclear weapons as a contrast to the existing strategy of deterrence through mutual assured destruction with nuclear weapons. Anyone who seriously desires a far-reaching reduction in the world's nuclear arsenals and has doubts about the strategy of nuclear deterrence, which is indispensable to us today and in the foreseeable future, should carefully ponder all alternative means of safeguarding peace and preventing war. Every opportunity to rid oneself of the somber threat of nuclear holocaust as the final means of preventing war merits conscientious examination. Nobody can yet judge with certainty whether President Reagan's SDI will prove to be a method of greatly reducing and ultimately outlawing nuclear weapons, however if this method proves feasible, Ronald Reagan will deserve tribute for a historical achievement.

Despite all our everyday political differences and the understandable varying viewpoints, we should retain the ability to discuss in a serious and far-sighted manner any political visions that can help us to achieve the vital goals of our policies. The SPD opposition's global rejection of the SDI before the necessary foundations exist for a decision and before the U.S. Administration has completed its assessment of the research program indicates not only a want of foresight, but also little sense of responsibility.

On the other hand, it came as no surprise to my Government and the Western alliance that the Soviet Union attacked and denigrated the SDI from the very outset. The sheer lack of credibility and moral justification of these Soviet attacks is borne out by the fact that for over a decade now the Soviet Union itself has, at considerable expense, been engaged in similar research into a large-scale anti-missile system. Of the two superpowers, it alone has an operative anti-missile system around its capital, which it is constantly upgrading.

Furthermore, the Soviet Union is the only country in the world possessing deployable anti-satellite weapons, i.e. so-called killer satellites. We know that in the summer of 1983 the Soviet Union tested such systems in space above Munich. By building a large radar at Krasnoyarsk—possibly in violation of the ABM Treaty—the Soviet Union is demonstrating its determination to keep open the option of strategic defense. The continuation of unilateral Soviet research into space weapons and of a build-up of such weapons would lead not only to the erosion of the ABM Treaty, but also to the emergence of dangerous instability.

The Soviet leaders themselves have never denied such research and developments. Yet until now we have not heard a single critical remark in this respect voiced by the opposition. As far as I have been able to see during the past few weeks, the same people who attacked the implementation of the NATO two-track decision in 1983 are today again in step with Soviet propaganda.

The SDI is a long-term research program reaching well into the 1990s. Even the United States does not expect to take any decisions on the development and deployment of weapons until the start of the next decade.

Research into space systems is compatible with the ABM Treaty. There will not be, nor can there be, an automatic succession of research, development and deployment of strategic defense systems. All decisions leading beyond the research program can only be taken on the basis of sound research findings. To my mind, President Reagan's resolve and moral entitlement in this matter are beyond doubt. In our view, the American research program is therefore

—justified,
—politically necessary, and
—in the interest of overall Western security.

My Government therefore basically supports the American research project on strategic defense.

2. On February 9, 1985, I for the first time spelled out the main elements of our position on the American project at the military science symposium in Munich. On that occasion, I stated quite clearly that the decisive criterion of our assessment of the SDI is as follows: can this initiative make peace in freedom more secure for us? Notwithstanding all the—in some respects complex—individual political, strategic and technological questions, the answer to this question will continue to govern our judgment and our action. In its decision of March 27, 1985, the Federal Security Council underscored this central point by viewing the SDI in the overall context of East-West relations, including the dialogue on arms control. Our goal of creating peace with ever fewer weapons and establishing more stable East-West relations remains valid, now as ever. It is the guiding principle of our policies, including our stance on the SDI.

3. The interests of the Federal Republic of Germany and its Western European allies are affected in various intricate ways by the SDI. The possible political and strategic implications inevitably have the greatest impact. They have a direct bearing on our vital political interests—our external security. We must from the outset voice a number of strategic demands deriving not least from our geostrategic situation. In Munich I already referred to them:

— Europe's security must not be decoupled from that of the United States. There must be no zones of differing security in the NATO area.

— NATO's strategy of flexible response must remain fully valid as long as no more promising alternative is found for preventing war.

— Instability must be avoided during any transition from a purely deterrent strategy to a new form of strategic stability that is more reliant on defensive systems.

— Disparities must be eliminated, and the emergence of new threats below the nuclear level avoided.

I can state with satisfaction that our American allies are increasingly aware and take account of vital German and European strategic demands.

4. To us the connection between political-strategic and arms control aspects in assessing the SDI is of special importance. In the short and medium term, observance of the ABM Treaty has priority. In the Federal government's view it is essential that before any decisions are taken that go beyond research, cooperative solutions should be sought which will ensure that

— strategic stability will be maintained and where possible improved,

— nuclear offensive potentials will be drastically reduced, and

— the relationship between offensive and defensive systems will be jointly defined to guarantee the largest degree of stability at the lowest possible level of armaments.

We are convinced that the Strategic Defense Initiative of the United States has already given an important impulse to the arms control dialogue. It has been conducive to the opening of the Geneva talks. And it can continue to have a favorable influence on the course of the negotiations.

It is in our interest that the superpowers should negotiate in Geneva on strategic defense systems in connection with the offensive nuclear weapons without blocking or impeding progress towards promising solutions by establishing one-sided and inappropriate links.

In seeking to give the necessary definite shape to the relationship between offensive and defensive weapons to ensure the largest degree of stability at the lowest possible level of armaments, all possible solutions must be explored without reservation.

I mentioned this connection in my address to the CDU party conference in Essen when I said that a drastic reduction of nuclear offensive weapons could have an influence on the need for and the extent of defensive systems in space.

I appeal in this connection to the Soviet Union to use the Geneva negotiations constructively in this sense and not to take the American Strategic Defense Initiative as a pretext for not showing the necessary flexibility in seeking to reduce nuclear offensive weapons.

5. The strategic initiative of the United States opens up opportunities for the North Atlantic alliance, but also involves risks.

The alliance's cohesion and solidarity must from the outset deny the Soviet Union any possibility of exploiting SDI to split the alliance and sow public mistrust in the West. The United States has begun to consult its allies on its new project. We welcome the offer of continuous consultations, both bilaterally and within the alliance. We shall make intensive use of this opportunity.

These consultations are indispensable for us. They are particularly necessary because the possible long-term adaptation of the alliance's current defensive strategy to new situations makes continuous dialogue absolutely essential, precisely in this field.

By together considering the American project, the members of the alliance have at the same time an opportunity to strengthen the alliance's solidarity and promote the transatlantic dialogue.

The Federal Government will make every effort to develop with its closest European allies a common stance on the SDI of the United States. This will give us an opportunity, together with European partners, to bring to bear more effectively our specifically European interests in our relationship with the United States.

In this connection the Federal Government welcomes the French proposal set out in a letter which Foreign Minister Dumas sent to Foreign Minister Genscher at the beginning of this week that the Europeans should without delay engage in closer cooperation on the technologies of the future. I share the view of the French Government that Europe's answer to the American SDI cannot consist in a policy of resignation, nor in uncoordinated rejection.

We are also in agreement with Prime Minister Craxi of Italy, Prime Minister Thatcher of the United Kingdom, and other European partners in our basic assessment of the American SDI.

We are receptive to the American suggestion that we together examine the possibilities of participating in this research project. Involvement by the nations of Europe would give them a historic opportunity to assert jointly their political, strategic and technological interests.

In this way the SDI of the United States could indeed mean a real opportunity for the NATO alliance and for Europe, and it could play a decisive role in strengthening and integrating both.

6. In view of the huge sum of about 80 billion marks which the American Government has assessed for its research program, it can already be said that it will produce important and far-reaching results, the significance of which will extend far beyond the sphere of strategic defense application.

It is not an exaggeration to speak in this connection of a broad-based, innovative technological thrust.

We shall and must be interested in putting at the service of our industry research findings that will have a revolutionary impact in their civilian applications. This economic and technological interest, however, will not be the sole factor in our decision on whether we take part in the research program. Nevertheless, we must ensure that the Federal Republic of Germany and Western Europe do not lose touch with technological developments and thereby become second-class powers. The joint security of the United States and Europe as demonstrated in their commitments to the alliance also requires a comparable state of economic and technological development in the United States and Europe.

Our economic system of a free and social market economy permits and promotes cooperation between enterprises across national frontiers. German and European enterprises and research establishments lead the field in several spheres.

Against this background, it is all the more necessary that we discuss with the American side the criteria and conditions of any research cooperation so as to gauge the framework for possible cooperation. In so doing, we shall set great store by ensuring that any future cooperation

— guarantees fair partnership and free exchange of findings,

— does not remain a technological one-way street,

— secures us, as far as possible, a self-contained sphere of research, and

— thereby permits us to exercise influence on the overall project.

Technological participation in the American research project would also make it easier for the Federal Republic of Germany and the other European allies to preserve and increase their influence on important questions regarding a possible new development in the alliance strategy.

7. In the foreseeable future, the Federal Government will have to decide on whether to participate in the U.S. research project. In this decision, it will not let itself be rushed but will establish all the preconditions required for such a decision to be taken. To this end, the following three basic moves are planned:

— The Federal Government will discuss with German business interest in and opportunities for participation in the research, giving particular consideration to cooperative European action.

— It will enter into consultations with interested European allies, particularly France, Italy and the United Kingdom, as well as other European partners, with a view to developing a common position and possibly joint participation.

— It will send a group of experts to the United States to find out at first hand about the conditions and spheres of participation in the research.

In addition, I shall take up the matter with President Reagan during his state visit.

8. Let me now sum up:

— The United States Strategic Defense Initiative presents an opportunity to develop in the longer term the currently indispensable strategy of deterrence based on the threat of mutual destruction into a more defensively oriented strategy that would permit large-scale nuclear disarmament. Nobody knows

164 / SDI and European Security

today whether this hope will be fulfilled. However, to give a negative reply at this point would not be in keeping with the responsibility we bear for the future of our country.

— Strategic stability between East and West and the political and strategic unity of the alliance must be guaranteed. The NATO strategy of flexible response will remain fully valid for as long as there is no alternative that better serves the purpose of preventing war.

— The arms control function of the Strategic Defense Initiative is of central importance to us. We shall steadfastly promote this view in our dealings with our American allies. A drastic reduction in the number of offensive nuclear systems on both sides remains our primary goal.

— An assessment of the American initiative in terms of alliance policy points to the task of averting risks and, through alliance solidarity and the exercise of increased influence by the European allies, of making determined use of the opportunities presented.

Whoever says no today will not avert any risk to the alliance and will be unable to make use of these opportunities.

— We shall take up the American suggestion and examine the possibilities of cooperation on the research program. In so doing we shall work closely together with our industry and our European allies.

I am sorry to see that the SPD has committed itself to rejection even before this examination has taken place. I ask you whether this attitude serves the interests of a leading economic and industrial nation.

9. Permit me to conclude by adding and reaffirming the following points:

Our consideration of the American Strategic Defense Initiative is fully in line with the overall concept of a policy in pursuit of peace. We remain as interested as ever in an improvement in East-West relations and hope that the arms control negotiations in Geneva provide a perceptible stimulus for the East-West dialogue in general.

I believe that East-West relations must not become restricted to questions of defense and arms control or even to a single issue such as the pros and cons of strategic defense.

Only a broad-based improvement in relations between the Soviet Union and the United States and between the states of NATO and those of the Warsaw Pact can lead to effective progress in disarmament and arms control. The Federal Government will continue to pursue steadfastly its policy of understanding and accommodation while at the same time endeavoring to protect its security interests.

6

In early 1985, the West German opposition Social Democrat Party released the following statement on SDI and Europe's Interests (as provided by the Friedrich Ebert Foundation).

At its Berlin congress in 1979, the German Social Democratic Party (SPD) called for early negotiations on space weapons with a view to banning them— that was long before either of the two nuclear superpowers broached the subject. The Soviet Union, which is today even proposing a research moratorium although it has for years now been intensively conducting research into space weapons, criticized the SPD's suggestion at the time.

Now the US President has declared that the development of space-based strategic defence is a central objective of the Western alliance.

The SPD is opposed to any plans aimed at militarizing space by deploying new weapon systems. Research programmes on this subject directly affect the interests of Western Europe. Just as we have always criticized the Soviet Union for its arms buildup, we cannot remain silent about the American programme for developing space-based strategic defence.

Western Europe must discuss in detail the possible consequences of the initiative so that it can then adopt a joint stance. If the Western European allies allow themselves to be divided on this matter of vital importance to peace, to the Western alliance and to East-West relations, one need in the future no longer speak of the necessity of Europe asserting itself in the Western alliance.

The erection of a strategic defence system in space will fundamentally alter NATO's defence strategy

The remark made by President Reagan in March 1983 that the strategy of deterrence based on mutual assured destruction must be superseded met with both the understanding and support of the Social Democrats. In fact, a great deal of what President Reagan said then and in subsequent speeches could be viewed as being directly connected with the demands of the peace movement: the need to replace the strategy of mutual destruction with a strategy of mutal assured security, the goal of making nuclear weapons superfluous with the aid of conventional weapons, the demand for offensive weapons to be superseded by defensive systems, and the need to elaborate joint security concepts with the Soviet Union—all of this can be regarded as moving towards the Social Democrats' demand that, for the sake of peace, today's balance of nuclear terror be replaced by security partnership between East and West, by partnership for survival.

However, the solutions offered by President Reagan for attaining these goals are unsuitable, in the SPD's view. They will probably lead to instability instead of stability, insecurity instead of security, an arms buildup instead of disarmament, and possibly to an increase in the number of offensive nuclear weapons. Unlike the Social Democrats, who want to achieve stability, security and a defensive capability not through weapons but primarily through dialogue, treaties and confidence-building, i.e. through political solutions, the US President relies on solving a political problem by technical means. This approach has never worked in the past, nor will it in the future.

Moreover, the original philosophy of the strategy of mutual assured destruction being substituted by one of mutual assured security has virtually been abandoned in the last two years. Today the US Administration assures us that the old strategy of deterrence is not to be replaced, but to be made more effective. A potential aggressor is to be deprived of the use of a military option against the United States in that its offensive nuclear weapons will be neutralized by non-nuclear defensive weapons. However, even at this stage it is clear that SDI will probably not result in offensive weapons being superseded by defensive space weapons. Instead, there will be a combination of offensive and defensive weapons. The overwhelming majority of American and European scientists do not consider the construction of a fully effective defence system in space to be technically feasible.

Strategic space defence calls the ABM Treaty into question

In 1972, the two superpowers signed the ABM Treaty, which greatly restricted the construction of an anti-ballistic missile system. The aim of the treaty was to prevent the deployment of defensive systems because it was rightly assumed that the deployment of a complete system would destabilize and jeopardize the approximate equilibrium of offensive weapons.

The US Administration's attitude towards the ABM Treaty is equivocal. On the one hand, the President and others state that the ABM Treaty will be respected and at best contractually updated with the Soviet Union. On the other, the United States accuses the Soviet Union of breaching the treaty and threatens to respond with violations of its own.

If the United States abides by its pledge of altering the ABM Treaty only in agreement with the Soviet Union, then the latter holds the key to the realization of the space defence programme. Without its consent, SDI systems can be neither developed nor deployed. Since research is not verifiable and controllable, the treaty makes a distinction between research on the one hand and testing, development and deployment on the other. Until now the US Administration has failed to answer the question of what will happen when the limits of research have been reached in the 5-year programme and the development phase starts. The plans for implementing SDI indicate that the limits of what is permitted under the ABM Treaty will be attained very soon. Washington is not dealing with a 5-year research programme costing approximately 26 billion dollars, but with a 10-year programme which embraces the testing and development of such weapons and whose total cost is estimated at 70 billion dollars.

Whoever participates in SDI research bears political
responsibility for the system's development and deployment

Mr Lawrence Eagleburger, former Deputy Secretary of State, has stressed that the Western Europeans must realize it is a question not only of participating in research, but also of sharing political responsibility for SDI development and deployment. Senator Lugar, the new Chairman of the Senate's Foreign Affairs Committee, has stated that the Western Europeans must not believe they can partake of the fruits of a technological programme without sharing political responsibility for the overall programme. It is thus quite clear that even at this stage it is no longer a question of participation in research activities, but of whether the Europeans want to share responsibility for the political and military consequences of the development and deployment of strategic space defence. Participation in research is merely an incentive to gain the support of the Europeans for the overall concept. Anyone who now says "yes" to SDI is, in the eyes of world, saying "yes" to an American space weapons programme and hence to the militarization of space.

Since the SDI programme encompasses not only research but testing and development, too, the question of the relationship between it and the ABM Treaty is directly raised. The superpowers are already accusing each other of violating the ABM Treaty. The Government of the Federal Republic of Germany has joined in some of the accusations against the Soviet Union. However, one should be careful in this context, considering the ambiguities existing in the interpretation of the treaty. What Foreign Secretary Howe of Britain said should be endorsed: Europe must on no account participate in any erosion of the ABM Treaty. Erosion or termination of the treaty by the United States would probably put an end to any arms control negotiations for a long time.

The implementation of SDI would probably
not improve the protection of Europe

Leaving aside the question of the technical feasibility of SDI, it can be stated that the implementation of this concept poses a number of security hazards for Europe.

The mobile deployment and far shorter flight times of short- and inter-mediate-range missiles rule out a graduated defence system in Europe of the kind envisaged by the Americans for their defence. Once the central strategic systems were neutralized by SDI, the nuclear weapons for the defence of Europe would acquire a different significance. A reliably functioning SDI system would call into question a basic element of NATO's strategy. The aggressor could dictate our actions. His conventional superiority would be fully felt by NATO. The risk of war would be lowered, and the readiness to take risks raised. Political control would no longer be guaranteed since a decision on war would have to be taken within minutes.

SDI might curb the threat posed by central strategic systems and, perhaps to a limited extent, that posed by intermediate-range missiles. However, SDI could certainly not eliminate the threat existing as a result of nuclear battlefield weapons or short-range missiles. In other words, the regionalization of a nuclear conflict, the confinement of a nuclear exchange to the battlefield would become a conceivable option. Consequently, a system of graduated security would arise in NATO. The frontline countries would be jeopardized even more than hitherto because they would on their own bear the burden of defence on their soil. A reduction of cohesion in the Alliance would be the outcome.

The realization of SDI would absorb the resources needed for stronger conventional defence

Even now it can be foreseen that the funds for SDI cannot be made available from new sources, but will largely be diverted from current items in the defence budget. In other words, the budget's priorities will have to be redefined for the sake of an expensive and questionable programme. The resources needed for strengthening NATO's conventional defence posture—the Alliance's declared target in the years ahead—will then no longer be available. However, if SDI is implemented it is precisely NATO's conventional capabilities that acquire particular significance. The elimination of the central strategic nuclear threat would result in the conventional imbalance accepted by NATO making itself fully felt.

General Rogers has stated the following in public: If the funds which NATO requires for Western Europe's conventional defence were used for the SDI programme, a situation would be approached where the United States can no longer ensure the protection pledged to the Western Europeans.

SDI will make the arms control talks at Geneva between the Americans and the Soviets even more difficult

The US Administration's attitude towards the relationship between the SDI programme and the Geneva negotiations is marked by a host of contradictions. On the one hand, the US and Soviet Union foreign ministers declared on 8 January 1985 that the prevention of an arms race in space is one of the objectives of the negotiations. In his explanatory paper, Mr Paul Nitze even hinted at a solution being found in co-operation with the Soviets, possibly including the transfer of American SDI technology to the Soviets during the so-called transitional phase. On the other hand, the government in Washington flatly refuses to allow the SDI programme to be eliminated through negotiation in Geneva. Representatives of the Administration publicly declare that defence systems in space must not only be investigated, but also developed, produced and deployed.

Such contradictions in the Reagan Administration are familiar to us in the context of the INF talks. The result is likely to be the same again: a new spiral in the arms race instead of arms control and limitation.

The Soviets will not await the outcome of the US programme, but step up their efforts to improve their offensive capacity once they feel that they are unable to keep abreast of the United States in space technology. In the event of termination of the ABM Treaty and other relevant arms control agreements, such as the Outer Space Treaty and the Nuclear Test Ban Treaty, the Soviets are free to deploy nuclear weapons against the American space defence system. "Denuclearization" of the arsenals existing on both sides cannot be achieved by one side only. Joint security cannot be attained unilaterally.

Chancellor Kohl has demanded that the talks in Geneva be conducted in such a way that a negotiated agreement renders space weapons superfluous. However, this cannot be accomplished by perpetually asserting that the negotiations are extremely complicated and will thus last many years. What is needed is an unequivocal confirmation by the US Administration and the Soviet leadership that not ABM-related research, but the development, testing and deployment of strategic space systems are from the very outset a subject of the Geneva talks. The aim of the talks must be to find a co-operative solution and thus "to prevent an arms race in space", as Secretary of State Schultz and Foreign Minister Gromyko pledged at Geneva on 8 January not only to each other, but also to the world at large. It should not be forgotten that the superpowers are duty-bound under the Non-Proliferation Treaty to hold such negotiations.

The SPD is weary of being consoled with the prospect of nuclear arms control and disarmament at some time in the distant future. In view of the growing arsenals of the superpowers and the existence of increasing instability, we call upon the superpowers to show a readiness for initiating without further delay concrete steps towards disarmament.

SDI will militarize basic research

The US Administration is trying at present to make participation in SDI palatable to the Europeans by pointing out the research advantages. There is, however, no reason at all why the Western Europeans should militarize their basic research and limit freedom of science by unnecessarily incorporating a substantial part of Western European research into a military programme. German scientific organizations and German industry should at long last speak out on this danger in public, too.

The question should first be asked as to why we have at all been invited to take part in the research activities only, and not in the development effort. The answer is obvious: The United States does not intend to share the systems or the control of them. The practical operation of the technological two-way street between the United States and Europe was pointedly demonstrated by the decision on the NATO Identification System (NIS) for friend-or-foe recognition: On the one hand, Defence Secretary Weinberger cites the advantages of NATO-wide research and armaments co-operation. On the other, out of national interests he makes the Europeans knuckle under, even when they objectively have a superior system to offer.

We cannot criticize the Americans for defending their own interests. Our American allies are naturally interested in incorporating our—i.e. German and Western European—knowhow and skills into their space defence programme and in also getting funds made available in Europe for this purpose. However, SDI will of course be subject to American secrecy regulations, irrespective of whether the Europeans take part. The Americans have made it quite clear that they intend to retain control of the overall programme. If one recalls the hindrances to the transfer of technology experienced by the Western Europeans in recent years—one need only mention COCOM—and if one bears in mind that military contracts awarded to US companies and institutes are even resulting in restrictions on free scientific interchange in the United States, then it is evident that SDI is surely the worst conceivable basis for co-operation by European industry and science with the Americans. The European Space Agency is an example showing that even in civilian co-operation in space matters it is difficult to induce the Americans to grant fair conditions. Military co-operation will be subject to far greater limitations.

Furthermore, it is wrong to believe that the civilian spin-off of military research is more significant than the direct benefits of civilian research. Japan, which uses only about 5% of its research budget for military research, is an example that refutes this preconception.

If we participate in the SDI programme, there is the danger that, as third countries, we ourselves get into conflict with the SDI. Article 9 of the treaty forbids the transfer of components of ABM systems to third countries. Such components include blueprints and technical descriptions, as declared in the Agreed Statement G annexed to the treaty. Once the research phase is ended and production starts, the question arises of whether the Americans can then still transfer to third countries the components and technology needed for manufacturing specific products.

Until now the government of the Federal Republic of Germany has failed to answer the question of how participation in the enormous SDI programme is actually to be funded. In the research ministry's budget there has until now not even been enough money to finance the civilian COLUMBUS project, not to mention the realization of France's proposals for concrete European co-operation in space matters, e.g. in the HERMES project or the construction of a European observation satellite. The defence ministry needs all of its budget to strengthen the conventional forces.

Western Europe must take up the American technological challenge and find a response of its own

The American challenge in connection with the creation of strategic space defence confronts the Western European allies with a new challenge. Western Europe must first of all define its own interests—both in terms of a long-term security concept and in the field of basic research.

The Western Europeans must develop a joint European response lying outside the sphere of co-operation in space weapons. The individual Western European countries must not go it alone and thus become an appendage of the US military-industrial complex. This does not by any means rule out co-operation with the United States on a case-by-case basis and in the field of basic civilian research. However, co-operation should be excluded which occurs on terms that would discredit Europe politically and/or cause it to be disadvantaged in the Alliance.

Co-operation can be accomplished by expanding the programmes already in existence: for instance, civilian space research in the fields of automation, robotics, guidance systems and new materials, or areas not belonging to space research proper, such as particle beams, lasers, ultrahigh-speed circuits, optics and sensors.

Europe must not allow itself to be persuaded that it is lagging behind in technological developments. In many domains, Western European research and technology are right up at the front. There is no reason why we should conceal our successes in key areas of technology, such as aircraft construction, carrier systems, sensors, optics and materials.

In view of its global commitments, the United States ought to be interested in Western Europe becoming a stronger pillar in its own right within the Alliance, instead of always splitting up.

The Western Europeans must at long last seek
closer coordination on major security issues

The Western Europeans should recall that, before the deployment of Pershing 2 and Cruise missiles, they never discussed this subject, even though President Giscard of France had made a proposal to that effect. This error should not be repeated in connection with SDI. We must frame a joint position; in the SPD's view, this should be: rejection of participation in the military programme. However, things must not be left at that. The Western Europeans should respond with a positive suggestion of their own: the development of a European research programme going beyond existing projects as well as the expression of a readiness to co-operate with the United States in precisely defined spheres of civilian research.

The Western European response must also relate to fundamental political and arms technology issues. The SPD shares President Reagan's desire for greater political stability in the world, for a world of hope instead of fear. However, this aspiration should not rest on military technology and arms programmes, but on political solutions. The aim must be to do away with East-West deterrence in a long-term process by qualitatively changing the conflict determined by power-political considerations and differences between the political systems. Unlike SDI, the concept of security partnership can actually lead to that goal because it seeks to supplement military deterrence gradually by means of security and disarmament agreements and to replace it ultimately.

The existing deterrence can be stabilized or destabilized by a reformed military strategy and new weapon technologies, can become more expensive or cheaper, can be reformed with primarily conventional or nuclear weapons, but it cannot be surmounted through the reform of military strategies.

Whoever wants to surmount the existing system of deterrence does not need to love his political adversary, but he must at least try to understand his motives. The notion that the system of mutual deterrence can be rendered obsolete by introducing new weapon technologies is a technocratic fallacy. Reconciliation cannot be enforced by means of technology, animosity cannot be overcome with technology.

The SPD calls for concrete steps towards disaramament at Geneva

The realization of the SDI programme will not lead to the abolition of nuclear weapons, but to the introduction of new types of weapon systems.

Chancellor Kohl has promised to safeguard peace with ever fewer weapons. He has not honoured his pledge until now. Only someone who is cynical or naive can support the development of new weapon technologies and at the same time assert that this brings us nearer the goal of peace with ever fewer weapons. Where questions concerning the survival of our nation are involved one must not adopt an approach based on purely tactical considerations.

We take the Chancellor at his word: The negotiations in Geneva must be conducted in such a way that a negotiated agreement renders space weapons superfluous. The SPD hopes that the US Administration will speak with one voice at the new Geneva talks in keeping with the negotiating objective of preventing an arms race in space by co-operative means.

What is needed at Geneva is an interim agreement comprising three elements: *First:* A ban of any testing of space weapons, including anti-satellite weapons. Such a ban is the precondition for at all [sic] reaching some day a substantive agreement on the non-development and non-deployment of space weapons. *Second:* A declaration by the two superpowers to the effect that the SALT II Treaty, which has in practice been complied with until now, will be observed even after the end of this year, which is the date when it would have expired, had it been ratified. *Third:* An agreement that imposes a ban of limited duration on the deployment of Eurostrategic missiles, coupled with an agreement for substantially reducing these weapons. The proposals tabled in the INF talks can be followed up in this context.

Such an interim agreement must retain the link between the three areas of the negotiations, namely strategic defence, intercontinental missiles and Eurostrategic missiles. Insistence on the implementation of SDI must not cause the interrelationship of these three topics to be dissolved. . . .

7

On March 15, 1985, Sir Geoffrey Howe, British Secretary of State for Foreign and Commonwealth Affairs, delivered the following speech at the Royal United Services Institute, London, in which he set forth the British government's view on nuclear arms control and the Strategic Defense Initiative (provided by British Information Services).

And now, with President Reagan's Strategic Defence Initiative . . . the strategic debate is focussing on new possibilities for active defence against the nuclear threat.

In our approach to these new issues the Government believe that certain well-tested premises retain their validity: the need for strong and credible military forces, the need to maintain deterrence, and the need to pursue arms control measures. The four points agreed last December at Camp David between the Prime Minister and President Reagan, and reaffirmed during their Washington discussions last month, are of prime importance in this context. These points are by now familiar. But as they represent the basis for the British Government's approach to the strategic future, their re-statement is in order.

As the Prime Minister has said, she agreed with the President that:

• the US and Western aim is not to achieve superiority but maintain balance, taking account of Soviet developments;

• SDI-related deployment would, in view of treaty obligations, have to be a matter for negotiation;

• the overall aim is to enhance, not undercut, deterrence; and

• East/West negotiation should aim to achieve security with reduced levels of offensive systems on both sides.

Thus our policy as we face the new challenge continues to be consistent. But what are the real problems to be resolved and the new questions to be answered?

President Reagan, in the historic address which launched the Strategic Defence Initiative almost two years ago, spoke of his vision that new technology might make it possible to create comprehensive defences against nuclear attack. These could render ballistic weapons impotent and obsolete, they could free the people of the world once and for all from the threat of nuclear annihilation.

From the start, such a vision was always recognised as subject to uncertainty. As the President himself said in March 1983, it will take years, probably decades of effort on many fronts. There will be failures and setbacks just as there will be successes and breakthroughs. Subsequent statements in Washington have underlined the tentative nature of the venture.

Weapons in Space

Nonetheless, the President's vision has already made a decisive impact in several respects. It has focussed interest on military activities in space, and on new weapons systems which might theoretically be deployed or aimed there. It has also drawn to public notice the very considerable research under way in the Soviet Union on a range of potential defensive measures.

Not enough attention has been paid to this Soviet research. It is extensive and far-reaching and has been going on for many years. Any discussion of future Western strategies must take full account of it. To ignore or to dismiss what is happening in the Soviet Union would be not only myopic; it would be dangerous.

Given the dimensions of space, it is hardly surprising that imaginative schemes for its military exploitation have been almost infinite, so too have been the misconceptions and distortions of what is happening now, and may happen in the future. To use terms such as Star Wars about either US or Soviet intentions is to distort the very real problems and their potential solutions.

Equally, in Soviet calls for the de-militarisation of space I see more propaganda than substance. Activities in space with military relevance are not by definition evil. It is neither feasible nor desirable to try to preclude all of them. Current Soviet rhetoric makes a less than serious contribution to a most serious debate. Greater precision and deeper thought are required. For a start we must distinguish between present military activities in space and those that may at some far-off point in the future achieve reality. And at all times we must keep in mind the key question: will new developments enhance or undercut deterrence? At present, space is used by a limited number of military systems, on both sides.

First, communications and surveillance satellites which add significantly to the effectiveness and credibility of Western defences, and thus to their deterrent effect. Efficient and cost-effective, they provide a unique contribution to the defence of the West.

Second, re-usable launchers. These pack-horses of the space age are equally valuable. Nor by their nature do they pose a real threat of aggression; the shuttle is too limited, too costly and too vulnerable a platform for that purpose.

Third, there is the potential use of space for the delivery of nuclear warheads by ballistic missiles. We must seek to ensure that this will always remain an unrealised potential.

Lastly, we face the problem of anti-satellite systems, exacerbated by the Soviet deployment over the past decade of a limited capability in this field. It would be a serious blunder if the West allowed the Russians to continue to enjoy their present monopoly.

The US intention to balance the established Soviet capability in this field is logical and prudent.

On the other hand, we must recognise the heavy Western dependence upon the existing utilisation of space technology and particularly upon satellites for intelligence purposes. We must also recognise that the prospect, at a time of crisis, of either side being faced with the loss of its strategic eyes and ears would be gravely de-stabilising. It could provoke a new and even more threatening stage in any East-West confrontation.

The West must therefore strive to make its satellites less vulnerable. But there may equally be good grounds for negotiating some constraints upon elements of anti-satellite activity. I welcome the readiness expressed by President Reagan at the UN last September to consider mutual restraint while the negotiations which have now been launched explore possibilities for concrete agreements.

One other factor must be recognised: the linkage between the development of anti-satellite capabilities and the potential development of defences against ballistic missiles. It could be argued that by imposing constraints on anti-satellite activity, decisions on the development of ballistic missile defences would be pre-empted before they could be properly considered. That however would be to ignore the important differences in the time-scales involved.

In the case of anti-satellite systems, the future is now. The Soviet Union has already deployed such a system at low altitude, and the United States is in the middle of a successful testing programme. By contrast, any development beyond the research state of defences against ballistic missiles, the most immediate nuclear threat, is in the Prime Minister's words many, many years away.

The Government take the view that, if negotiations were to succeed in imposing mutual constraints on anti-satellite systems, these could have a helpful impact over a period of years. We should take that opportunity now, if it is in the Western interest. Any such ASAT Agreement could be limited if necessary to a fixed period, in order not to prejudice the future.

Against that background of present space activities, I should like now to consider the longer-term issue of active defences against ballistic missiles, and particularly defences which might be deployed in or into outer space. By active defences I mean systems specifically designed to prevent enemy missiles getting through, rather than deterrence based on the threat of retaliation.

Much has been said and written about President Reagan's Strategic Defence Initiative. The first point to make is that, as US spokesmen have made clear, this is a research programme, conducted in full conformity with the limits of the ABM Treaty. As a research programme, it is also full of questions. The answers may be clear or obscure. They may not even emerge at all. As the US Administration themselves recognise, the programme is geared to a concept, which may in the end prove elusive.

The second point is that treaty obligations specifically allow for research to continue into defensive systems. Evidently, it is pointless to try to impose constraints which cannot be verified. Most activities in laboratories or research institutes comes into that category. The ABM Treaty recognised this when it drew a distinction between research on the one hand and development, testing and deployment on the other.

The third, equally important point is that a balance must always be maintained between US and Soviet capabilities, in research as in other aspects. Given what we know of Soviet activities in the research field over a number of years, there is a clear need for the United States to match the present stage in Soviet programmes. It is for this reason that the Prime Minister has repeatedly expressed our firm conviction that US research should go ahead.

SDI: Implications of Deployment

But what should happen if and when decisions are required on moving from the research to the development stage?

In evaluating the results of research, and in taking any such decisions, we shall need to ask ourselves some very basic questions about the future nature of Western strategy. In particular, we shall have to consider how best to enhance deterrence, how best to curb rather than stimulate a new arms race. At that stage, the judgements to be made will only partly depend upon technical assessments about the feasibility of defences. Even if the research shows promise, the case for proceeding will have to be weighed in the light of the wider strategic implications of moving down the defensive road.

But can we afford even now simply to wait for the scientists and military experts to deliver their results at some later stage? Have we a breathing space of five, ten, fifteen years before we need to address strategic concerns? I do not believe so. The history of weapons development and the strategic balance shows only too clearly that research into new weapons and study of their strategic implications must go hand in hand. Otherwise, research may acquire an unstoppable momentum of its own, even though the case for stopping may strengthen with the passage of years. Prevention may be better than later attempts at a cure. We must take care that political decisions are not pre-empted by the march of technology. Still less by premature attempts to predict the route of that march.

The questions to be faced are complex and difficult. I want to emphasise that they are questions and not prior judgements. The answers will only emerge in time.

There would inevitably be risks in a radical alteration of the present basis for Western security. How far would these risks be offset by the attractions of adopting a more defensive posture: that is to say, of developing what might prove to be only a limited defence against weapons of devastating destructive force. Could the process of moving towards a greater emphasis on active defences be managed without generating dangerous uncertainty?

Let us assume that limited defences began to prove possible, and key installations began to be protected by active defences. In his 1983 address President Reagan himself acknowledged that a mix of offensive and defensive systems could be viewed as fostering an aggressive policy. Uncertainty apart, would the establishment of limited defences increase the threat to civilian populations by stimulating a return to the targeting policies of the 1950s?

Most fundamental of all, would the supposed technology actually work? And would it, as Mr Paul Nitze has noted, provide defences that not only worked but were survivable and cost-effective? These are the key questions to be answered by the research that is being undertaken on both sides.

It would be wrong to underestimate the enormous technological expertise and potential of the United States; but, as we all recognise, there would be no advantage in creating a new Maginot Line of the 21st Century, liable to be outflanked by relatively simpler and demonstrably cheaper counter-measures. If the technology does work, what will be its psychological impact on the other side? President Reagan has repeatedly made it clear that he does not seek superiority. But we would have to ensure that the perceptions of others were not different.

What are the chances that there would be no outright winner in the ever-lasting marathon of the arms race? And if the ballistic missile indeed showed signs of becoming, in President Reagan's words, impotent and obsolete, how would protection be extended against the non-ballistic nuclear threat, the threat posed by aircraft or Cruise missiles, battlefield nuclear weapons or, in the last resort, by covert action. What other defences in addition to space-based systems would need to be developed, and at what cost, to meet these continuing threats?

If it initially proved feasible to construct only limited defences, these would be bound to be more vulnerable than comprehensive systems to counter-measures. Would these holes in the dyke produce and even encourage a nuclear flood? Leaving aside the threat to civilian populations, would active defences provide the only feasible way of protecting key military installations? Might we be better advised to employ other methods of protection, such as more mobile and under-sea forces?

Finally on the technology side, could we be certain that the new systems would permit adequate political control over both nuclear weapons and defensive systems, or might we find ourselves in a situation where the peace of the world rested solely upon computers and automatic decision-making?

Then there is the question of cost. The financial burden of developing and deploying defences goes far beyond the additional cost of providing defences against the non-ballistic missile threat. No-one at present can provide even a guestimate of the total sums involved. But it is fair to assume that these will run into many hundreds of billions of dollars.

We know only too well that our defences must be cut to the cloth of our financial resources. We shall have to ask ourselves not only whether the West can afford active defences against nuclear missiles. We must also ask whether the enormous funds to be devoted to such systems might be better employed.

Deterrence

Are there more cost-effective and affordable ways of enhancing deterrence? Might it be better to use the available funds to improve our capability to oppose a potential aggressor at a time of crisis with a credible, sustainable and controllable mix of conventional and nuclear forces? In short, how far will we be able to impose new burdens on defence budgets already under strain? And what would be the effect on all the other elements of our defences, on which Western security will continue in large part to depend?

The implications for arms control must also be carefully considered. Would the prospect of new defences being deployed inexorably crank up the levels of offensive nuclear systems designed to overwhelm them? History and the present state of technology suggest that this risk cannot be ignored. Or could the same prospect—the vision of effective defences over the horizon—provide new incentives to both sides to start at once on reducing their present levels? This explains the importance of the second point agreed at Camp David last December.

In his statement to Congress last month President Reagan spoke of the need to reverse the erosion of the ABM Treaty. It represents a political and military keystone in the still shaky arch of security we have constructed with the East over the past decade and a half. But to go beyond research into defensive systems would be inconsistent with the terms of the ABM Treaty as it stands. It was agreed at Camp David last December that any deployment beyond those limits would have to be a matter for negotiation. We would have to be confident that that formidable task could actually be managed on a mutually acceptable basis.

We have heard recently from Moscow a lot of dogmatic statements and pre-conditions for the success of the new talks. I discount much of these. But I do attach importance to convincing the Soviet leadership that we in the West are indeed serious in our aim of maintaining strategic stability at significantly lower levels of nuclear weapons. We do not want to give them the impression that we have something else in mind. We are serious about arms control. And we must be seen and heard to be so.

Finally, as members of the Atlantic Alliance, we must consider the potential consequences for this unique relationship. We must be sure that the US nuclear guarantee to Europe would indeed be enhanced as a result of defensive deployments. Not only enhanced at the end of the process, but from its very inception.

Many years of deployments may be involved. Many years of insecurity and instability cannot be our objective. All the Allies must continue at every stage to share the same sense that the security of NATO territory is indivisible. Otherwise the twin pillars of the Alliance might begin to fall apart.

Other things being equal, we welcome any cost-effective enhancement of deterrence to meet palpable weaknesses on the Western side. But we also have to consider what might be the offsetting developments on the Soviet side, if unconstrained competition in ballistic missile defences beyond the ABM Treaty limits were to be provoked. In terms of NATO's policy of forward defence and flexible response, would we lose on the swings whatever might be gained on the roundabouts?

I have posed a lengthy list of questions, to which the answers cannot be simple. Some do not admit of answers now. But that does not acquit us of the duty to pose them. They are questions so vital to our future that we cannot afford to shrug them off. It is right to ponder and debate them as research continues. In this way we stand the best chance of reaching the right policies. The attractions of moving towards a more defensive strategy for the prevention of war [are] as apparent as are the risks. It would be wrong to rule out the possibility on the grounds that the questions it raises are too difficult.

But the fact that there are no easy answers, that the risks may outweigh the benefits, that science may not be able to provide a safer solution to the nuclear dilemma of the past 40 years than we have found already—all these points underline the importance of proceeding with the utmost deliberation. Recent testimony to the US Congress by Secretary Shultz and Mr Nitze, and the continual process of Alliance consultation, confirm the Prime Minister's statement last December that the US Administration see matters in very much the same light.

Deterrence has worked; and it will continue to work. It may be enhanced by active defences. Or their development may set us on a road that diminishes security. We do not know the answer to that question. Meanwhile, four clear points emerge.

First, as the Prime Minister reminded the United States' Congress last month, in the words of Sir Winston Churchill: Be careful above all things not to let go of the atomic weapon until you are sure, and more than sure, that other means of preserving peace are in your hands.

Secondly, impressions can be created by words as well as deeds. Policies, aims, visions—all these can and must be clearly stated. Without the approval of an informed public, the governments of the West are wasting their breath. But we must be especially on our guard against raising hopes that it may be impossible to fulfil. We would all like to think of nuclear deterrence as a distasteful but temporary expedient. Unfortunately we have to face the harsh realities of a world in which nuclear weapons exist and cannot be disinvented. Words and dreams cannot by themselves justify what the Prime Minister described to the United Nations as the perilous pretence that [no] better system than nuclear deterrence [can be reached] at the present time.

Thirdly, any deployments of space-based or other defences must be a matter for negotiation. The Prime Minister agreed this with President Reagan at Camp David, and they reaffirmed it in Washington. In the words of the White House statement of 3 January, deployments of defensive systems would most usefully be done in the context of a cooperative, equitable and verifiable arms control environment. A unilateral Soviet deployment of such defences . . . would destroy the foundation on which deterrence has rested for 20 years. I warmly welcome the clear statements of the US Administration's view that deployments would need to be a cooperative endeavour, to be embarked upon in an arms control context.

Fourthly, the linkage between offensive and defensive systems. The White House statement of 3 January recognised the merit in controlling both the offensive and defensive developments and deployments on both sides. If defensive systems are to be deployed, they will be directed against the then levels of offensive forces. If the latter can be lowered dramatically, then the case for active defences may be correspondingly strengthened. Conversely, radical cuts in offensive missiles might make the need for active defences superfluous. Equally, the effectiveness of missiles and warheads which they are intended to destroy. If the levels rise dramatically, then the effectiveness of defences may not be adequate.

It is therefore clear that there is and will continue to be an integral relationship between measures to control offensive forces and any decisions to move to the development of active defences. The US Administration have always recognised such a linkage. Belatedly, the Russians now seem to have reached the same conclusion. As the new negotiations, finally launched this week, get underway, a key question for all our futures will be the extent to which reductions in offensive forces prove possible and the impact this will have upon the incentive to develop defences. . . .

8

The British Secretary of State for Defense, the Rt Hon Michael Heseltine MP, made the following statement on British participation in the Strategic Defense Initiative to the House of Commons on December 10, 1985 (as provided by British Information Services).

The British Government's policy towards the Strategic Defense Initiative remains firmly based on the four points agreed between the Prime Minister and President Reagan at Camp David in December 1984: that the Western aim is not to achieve superiority, but to maintain balance taking account of Soviet developments; that SDI-related deployment would, in view of treaty obligations, have to be a matter for negotiation; that the aim is to enhance, and not to undermine deterrence; and that East-West negotiation should aim to achieve security with reduced levels of offensive weapons on both sides.

It was in that context that, at Camp David, the Prime Minister told President Reagan of her firm conviction that the SDI research program should go ahead as a prudent hedge against Soviet activities in the same field.

Earlier this year, the United States invited her NATO and certain other allies to participate in the SDI research program.

Following that invitation, we have engaged in detailed discussions with the United States Government on the nature and scope of the research which could sensibly be undertaken by United Kingdom firms and institutions.

Those complex discussions have now been completed and agreement has been reached on an information exchange program, on the areas where British companies and institutions have enterprise which might form part of the United States-funded SDI research program, and on the mechanisms to facilitate that cooperation.

The confidential memorandum of understanding reached between the two Governments safeguards British interests in relation to the ownership of intellectual property rights and technology transfer, and provides for consultative and review mechanisms in support of the aims of the memorandum.

The SDI research program goes to the heart of the future defense technologies. Participation will enhance our ability to sustain an effective British research capability in areas of high technology relevant to both defense and civil programs.

Now that agreement has been reached on the memorandum, British companies, universities and research institutions have the opportunity to compete on a clearly defined basis for the research contracts which are on offer from the United States Government, as well as to participate in an information exchange program on a fully reciprocal basis for the mutual benefit of the United Kingdom and the United States.

To act as a focal point for British participation, and to liaise with the United States SDI participation office, I am establishing immediately within the Ministry of Defence an SDI participation office with representation from other interested departments. That office will work in the closest concert with British firms and institutions interested in such participation.

This agreement opens for Britain research possibilities which we could not afford on our own in technologies that will be at the center of tomorrow's world. It will bring jobs that would otherwise be created abroad, and I commend it to the House.

Press Conference

Earlier at a joint press conference with the U.S. Secretary of State for Defence, Mr Caspar Weinberger, Mr Heseltine was asked whether Britain had a commitment from the United States covering a certain sum of contracts. He replied:

When I first got into the detailed discussions with Mr. Weinberger, I had two points that I wanted to put to him. First of all, the program of research was important, not just in the context of SDI, but in the wider exploration of the technologies that go to build it up. Therefore the understandings we needed to achieve on technology transfer—on the legitimate protection of industrial property rights—were very fundamental.

The second point I wanted to make was that in order to address the fundamental issues of the maintenance of high technology base in a country like the United Kingdom—which is advanced but not on the scale of the United States—it was necessary for us, if we were going to play a part in the research program, to do so on a scale that was commensurate with our industrial base and our industrial expertise and technological knowledge. I therefore gave very clear indications that we did not want to come in on a sort of penny packet basis. It had to be done on a significant basis, where there were real opportunities and real contracts and real jobs, and I illustrated the sort of scale that I had in mind.

I fully understood that in saying that there was not going to be a series of blank dollar cheques handed over on a regular cash-flow basis. There has to be a process of making the awards and concluding the contracts, and that has to be a process of competition.

Britain has got to be able to deliver to the United States the results the United States is entitled to get in terms of quality and price.

What has happened as a result of the discussions that followed from that early visit I made in the mid-summer to Washington is that we have now concluded a memorandum of understanding, and on these two fundamental issues it actually addresses the concerns I expressed. And I have made it clear that I think the aspirations I had for the British defense industry have been fully met.

That does not mean that there is an expressed commitment in terms of a finite figure. That was not appropriate to the final conclusion of the document. What there is, is an understanding about the scale of the commitment and the scale of the resource in the United Kingdom, and of the American intentions to ensure that we have a real opportunity to win contracts which are commensurate with our industrial organizations.

Mr. Weinberger added:

I think that is exactly correct. Everybody knows that we are not able to guarantee in advance the award of a specific contract to any particular applicant or any particular candidate. But there is a very strong desire to have major British participation in the program. That has been expressed by me many times and by our Government, and that I am sure will prevail. I do not have any doubt at all, knowing the state of industry and the state of research and development of laboratory, scientific work here, that there will be major awards as we continue to go ahead with the program—major awards here in Britain.

In response to a question concerning guarantees to prevent British scientists or technologists being "drained away" to the United States, Mr Heseltine said that in a free society, individual technologists, scientists, and engineers, could not be prevented from living and working where they wished. But one of the initial concerns about which he had approached Mr Weinberger was to ensure that there was sufficient work in the program in the United Kingdom to make sure that those involved had opportunities which would persuade them to stay in Britain.

Mr Weinberger added:

We think it is to everyone's advantage that there be this strong scientific, educational and commercial productive capability in all of the allied countries, so it is to everybody's advantage that that strong capability that is here now continues here.

About the Authors

F. Stephen Larrabee is Vice President and Director of Studies of the Institute for East-West Security Studies, New York. Formerly, Dr. Larrabee co-directed the Soviet and East European Research Program at the Johns Hopkins University School of Advanced International Studies. From 1978 to 1981, he served on the U.S. National Security Council staff as a specialist on Soviet-East European affairs and East-West political-military relations. He is the author of *The Challenge to Soviet Interests in Eastern Europe* and co-author of "Gorbachev: The Road to Reykjavik" (*Foreign Policy*, Winter 1986/87).

Regina Cowen was a Resident Fellow at the Institute for East-West Security Studies, 1985-1986. She is presently a researcher at the Stockholm International Peace Research Institute, where she is editing a study on the future of the ABM Treaty. She has been awarded fellowships at the Center for Arms Control, University of Lancaster, England, and the Center for International Security, Stanford University. Dr. Cowen's publications include the book *Defense Procurement in the Federal Republic of Germany* and various articles on arms control and policy-making in Western Europe.

Peter Rajcsanyi, Resident Fellow at the Institute for East-West Security Studies, 1984-1985, and a specialist on U.S. domestic and foreign policy and arms control, is currently a member of the Central Committee staff of the Hungarian Socialist Workers' Party. He also holds the position of Secretary of the Presidential Board of the Hungarian Political Science Association. In addition to numerous published articles, Dr. Rajcsanyi is the author of two books, *The Scientific-Technological Revolution and the Correlation of World Forces* and *The American Challenge 1980-1990*.

Vladimir Bilandzic was a Resident Fellow at the Institute for East-West Security Studies, 1984-1985. He is presently a Senior Researcher at the Department of International Relations of the Institute of International Politics and Economics in Belgrade, which he headed from 1981 to 1983. He is co-author of the book *Disarmament in Europe* and other articles on international security and disarmament. Dr. Bilandzic also participated as a member of the delegation of Yugoslavia in the CSCE conference in Geneva, Belgrade, Madrid and in the CDE in Stockholm.